"Software piracy remains a major problem around the globe, negating literally thousands of person-years of intellectual effort. This book provides a thorough and detailed analysis of the economic damage that piracy causes both to local economies and the technology industry. Gantz and Rochester describe how technology, society, and globalization have evolved to make piracy easier than ever and highlight the challenges faced by industries trying to adapt to this change and enforcement organizations trying to stem the tide. This is an important read for media executives, college students, parents, intellectual property lawyers, and, of course, would-be digital pirates."

*Brad Smith, Microsoft Senior Vice President,*
*General Counsel, and Corporate Secretary*

"The pirates in this book include both teenagers working in their bedrooms and corporate executives in their offices, hijacking the gift of digital technology. This is a well-researched and engaging work on a subject of great importance now and for the future."

*Tracy Kidder, author of the international best seller,*
The Soul of the New Machine

"Pirates, like any predator, are agents of Darwinian evolution, forcing adaptations and driving next-generation innovations. Gantz and Rochester do a masterful job of analyzing this process and the impact piracy is having at the intersection of business, technology, and society. The moral? What doesn't kill us will make us stronger."

*Geoffrey Moore, author of* Crossing the Chasm, Inside the Tornado, *and*
Living on the Fault Line, *founder of The Chasm Group, and Managing*
*Director of TCG Advisors*

"In *Pirates of the Digital Millennium*, Gantz and Rochester zero in on the critical issue of protection for intellectual property in a way that everyone— parents, business people, media executives, and artists—can understand. We have entered the digital millennium, and this book looks at not only how we got there but, more importantly, where we are going when it comes to digital piracy. It's entertaining and serious at the same time, offering a 360-degree view of the issue with fresh research and compelling insights!"

*Pat McGovern, Chairman and Founder, IDG*

"Much has been written about the legal theories surrounding technology and piracy. What has been lacking is the empirical research to explain the practical impacts of piracy and the legal efforts to stamp it out. *Pirates of the Digital Millennium* does just that, and more. John and Jack have taken a problem that's been with us for 500 years and put it into a 21$^{st}$ century context. Technology advances have always affected the rules for copyright protection—and the ease with which those rules can be circumvented. John and Jack show that downloading pirated music from a P2P network, justified on the grounds that 'monetary interests precede art' in the recording industry, potentially stunts the development of diverse music and movie industries around the globe. At the same time, the legal response is heavy-handed, denying access for all to digital works to prevent the illegal behavior by some, making criminals out of our children for culturally accepted behavior. An important work for legal, business and sociological scholars alike, not to mention parents, teachers, and kids."

*Lars S. Smith, Assistant Professor of Law, Trademarks and Intellectual Property, Louis D. Brandeis School of Law, University of Louisville*

"I ate, drank, lived, and loved the music business for 25 years. Today, I see a business that has done its best to kill itself—first creatively, and now technologically. The music business, big and small, could have owned the downloading business, were it not for the collective of aging Luddites who run things, who are holding on desperately to a system that has sustained them for so long that their drive to innovate, educate, and entertain has ossified. There is so much music—new and old—out there that people either have no access to or have to jump through increasingly costly hoops to find. As a former artist who owns copyrighted music, I am convinced people will pay for it—if it is priced right and so easily available in this digital age. But, like artists and like music itself, the business needs to change and grow. Now as a teacher, I concentrate on teaching students the rigors and art of critical thinking, how to distinguish between fact and fiction. Jack and John's book is essential reading for anyone who wants or needs the music industry to have any sort of viable future. In these pages readers will find clear information that allows them to make the distinction between the facts and the overwhelming fiction on this great subject, to make informed decisions. The reader will find not just the seeds of change, but the leaves (and stems) as well."

*Hugo Burnham, New England Institute of Art, Brookline, Massachusetts, founding member of English post-punk band Gang of Four, whose debut album* Entertainment, *released by Warner Bros. Records in 1980, was named one of the 500 greatest albums of all-time by* Rolling Stone *in 2004*

# PIRATES OF THE DIGITAL MILLENNIUM

## How the Intellectual Property Wars Damage Our Personal Freedoms, Our Jobs, and the World Economy

JOHN GANTZ AND JACK B. ROCHESTER

**FT** Prentice Hall
FINANCIAL TIMES

An Imprint of PEARSON EDUCATION
Upper Saddle River, NJ • New York • London • San Francisco • Toronto • Sydney
Tokyo • Singapore • Hong Kong • Cape Town • Madrid
Paris • Milan • Munich • Amsterdam

www.ft-ph.com

A CIP record of this book can be obtained from the Library of Congress

Author Photos: *Adam Gooder*
Editorial/Production Supervision: *Donna Cullen-Dolce*
Cover Design: *Nina Scuderi*
Cover Design Director: *Jerry Votta*
Interior Design: *Gail Cocker-Bogusz*
Manufacturing Buyer: *Alexis Heydt-Long*
Vice President and Editor-in-Chief: *Tim Moore*
Editorial Assistant: *Richard Winkler*
Development Editor: *Russ Hall*
Marketing Manager: *John Pierce*

 © 2005 Pearson Education, Inc.
Publishing as Financial Times Prentice Hall
Upper Saddle River, NJ 07458

**Financial Times Prentice Hall offers excellent discounts on this book when ordered in
quantity for bulk purchases or special sales. For more information, please contact:
U.S. Corporate and Government Sales, 1-800-382-3419,
corpsales@pearsontechgroup.com. For sales outside of the U.S., please contact:
International Sales, 1-317-581-3793, international@pearsontechgroup.com.**

Printed in the United States of America

First Printing

ISBN0-13-146315-2

Pearson Education LTD.
Pearson Education Australia PTY, Limited
Pearson Education Singapore, Pte. Ltd.
Pearson Education North Asia Ltd.
Pearson Education Canada, Ltd.
Pearson Educación de Mexico, S.A. de C.V.
Pearson Education—Japan
Pearson Education Malaysia, Pte. Ltd.

Dedicated to our wives and sons, without whose love, support, and frank appraisals we wouldn't have made it this far.
In this book or in life.

In an increasingly competitive world, it is quality
of thinking that gives an edge—an idea that opens new
doors, a technique that solves a problem, or an insight
that simply helps make sense of it all.

We work with leading authors in the various arenas
of business and finance to bring cutting-edge thinking
and best learning practice to a global market.

It is our goal to create world-class print publications
and electronic products that give readers
knowledge and understanding which can then be
applied, whether studying or at work.

To find out more about our business
products, you can visit us at www.ft-ph.com

# FINANCIAL TIMES PRENTICE HALL BOOKS

*For more information, please go to www.ft-ph.com*

## Business and Society

John Gantz and Jack B. Rochester
*Pirates of the Digital Millennium: How the Intellectual Property Wars Damage Our Personal Freedoms, Our Jobs, and the World Economy*

Douglas K. Smith
*On Value and Values: Thinking Differently About We in an Age of Me*

## Current Events

Alan Elsner
*Gates of Injustice: The Crisis in America's Prisons*

John R. Talbott
*Where America Went Wrong: And How to Regain Her Democratic Ideals*

## Economics

David Dranove
*What's Your Life Worth? Health Care Rationing...Who Lives? Who Dies? Who Decides?*

## Entrepreneurship

Dr. Candida Brush, Dr. Nancy M. Carter, Dr. Elizabeth Gatewood, Dr. Patricia G. Greene, and Dr. Myra M. Hart
*Clearing the Hurdles: Women Building High Growth Businesses*

Oren Fuerst and Uri Geiger
*From Concept to Wall Street: A Complete Guide to Entrepreneurship and Venture Capital*

David Gladstone and Laura Gladstone
*Venture Capital Handbook: An Entrepreneur's Guide to Raising Venture Capital, Revised and Updated*

Thomas K. McKnight
*Will It Fly? How to Know if Your New Business Idea Has Wings... Before You Take the Leap*

Stephen Spinelli, Jr., Robert M. Rosenberg, and Sue Birley
*Franchising: Pathway to Wealth Creation*

## Executive Skills

Cyndi Maxey and Jill Bremer
*It's Your Move: Dealing Yourself the Best Cards in Life and Work*

John Putzier
*Weirdos in the Workplace*

## Finance

Aswath Damodaran
*The Dark Side of Valuation: Valuing Old Tech, New Tech, and New Economy Companies*

Kenneth R. Ferris and Barbara S. Pécherot Petitt
*Valuation: Avoiding the Winner's Curse*

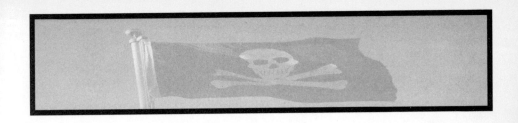

# CONTENTS

# ACKNOWLEDGMENTS

The studies and thought of many people have found their way into this work, either directly or by reflection, leaving their imprint upon our ideas. We gratefully acknowledge all these influences; as you read, you will know who you are.

Our thanks to our literary agent, Karen Warner-Kurtzman of the Helen Rees Literary Agency, Boston, who was quick to see the potential for a work on digital piracy and equally prompt in getting us a contract.

Liya Escalera put her keen mind together with her English degree from Stonehill College and made a major contribution to this work, beginning as our permissions editor but quickly graduating to content editing. Because of Liya, this is a better book. We are grateful.

Todd Mitchell, head honcho at the Mitchell Creative Group in Sutton, Massachusetts, did a mind-merge with us and our content to create the outstanding graphics in these pages. We think the graphics do a great job of conveying the quantitative information that often gets overlooked.

Laurie Seymour, program manager for software and services at IDC, provided us with an unending stream of source material. She was so often on top of breaking stories in this fast-moving subject area that we thought she might be a reporter for *The New York Times.*

Joshua Line, the research librarian at Jack's college, the New England Institute of Art, proved on a number of occasions that you can't find everything with Google and that his trade is not only a skill but at times an art.

Hats off to Tim Moore, vice president and editor-in-chief at Financial Times Prentice Hall, for his steadfastness and Sunday night emails as we struggled toward the finish line. (It is so hard to finish a book!) Go Red Sox!

Our appreciation to Russ Hall, developmental editor extraordinaire and a publishing pro if we ever saw one (and we've seen a few). You kept us on target and on schedule with your professionalism, email nudges, and good spirits. Besides that, we're so jealous of you, writing novels from your Texas lakefront.

This book generated considerable interest and dialogue among our families, friends, and colleagues, and even the kids in our focus groups. It seemed like someone was always asking us how the book was going or how they ought to deal with downloading. Was it right, was it wrong? We thank all those people for their encouragement and helpful suggestions while writing this book, but in the final analysis, the thoughts and opinions, facts and errors, hyperbole and omissions, are ours alone.

John Gantz
Wayland, Massachusetts

Jack B. Rochester
Lexington, Massachusetts

March 2004

# PREFACE

It was a quintessential New England fall morning—crisp, sunny, cold—that day in November 2002. We were two old friends and colleagues, getting together for breakfast to catch up, talk about our work, our children, our lives.

John, the researcher, was just finishing up a massive project at IDC on the economic impact of worldwide software piracy. Jack, the writer, smelled an important story in the making. We were both amazed at the extent of worldwide copyright violation, astounded at how fast Napster had grown, sad at its demise and the loss of one of the easiest to use software programs we'd ever seen, and amused at how quickly KaZaA had filled its shoes.

Little did we know that the casual activity known as file-sharing, or downloading MP3s, would explode in the news six months later when the Recording Industry Association of America began issuing takedown orders on college students. And even though we knew our kids—boys in high school, college, and beyond—were downloaders, we didn't really understand how they felt about what they were doing, about what the music industry was doing, or about copyright infringement in general.

Nor, when we met, did we understand the wildly complex facets of copyright law—for example, how it was rewritten 11 separate times during the 1900s, each time granting longer and longer terms of copyright. We had no idea that Mickey Mouse's copyright (1928–2023) would outlive his creator, Walt Disney (1901–1966), by 57 years. We had yet to grasp the full extent of worldwide media piracy and its impact on the global economy.

Before we left the breakfast table, we were talking about working together on another book, 20 years after our first collaboration—a widely popular book called *The Naked Computer*—was published. Our agent and publisher shared our enthusiasm for this new book, and soon we were once again writing together.

We have entered the digital millennium, where most, if not all, of our media have been (or soon will be) rendered into the strings of ones and zeroes a computer chip understands. The world is awash in media and entertainment devices, personal computers, Internet connections, and broadband transmission. We're surrounded by MP3 players, TiVo, Personal Video Recorders, CD burners, iPods, laptops, Playstations, and more.

Technology has unsheathed a sword of Damocles that makes it possible for us to enjoy media—software, computer games, music, movies—in ways that were not possible 20 years ago. At the same time, it threatens the long-held right of artists and copyright owners to expect a fair return for their intellectual capital and the sweat of their brows. Yet as the media for gaming, music, movies, and computers become ever more interchangeable, so will the public's expectations that they ought to have the right to use them in all the new and different ways they choose.

These two viewpoints are in serious conflict.

When we began writing *Pirates of the Digital Millennium*, we held some cherished, all-American beliefs. We believed business is entitled to a profit. We were convinced that black marketeers in other countries are hurting the world's economy by stealing and replicating computer software and games, movies, and other forms of intellectual property. We assumed kids don't really understand copyright and that they're stealing from record companies and artists.

But after a year of researching and writing, we didn't end up in quite the same intellectual place we started. This book was a journey of personal discovery. We hope it will be the same for you. We have been forced to scrutinize our personal philosophies and our understanding about what motivates people. We've had to travel the timeline of copyright protection from the Middle Ages until now to see how it has evolved. We've had to understand how business, politics, and law mix in today's information society. We've had to ask: What freedoms have we given up in the name of copyright protection?

Our discussion concerns intellectual property: its use and its value. On one hand are those who believe that anything they conjure up, anything that transforms an idea into form, is intellectual property. On the other are the individuals who believe just as passionately that the entire notion of intellectual property is at best a farce, at worst just another way to suck profits out of the ether. In between these two extremes is a spectrum of social, legal, and ethical points of view.

"There's a battle outside and it's ragin'," sang Bob Dylan in "The Times They Are A-Changin'." This battle pits media conglomerates against teenagers, artists against artists, technology providers against content providers, nations against nations, Internet service providers against entertainment companies, media companies against their best customers—and even law enforcement against organized crime.

The ownership of intellectual property has been passing from the minds of artists and into the bank accounts of media businesses for at least 200 years. Yet since the passage of the Digital Millennium Copyright Act of 1998, some of those in the media business have developed a lockdown mentality that many people feel threatens their right to enjoy the media they buy however they see fit, as well as the public right of fair use. The concerns discussed in this book rise way beyond simply being able to legitimately download a song from the Internet: They extend all the way to your right to not sit through commercials when you watch a recorded television show. There are those who believe the

American model of capitalism, along with American intellectual property, should be promulgated throughout the world economy, with the same terms of sale and use for their products as in the United States, regardless of disparities in economic status or local customs regarding ownership and copying. And there are those who don't.

We found ourselves asking a number of these questions as we traveled the road from blank page to completed manuscript: Do we have a right to use media we license or buy in any way we see fit? Do the media publishers have a right to profit for decades from their acquired intellectual property? Is downloading stealing or civil disobedience? Is enforcement curtailing piracy or making it worse? Can we expect to change the hearts and minds of the global citizenry to a capitalistic point of view? Could the software companies and media firms do something different to alleviate the problem? How bad is the problem? Whose problem is it? Why do pirates pirate? And why don't others?

This is our invitation to you to take a journey into the heart of intellectual property darkness with us.

## WHAT'S IN THIS BOOK?

Here's a roadmap for the 10 chapters of the journey you're about to embark upon with us:

Chapter 1, *Are You a Digital Pirate?*, presents an overview of the ideas and social situations regarding the licit and illicit use of copyrighted intellectual property. We ask you to evaluate your own behavior, or that of people close to you, to determine if you, or they, are pirates of the digital millennium.

Chapter 2, *Is it Copyright or the Right to Copy?*, presents a history of modern copyright in what we generally regard as Western civilization, beginning with monks in the European Dark Ages and moving (somewhat regressively) through English law to American issues of fair use and the sanctity of ideas. A table of the political history of copyright concludes the chapter.

Chapter 3, *Us Against Them?*, explores the war over intellectual property use, providing a fair and balanced perspective of all the competing camps. It's the scorecard—the playbook—of the conflict.

Chapter 4, *Inside the Corporate Intellect: A Day at Microsoft*, explains just what goes into software development, in terms of human intellectual capital and corporate resources. Next time you think how cheap it is to make a CD, remember this chapter and that the aluminum and plastic disc is a very small part of the cost.

Chapter 5, *Inside the Sausage: The Making of the Digital Millennium Copyright Act*, sets out what led to the creation and passage of this piece of legislation, which has caused one of the most pitched battles between copyists and capitalists in the history of copyright.

Chapter 6, *Global Fallout*, explores the worldwide effects and aftereffects of digital piracy. We're not talking about kids downloading tunes here. In some cases, organized crime is a major player. We explore what it takes for a less privileged country to gain economic footing with our intellectual property.

Chapter 7, *Dude, Where's My MP3?*, focuses on youth, primarily American, who regard access to the Internet as an ordained right and anything on it as fair and free game. Yes, a game: If the copyright holders find a way to protect their intellectual property, the game is to crack it.

Chapter 8, *Eliot Ness or Keystone Kops?*, looks at the attempts— and we do mean attempts—to stem the tide of international piracy and download thievery. While the RIAA did put the fear of God in America's downloaders for a short while, most have come to believe that detection and punishment are unlikely—and it appears they may be right. Ditto for the rest of the digital planet.

Chapter 9, *Angel on My Shoulder: What's in It for Me?*, asks you to examine your own beliefs and ethics in making a personal determination about what's right and what's not, what the other guy does be damned. We all have to take our own ethical stand.

Chapter 10, *Through the Fog: The Future of Intellectual Property*, sums up what we've learned in the foregoing nine chapters, and extrapolates from that some solutions to the problem. Here you can test our logic and vision, and add your own.

The Afterword, following Chapter 10, describes each of our personal journeys, where we reveal our views to you. Don't peek until you've read the book, though!

# ARE YOU A DIGITAL PIRATE?

At this precise moment, movies and other visual entertainment works are in ever-multiplying numbers swarming illegally throughout the so-called file-sharing sites (a more accurate description would be "file-stealing" sites)....There is one truth that sums up the urgency of this request to Congress....if you cannot protect what you own, you don't own anything.[1]

**Jack Valenti, president and CEO, Motion Picture Association of America**

It is essential to understand that copyright in the American tradition was not meant to be a "property" right as the public generally understands property. It was originally a narrow federal policy that granted a limited trade monopoly in exchange for universal use and access...copyright issues are now more about large corporations limiting access to and use of their products and less about lonely songwriters snapping their pencil tips under the glare of bare bulbs.[2]

**Siva Vaidhyanathan, Assistant Professor, Culture and Communication, at New York University**

---

1.  From testimony before the U.S. Senate Committee on Commerce, Science, and Transportation during a hearing on February 28, 2002, on whether the government should mandate specific controls against piracy be built into video receivers and computers. Full testimony available at http://commerce.senate.gov/hearings/hearings0202.htm.
2.  From *Copyrights and Copywrongs, The Rise of Intellectual Property and How It Threatens Creativity*, by Siva Vaidhyanathan (New York: New York University Press, 2001), 11–12. Vaidhyanathan is a writer, former journalist, and professor at New York University with a doctorate from the University of Texas. You can read his Web blog at http://www.nyu.edu/classes/siva/.

Darren (not his real name) is a first-year student at a large, well-known Eastern university, where his computer is connected to the college's high-speed Internet connection. He's a nice kid: tall, curly hair, clean-shaven, no piercings or tattoos, a shy smile. In his dorm room, Darren opens his browser application and types in www.kaaza.com and immediately connects to a vast network of computers around the globe. Millions, in fact: As many as 300 million copies of the KaZaA file-sharing software have been downloaded.

Collectively, these computers hold a vast repository of music, movies, computer games, and software on their hard drives. As participants on the KaZaA peer-to-peer (P2P) network (a network where all connected computers are equal), they are like buyers and sellers at an enormous swap meet, sharing their wares with each other. Except nothing is bought or sold, no money changes hands, and there are no terms or conditions to the transactions. Instead, KaZaA opens a portal to media files that are free for the copying from all the computers connected to each other on KaZaA's P2P network. You can download selected files from others' computers, while permitting others to upload files from yours at the same time.

Darren searches for the group Coldplay and finds a number of cuts available. He sees "Clocks," the one he wants; 12 people have it available. He clicks on one and begins downloading the MP3 file to his computer's hard drive. He clicks on it again, and the tune begins to play. He clicks over to his word processing program and desultorily begins typing up his lab notes from astronomy class. While he listens and types, KaZaA continues working in the background, making the 2,455 files Darren has stored on his computer from downloads and copies of his and other people's CDs available to others for downloading. He mostly listens to music on his computer, but he has also made his own personal mixes of his favorite tunes and burned them on CDs to play in the car and elsewhere. He keeps his CD collection in a carrying case resembling a briefcase—there are probably 120 CDs in there. About 20 have labels on them from the music company. Most just have writing in a felt tip pen.

Darren's a nice kid and a good student. He's never been in trouble. He wouldn't think of plagiarizing somebody else's work for an assignment, cheating on a test, or shoplifting. In his *mind*, he's pretty sure downloading copyrighted songs from KaZaA is wrong, but in his *conscience*, he feels only the lightest of twinges: It's not a very big wrong.

# INTELLECTUAL PROPERTY AND THE CONCEPT OF COPY RIGHTS

Darren, along with about 60 million other people around the globe, is a pirate of the digital millennium. What Darren doesn't know is that the recording industry is in all probability watching him, tracking his downloading activities on the Internet and preparing to issue what is legally termed a *takedown order* against him to his college Information Technology administrator. If he's downloading software or movies, those industries are on the lookout for him, too.

Perhaps you're a pirate, too, cherishing a bit of roguishness in your personality. It's okay; we've done some pirating ourselves and have talked to numerous others who have confessed. We're not going to turn anyone in or even suggest you find a Digital Pirates Anonymous meeting. We view this as a dialog, one as interactive as the print medium allows, in which we can satisfy your desire to understand what's going on with digital piracy, help you define your intellectual and ethical arguments, and proffer some suggestions as to how each of us can—or should— take action.

Honest.

As we begin our dialog, this chapter introduces the long and illustrious history of copying throughout the ages, paying particular attention to how the digital age in which we live has changed the nature and perception of copyrighted materials. For example, it is unlikely that the framers of the U.S. Constitution anticipated downloading movies from the Internet when they established our copyright laws. We'll discuss a few examples and problems having to do with what is commonly termed intellectual property and ask you to reflect on your own attitudes.

Elsewhere in the book, we'll look at the history of copyright and the swinging pendulum between the interests of copyright holders and the public, and the ensemble cast of players in our digital millennium drama and their roles. You'll learn about the economic impact of piracy, the current state of the law and its sometimes comical enforcement, and the personal and ethical tradeoffs that surround piracy. We'll discuss whether what we're talking about should even be called piracy.

But one main point we have to agree upon at the outset is that *any* copyrighted media—whether a book, movie, song, computer game, or software program—is someone's *intellectual property*. Ah, but what, exactly, is intellectual property? Here are two complementary definitions:

> A product of the intellect that has commercial value, including copyrighted property such as literary or artistic works, and ideational property, such as patents, appellations of origin, business methods, and industrial processes.[3]

> The ownership of ideas and control over the tangible or virtual representation of those ideas. Use of another person's intellectual property may or may not involve royalty payments or permission, but should always include proper credit to the source.[4]

So what we conclude is that intellectual property is an original idea that someone thought up, and then realized in some tangible form, making it his or her possession—to hoard, sell, license, rent, sign away, or share freely. This book you're reading is our intellectual property (assigned as is the custom for

3. *The American Heritage® Dictionary of the English Language*, Fourth Edition (New York: Houghton Mifflin Company, 2000).
4. *The Free On-line Dictionary of Computing*, © 1993–2003, Denis Howe, available at http://wombat.doc.ic.ac.uk/foldoc/.

most authors to the publisher), protected by copyright law. For the purposes of our discussion in this book, we commonly regard music, movies, software programs, and computer games as intellectual property.[5]

We can all probably agree that original works such as these are the intellectual property of their creators (or their assigns), as we do with written works such as books. We must also agree, however, that nine-tenths of the people on the planet are from cultures or political systems that don't have a concept of or laws regarding intellectual property—in fact, many don't recognize individual property ownership. Chances are if you are reading this book, you're in that other 10 percent, but this difference over something as fundamental as the very concept of intellectual property will add flavor to our dialog. We'll need to dip into the swirl of competing views, complex positions, subtle distinctions, and legitimate debate that surrounds this worthy topic.

Copyright law, in its essence, grants the owner of a piece of intellectual property the *right* to determine who can have a *copy* of it. Hence the term, which has been in use for over 300 years. You may argue, as some do, that the "right" being protected is actually a monopoly granted by the government, but the law does the same thing regardless of the semantics. Copyright does not protect an idea; rather, it protects the unique expression of that idea.[6]

As originally conceived, it was a way to reward copyright owners for their labors over a fixed length of time, after which the copyrighted works would enter the public domain to be disseminated to and reinvented by anyone. An original idea could be

---

5. There is fair disagreement about what constitutes intellectual property, yet the social trend is to regard more and more creative artifacts as such. For example, the National Football League regards its logo, its name, and the term "Super Bowl" as intellectual property requiring prior authorization for use. (And yes, we had to get permission.) An entire Web site devoted to tracking IP issues can be found at www.ipwatchdog.com.

6. A good explanation of copyright and copyrightable material can be found at www.ipwatchdog.com/copyright_basics.html.

reconceived or reformatted, if you will, into another unique expression.[7]

Let's also assume that it's wrong to steal something, for example a book or a CD, that belongs to someone else. But when it comes to a song or movie or game or software program that we've copied from a friend or downloaded from the Internet, we say, "I'm not really *stealing* it." Is it somehow different because you're simply making a *copy*, not absconding with the original? Is it somehow different because you have the owner's permission? Consider the following brief comparative scenarios and ask yourself what, if anything, is unethical or illegal about each:

1. You borrow a book from the public library, read it and return it.
2. You borrow a book from the public library, make a copy at Kinko's, and return it.

1. You copy the new Norah Jones CD onto your computer so you can listen to it while you do your homework.
2. You copy the new Norah Jones CD onto your computer then burn five CD copies to give to your friends.

---

7.  An interesting case of copyright law demonstrating this point was brought to court in 2001. The estate of Margaret Mitchell (1900–1949), who wrote the best-selling novel *Gone with the Wind,* charged Alice Randall, who had written a parody novel entitled *The Wind Done Gone*, with copyright infringement. The Mitchell estate claimed that, because Randall used plot lines and characters from Mitchell's work (her novel portrayed a fictional slave at Scarlett O'Hara's plantation), she had written a sequel, therefore infringing the Mitchell copyright. The 11th U.S. Circuit Court of Appeals lifted a lower court injunction against the publication of Randall's parody, ruling that "copyright does not immunize a work from comment and criticism" and that the injunction was an "extraordinary and drastic remedy" that "amounts to unlawful prior restraint in violation of the First Amendment." In the words of Dr. Matthew Rimmer, lecturer, Faculty of Law, the Australian National University, the appeals court "emphasized that the decision upheld the main objectives of copyright law: the promotion of learning, the protection of the public domain, the granting of an exclusive right to the author, and the prevention of private censorship." See http://alia.org.au/publishing/incite/2003/04/wind.gone.html.

1. You record a TV program on your TiVo, then make a digital copy and upload it to KaZaA.
2. You record a TV program on your TiVo, then invite a bunch of people over and charge them a dollar apiece to watch it.

Did you find a few that were tough to call? Let's review:

■ In the first example, there's a huge legal distinction between borrowing a book (legal) and making your own copy (illegal).

■ In the second, you can legally burn a copy for your own *personal use* (it's like making a cassette tape of a record), but not for others.

■ In the third example, while you can share a copy without breaking copyright law, under the rules of *fair use*, you can't upload it to another medium such as the Internet because now you're distributing it without a license. Moreover, you can't charge others to watch a copyrighted recorded program with you.

Actual case law on the doctrine of fair use (see sidebar) splits even more hairs than we have here. The portrait of a church quilt used in the background of a TV series for only 27 seconds was not fair use, while the use of 41 seconds of a boxing film in a biographical movie of Muhammad Ali was. A sculptor using a copyrighted photograph as the basis for his sculpture violated copyright, while Google rendering thumbnail images on its search engine for millions of viewers was considered fair use.

So you see, the problem is there's a gray area here between what's a legitimate use and what is not; when it's okay to make a copy for personal use and when it is not; and when it's for personal use, or if it's fair use, and when it isn't. There may even be a gray area between what's morally or ethically wrong and what's illegal.

## WHAT IS "FAIR USE"?

The doctrine of fair use was a right granted under Section 107 of Title 17, The United States Copyright Act, to permit the use of copyrighted property for criticism, commentary, news reportage, academic research and scholarship, and teaching, to name the most common. Section 107 set out four factors for determining fair use:

1.   The purpose and character of the use, including whether such use is of commercial nature or is for nonprofit educational purposes.
2.   The nature of the copyrighted work.
3.   The amount and substantiality of the portion used in relation to the copyrighted work as a whole.
4.   The effect of the use upon the potential market for or value of the copyrighted work.

Fair use has always been tough to interpret: What the user thinks is fair use is not always what the copyright holder regards as fair. For this reason, a mechanism was created for formally requesting *permission* to use copyrighted material. In this way, the person requesting the use makes sure it's proper and authorized use, and the copyright holder can determine if the interests (both intellectual and financial) of the copyrighted material are being honored.

Given this interpretation, it would appear that fair use of recorded music would only be for a few seconds, or a small percentage, of the work's length—in other words, not the entire CD, as most people assume is legal. By way of comparison, you don't "archive" a book you bought by making a photocopy of the entire thing.

The Digital Millennium Copyright Act of 1998 (DMCA) considerably tightened up the interpretation of fair use as it applies to digital intellectual property—too much so, in the eyes of many civil rights advocates and legal scholars. Several bills have been introduced in Congress to restore some of the fair-use rights accorded consumers prior to passage of the DMCA. This law, and its ramifications, is discussed at length in Chapter 5, *Inside the Sausage: The Making of the Digital Millennium Copyright Act.*[8]

By the time you finish this book, we hope the gray areas won't be quite as gray. In fact, they ought to be a lot more black and white. We want to lay out the arguments—on all sides by all parties—regarding the piracy of digital intellectual property and to chart a course through them to help establish a set of behaviors that work for you and every concerned individual. You'll learn a lot more about these issues in the following chapter on copyright law.

## COPYING AND VIRTUE: A SHORT HISTORY

What was the first thing humans ever copied? Was it duplicating cave paintings onto an animal hide? Did they copy to transport art from one place to another, or perhaps as a means of communicating information or knowledge to others? Whatever the original causes and effects, copying has a long and often virtuous lineage. Without a doubt, copying has made learning across time, space, and even different media, possible. During the Dark Ages, ca. 450–800 C.E., monasteries held the world's accumulated knowledge in one-of-a-kind books. If a monk at, say, the Fountains Abbey in Yorkshire, England, wanted to read a particular work that was at the Iona monastery on the Hebridean island off the coast of Scotland, a monk (such as the redoubtable Adomnan, ca. 624–704 C.E.) would laboriously replicate it with exacting precision, the copy nearly indistinguishable from the original.

---

8. The Stanford Law School and Nolo Press have jointly (with others) sponsored a Web site with a detailed examination of current application of the doctrine of fair use at http://fairuse.stanford.edu/Copyright_and_Fair_Use_Overview/chapter9/index.html.

The German Johannes Gutenberg made copying books much easier by mechanizing the process with his printing press. The first book he published was the Bible in 1455. But the printing press moved knowledge and learning out of the Church and into the halls of secular learning. The printing press's role in disseminating information added momentum to the flowering of European learning known as the Renaissance. Sir Francis Bacon commented at the turn of the 17th century that "Knowledge is power." Hoarding knowledge had been a way for certain individuals to maintain control, but during the Renaissance, that all began to change, culminating in the global dissemination of information and knowledge today over the Internet.

Even the monks finally caught on to copying. In the early 1980s, Patrick J. McGovern, Chairman of the Board of International Data Group and co-author Gantz's boss, was traveling in Nepal when he visited a monastery where he was shown handwritten sacred documents stored on stone shelves. He discussed their importance with the lama, who said it was difficult for monks from distant monasteries to travel the great distances to read the books. The lama said they had plans to begin making copies. Would scribes copy them in longhand? McGovern asked. "Oh, no," the lama replied. "We use a Xerox 9200."[9]

Copying is an even more interesting phenomenon in Asia, where to copy or emulate is often seen as a sign of respect. Some cultures, such as Japan's, are an amalgam of what they have learned and observed from others. The noted Japanese economist and author Michio Morishima tells the story of how in 1871 a contingent of Meiji government officials studied the social, economic, and military systems of the Western world for seven months. The result was patterning the Japanese education system on the French, their universities after those in America, and the telegraph and railways on the British. The Meiji Constitution and the Civil Code were of German origin, the Criminal Code was French,

9.  Jack B. Rochester and John Gantz, *The Naked Computer* (New York: William Morrow, 1983).

and the Imperial Japanese Navy was patterned on the British Royal Navy.[10]

To this day, we say "I want to get a copy of John and Jack's new book," for indeed, that is what it is: a typeset, printed, and bound copy of an original manuscript, owned and copyrighted by its author or owner. What we understand today as copyright is, at its core, a legal and legislative dictate intended to protect the economic rights of the copyright holder. That makes copyrighted work your property, with attendant rights of possession, distribution, and levying a charge for use. Through the 19th century, the right of copyright primarily applied to written work: journals, books, sheet music, and so forth.

## I SING THE COPY ELECTRIC

As we entered the 20th century, it became possible to record and play back sounds and motion on media. The great American inventor Thomas Edison, known as "the Wizard of Menlo Park," introduced media recording to the world: first, the recordable cylinder, then the disk-shaped record and celluloid film for motion pictures. Indeed, Edison copyrighted the first full-length movie, *The Great Train Robbery*, in 1903. It was just under 11 minutes long. You can watch it on your computer today by downloading it from the Library of Congress Edison Web site.[11]

Edison's recordable media were invented for dictation and recording telephone messages. Indeed, most consumer electronics devices were conceived to answer a business, industry, or military need. Edison would have been proud of the engineers at Ampex in San Carlos, California, who designed and built machines that would record audio and video on magnetic tape. In 1948, an Ampex tape recorder was used for the first time to tape-record, or transcribe, *The Bing Crosby Show* for later broadcast

---

10. Michio Morishima, "Why has Japan 'Succeeded'?" in *Western Technology and the Japanese Ethos* (Cambridge, England: Cambridge University Press, 1982), pp. 88–89.

11. See http://memory.loc.gov/ammem/edhtml/.

on the radio. Prior to that, radio programs were transcribed to 16" acetate platters (with all their attendant pops, scratches, and tics). Ampex tape recorders later became available to the general public as tape recording machines, in large part popularized by the Japanese companies Sony and Teac.

When the Philips Compact Cassette was introduced in the early 1960s, it was intended for use as a portable medium for dictation (the tape moved so slowly that it was not at first thought to be of acceptable quality for music recording). But recorder technology improved, and soon companies began releasing LP (long playing) record albums for sale on cassette. But Philips did not anticipate that so many *blank* cassettes would be purchased—clearly for home recording. The 1970s were great days for home recording aficionados. You could record a record on a cassette; that was easy. But if you were really into your music, you could buy a high-end cassette recorder that had the juice to make recordings of the same quality as a reel-to-reel tape recorder, hook it up to your stereo receiver along with a mixer and a couple of turntables, and make your own custom music collages. Add a microphone and you became your own radio station. You could fade in and out of tunes and even do your own voiceovers. You could *really* make your music collection your own.

It was the beginning of the culture shift from media massification to personalized media: my choices, my order, my time and place.

## RECORDING, FROM A TO V

Reel-to-reel and cassette *audio* recording machines were followed by *video* recorders. Ampex also invented the first VTR, or video tape recorder, in 1956, but it would have to wait for another 20 years to become a consumer product. Sony introduced its Betamax video cassette recorders and tape cassettes in 1976 and, after a fashion, repeated what had occurred with home audio cassette recording. In an attempt to boost sales of both VCRs and cassette tapes, Sony advertised that consumers could tape-record television programs or rental movies, prompting a copyright infringement lawsuit from MCA/Universal and Disney. The first judge ruled for Sony, but the appeals court reversed that decision—then the Supreme Court reversed it again. Two important precedents were set:

1. The consumer's right to make a copy of copyrighted media *for his or her own personal use*.
2. The Doctrine of First Sale, set forth in the Copyright Act of 1976, which states that if you purchase something, you have the right to use it any way you see fit *so long as copyright is not violated*.

## IS IT LIVE OR IS IT MEMOREX?

Remember the classic Memorex tape commercial on TV? Jazz vocalist Ella Fitzgerald hits a note that breaks a champagne flute while her voice is recorded on Memorex tape. Then the tape is played back and it, too, breaks glass! These days, it can be awfully difficult to discern live from recorded: Witness a Britney Spears concert where she dances and lip-syncs her little heart away.[12] But 30 or 40 years ago, recording was done on analog machines, meaning you played back content as it was originally recorded, sequentially and with some degradation in fidelity during to the transfer from the original, or master, to the copy medium (tape). That's why the Memorex demonstration was such a big deal.

In point of fact, all analog recorded media are subject to loss of quality. So records wore out. Tape stretched. One of the great Edsels of recording media was the eight-track tape cassette: hard to use, subject to constant mechanical failures, lousy sound quality. The slow speeds used by compact cassettes and videotape resulted in quality degradation as well.

---

12. "Lip-Syncing Gets Real," *The New York Times*, Section 2, Arts & Leisure, February 1, 2004, p. 1.

## COPYING AND CONVENIENCE

Maybe that's why the recorded music and movie industries initially looked askance at the small percentage of people who were making copies for themselves and their friends. By the letter of the law, such copying was legal. But how about making a copy of an entire record album or a feature-length movie? Could that be construed as fair use? And even if it's legal, is it fair? Well, the Doctrine of Fair Use also said that as long as you weren't using the copyrighted material for other than personal enjoyment—in other words, you weren't inviting neighbors in and charging them to watch a movie or TV show (or even a recorded musical work, for that matter) you had copied—it was still legal. It still is today.

When the earth's tectonic plates move, it's called a seismic shift. Media copying for personal use changed the rules of the media business because of three seismic social shifts: time, space, and cost.

*The time shift*. This was one of the benefits Sony pushed with its Betamax VCRs: You can record a television show that's on at an inconvenient time and view it whenever you want. Little did the VCR industry know that time-shift recording—indeed, even setting the clock time—would be beyond the expertise of most consumers. Nevertheless, people did record TV programs and cable movies for later viewing, many amassing huge collections of videotapes. It got so crazy that software companies developed videotape cataloguing programs. Today that time shifting has moved into the digital world, with TiVo pioneering a digital video recording technology that does on a hard disk what the VCR did on tape; cable TV companies followed, building the same technology into their cable boxes.

*The space shift*. Media has always been somewhat location-bound. To watch TV, you must be in front of a television set (usually in your living room). To listen to a record, you need to have a stereo and turntable. It was, let's say, impractical to listen to a record in your car (before you laugh, there was in fact a 45RPM record player for autos in the early 1960s—briefly, very briefly). However, once cassette tapes were introduced, consumers realized they could tape a record to listen to in their car stereo or on a personal cassette player.

Music lovers soon realized there was an incredible congruence between time- and space-shifting: the two went hand-in-hand. They—you—probably didn't think of it as the confluence of the time-space continuum. If you had thought about it at all, you probably would use the word *convenience*. It gave us the media our way, when and where we wanted it. Television followed suit, with personal and portable TVs. Today, we take this convenience for granted. Now we can even download songs and special ring tones onto our cell phones.

*The cost shift*. The other benefit to making a copy of your tunes or movies is the economic savings. You don't have to buy multiple copies of a CD: one to listen to at home, another for the car or Walkman. And you can load up your computer's hard drive with all your favorite CDs, thus replicating your entire home music collection. Then you can copy the music stored on your computer back onto blank CDs for your friends and family, or to make your own mixes. This economic reality is hard to argue with, and what's more, you say, "This CD *is* my property. I bought it, and I can do anything I want with it."

Well, not quite. Can you share it with your friends, for instance? Can you share it with a million other people?

Unfortunately, we often take copying for granted, whether it's running to the copy machine to reproduce sheet music or compiling a CD as a gift. If we think about it at all, our thoughts probably go something like this: *I'll only do it this once*, or *My occasional copying can't be hurting the big old music business **that** much. I don't litter, and I recycle, so I can't be doing anything very wrong here*. I'm John Q. or Jane Public, after all.

## THE EMPIRE STRIKES BACK

Of course, if you follow the news you know the music business is hurting. CD sales are down, sales of new releases are weak, and

**Figure 1–1**    Every recorded movie carries the FBI warning, sometimes even in multiple languages. As of 2004, CDs, DVDs, and other digital media will carry FBI warning labels as well.

the industry is suing and fining its own customers for copyright violations, using a provision of the DMCA.

Entertainment companies have long been aware that customers copy their tunes. Back in the analog days, they simply decided it wasn't worth pursuing beyond a certain point, as long as people were just making copies for personal use. Besides, the copies just weren't that great. The movie industry, having anticipated copying better than the music industry, decided (and hoped) a warning, shown in Figure 1–1, would suffice:[13]

But everything changed with the advent of digital media. Ted Cohen, an EMI senior vice president and a guest on TechTV's "Music Wars" television special, was asked what the difference

---

13.  There is debate about whether this warning, in fact, holds any meaning for the typical home VCR or DVD user, and it is certainly pretty much unenforceable except in egregious situations. What's egregious? We've seen movies playing in fashionable coffee bars on wide-screen plasma TVs. Fred von Lohmann, an attorney for the Electronic Frontier Foundation, says he is "under no illusions that this kind of label is going to change public perceptions," and adds that the warning doesn't clearly explain legitimate copying rights. Source: AP News Service, February 20, 2004.

was between taping a song off the radio and copying it on a computer. He said this harkened back to the days of the 1970s, when "usually the quality of what you ended up with was not of the level of something you would want to keep." John Perry Barlow, lyricist for the Grateful Dead and co-founder of the Electronic Frontier Foundation (EFF), rejoined Cohen, asking "Are you actually saying that it's not stealing if it's low-quality and it is stealing if it's high-quality?" Cohen replied that allowing radio to play songs was intended to create more demand, but that downloading from the Internet apparently is not serving the music industry as a suitable marketing vehicle—a point with which a great many people we interviewed would take issue.[14]

## EVEN BETTER THAN THE REAL THING?

Several events in the early 1980s changed the ballgame. One was the introduction of the personal computer (PC), a machine that worked with digital rather than analog media: Fast, tiny ones and zeros replaced undulating (and often truncated) modulations to do the same things better—including store audio and video signals. The Compact Disc (like the Compact Cassette, invented by Philips), which recorded music digitally, was introduced about the same time as the IBM Personal Computer, although the two technologies were incompatible at the time. A decade later, however, software publishers realized they could use CDs as a delivery medium for their applications: Instead of 10 or 20 floppy disks, a single CD could be used to store an entire program.

At first, personal computer software programs and applications were assiduously copy-protected; often, they could only be installed once on a single computer. But consumers complained, sometimes because an installation failed and they weren't permitted a second chance, other times because they wanted to use the same program on a second computer they owned—for example their laptop—and sometimes simply because they wanted a backup copy. So the software industry relented, took the inten-

---

14. "Music Wars," broadcast on TechTV, September 12, 2003.

sive copy-protections away, and asked people to honor the license agreement.

## THE END-USER LICENSE AGREEMENT

The convoluted legalese of the "end-user license agreement," or EULA, seems designed to discourage the customer from actually reading it and simply accepting the terms. Accepting an online license agreement is made as easy as possible: Just click on the "Accept" button. However, by accepting the EULA for Microsoft Office 2003,[15] consider what you are agreeing to:

- You can install a copy on two personal computers if both are for your personal use. (And if you own three computers?)
- You can use "Media Elements" that are part of the software package (such as clip art) but "You may not sell, license or distribute copies of the Media Elements by themselves or as part of any collection, product or service if the primary value of the product or service is in the Media Elements." (Uh, and who decides this value thing?)
- Activation of the software is "mandatory." If you do not activate it, or if you do not legally own the software, you will not be permitted to use it. Activation also includes mandatory registration. (Activation? Sounds like something Dr. Frankenstein did to his monster.)
- You don't own the software, even though you paid for it: "Microsoft reserves all rights not expressly granted to you in this EULA. The Software is protected by copyright and other intellectual property laws and treaties. Microsoft or its suppliers own the title, copyright, and other intellectual property rights in the Software. The Software is licensed, not sold. This EULA does not grant you any rights to trademarks or service marks of Microsoft. (So it's a loan, right?)
- You may not reverse engineer, rent, lease, or lend the software. You may transfer your copy if you cease using it thereafter. (What if I have two heirs?)

15. Found at http://download.microsoft.com/download/1/2/5/12538ba0-3d24-4f00-aab1-dd9ff4aacfc9/en_client_eula.pdf.

■   You agree to allow Microsoft to collect technical data on how you use the software. (And how do they do that, with secret probes or something?)

And there's more, pages more. Microsoft's EULA is quite similar to that of other software publishers; what often comes as the greatest surprise to people is that they have not bought the software, only the right or privilege to use it, and that only so long as they respect the terms of the licensing agreement. But consider the consequences if the software was sold: Others could then modify it however they saw fit and sell a dozen, a hundred, a thousand different versions, creating just as many different versions to confuse and obfuscate the market.

---

However, once clever computer users realized they could copy the entire contents of one CD to another, software piracy became commonplace. They not only installed software on all their machines, but they let their friends do the same. Then they took their CDs to their computer club meetings and swapped copies with other members. Others started little businesses copying software and reselling it—until pirating software became an industry unto itself (see Chapter 6, *Global Fallout*).

Thus does one of the great conundrums of computing emerge: While computers become more trouble-free and easier for people to use, they also become more vulnerable to abuse and crime. In a trice, the software industry discovered there were a lot more copies of software installed than had actually been sold. Now the industry has an entire infrastructure built around lowering piracy—and of course the cost of that infrastructure is built into the price of the products, which, in a Catch-22, is an incentive to pirate even more.

Inexorably, digital convergence has made digital copying more commonplace. Consumers copied CDs to cassette tapes in the '80s, with the resultant degradation in quality from digital to analog and CD to tape, but they didn't much think about copying

CDs to CDs—until, that is, they realized they could do it on their PC. CD drives were introduced around 1990. In just eight years, PCs would have DVD drives as well. Suddenly digital convergence began drawing the personal computer system and the home entertainment system closer together. Soon, pundits crowed, the two would become one.

And they're getting there.

While the software industry was grappling with the illicit copying, music business executives began worrying themselves sick over it as well. It hadn't been such a big worry in the analog age, but now the shift to digital was making it very, very easy to make a perfect copy, and another, and another. The movie industry, having had experience with videotape copying and watching what was going on in the music industry, determined that the emerging DVD would be copy-protected from spindle to edge. To sweeten the pot, the movie industry decided to price them low, getting the DVD player makers to go along in the hope that soon everybody would be buying DVDs like crazy.[16]

It worked.

In fact, the market for DVD and VHS players now rivals the market for movie box office receipts or rentals. What's more, moviemakers have two markets for recorded movies: the rental stores and online retailers, and directly to the home.[17] Indeed, some movies that flop at the box office are wildly successful in the home viewing aftermarket. And because they are priced so low (and perhaps because video rentals are, by and large, still expen-

---

16. The movie business is also lucky. While it can only take a few minutes to download a song using MP3 compression and a dial-up modem, it can take hours to download a movie. And many downloaded movies are actually filmed by someone with a camera in a movie theater, so the quality of the downloaded movies is generally low. They're twice lucky, because it's easier to track illicit downloads that take a long time.

17. Julie Mortimer, an economist at Harvard University, has written an interesting analysis of this subject, "Price Discrimination and Copyright Law: Evidence from the Introduction of DVDs," that is well worth reading. It can be found at http://www.econ.yale.edu/seminars/apmicro/am03/mortimer-030508.pdf.

sive at an average of four bucks a pop, not counting the inevitable late fees), people simply buy them.

## MEANWHILE, BACK ON THE PC

Then along came the Internet and the World Wide Web in 1993, rattling the digital paradigm to its core. One of the earliest uses for the Internet was transferring files between computers, using a system called the File Transfer Protocol or FTP. It wasn't difficult, but it was often time-consuming. Technologies to compress files—make them smaller and more compact so that they could be uploaded and downloaded more quickly—emerged.

Today's gold standard is the MP3 file, which compresses, or shrinks, a sound or video media file to one-tenth to one-fourteenth of its original size while preserving most, but not all, of its fidelity. People began copying their CDs to their computer's hard disk, using a program to compress the tunes into MP3 files, like that shown in Figure 1–2. Now they could share the files with friends and strangers alike. Several Web services emerged to make it even easier: Bulletin boards and peer-to-peer Web sites, such as Napster, made downloading files as easy as ordering from a restaurant menu—although technically in these networks you are actually *sharing* music, since others have access to your stored songs.

The MP3 player, CD burner, and blank media market is bigger than the entire market for music CDs. Soon, DVD burners will be relatively inexpensive and commonplace in PCs as well. The entire entertainment industry is inexorably moving toward an online distribution and acquisition business model designed to satisfy a highly personalized market.

My media, in my chosen format, on whatever playback device I choose, wherever I want to enjoy it.

The record companies fought the growing P2P networks, while at the same time making desultory efforts to create their own pay versions. First, they sued the organizers and companies that ran

**Home**

### MP3 WAV Converter 2.68

When it comes to digital music, sometimes you want the compactness of MP3s, and sometimes you want the quality of a CD. MP3 WAV Converter makes it easy to have both. The program converts .wav music files to .mp3 format to reduce the size of the files by roughly a factor of 10, and it changes MP3s to .wav files for playback on standard CD players. It also doubles as an audio player, minus the fancy skins and light shows most players have these days. The program completes conversions in seconds, and you can convert and play batches of files at a time. Any .wav files converted to MP3s are automatically normalized to a consistent volume level.
MP3 to WAV Converter software works on any Windows platform.

**Screenshot**

**read comments**

**Download a free trial version. Buy it now for only $19.95.**
**Buy one Get one free**

**Figure 1–2**    Utility programs such as this one, which are either free or sell for just a few dollars, can be used to turn digital music files into MP3s. Courtesy of American Shareware Technologies, Inc. (www.americanshareware.com).

the free sites, but every time they shut one down, two more would pop up. Then, in 2003, they adopted a new strategy and launched a major offensive against *individual* digital pirates, targeting especially those who upload over 1,000 files (ostensibly all music). The price of digital piracy is high: fines up to $150,000 per song and possible jail sentences. It seems to us that paying 99 cents to download a favorite tune is a better bargain.

Still, some people think that's too expensive.

They say it ought to be free.

Well, it's free until you get caught. College students fined by the Recording Industry Association of America (RIAA) in 2003 paid anywhere from $2,500 and $17,000 in out-of-court settlements. At a buck a tune, did they have between 2,500 and 17,000 downloaded songs on their computers? Who got the better of the deal?

# THE DIGITAL BLACK MARKET

By the numbers, most digital pirates are home consumers. But there are those who make a living at it—with some now living in jail. They fuel a huge black market around the world, with their activities running the gamut from operating duplication factories in places like Paraguay and Thailand to "cracking" the latest software programs and distributing them free over obscure sites on the Internet to copying CDs on home computers, forging CD covers using laser printers, and selling the fakes in the subways of Boston, Moscow, London, and Bangkok.

We asked a Harvard graduate student friend, who had gone home to Hong Kong for Christmas 2003, to give us a firsthand view of the black market in this, one of the world's great cities:

> The place I went to was called '298 Computer Zone' in Wanchai, Hong Kong. The general layout of all these places is quite similar—it's a shop inside a computer shopping mall that is, save for a few aluminium bars on the walls acting as CD holders, completely empty inside. There are plenty of legitimate software and hardware vendors in the mall as well. When the shop opens, the seller puts numbered covers of CDs wrapped in plastic on the racks. The buyer copies down the catalog numbers of the CDs he/she is interested in purchasing onto a sheet of paper, and hands it over to the seller. After half an hour, the CDs are ready for collection. The CDs are unmarked and look like they were burned on the fly.

> The CDs for sale range from the latest versions of software to computer games. The software selection is quite extensive; aside from usual packages such as Windows XP and Adobe Photoshop, there are more specialized applications such as Matlab, Mathematica (software for scientific computing), and Finale (a professionally used music notation software). The game collection is quite up-to-date, and includes games like Star Wars Jedi Academy, Warcraft III Frozen Throne Expansion Pack, and even an

**Figure 1–3**    Software piracy is common in the high-tech marketplace in Taipei, Taiwan. Next to the brick column, two young men sell software out of a three-ring binder menu. The CDs are burned in the back of the computer shop to the left. Photo courtesy of Jack B. Rochester.

alpha-version of the unreleased Doom 3 (scheduled for release in the year 2004).

Hole-in-the-wall shops like those our friend described pepper the urban landscape around the globe (see Figure 1–3), spawn perhaps of the globalization of software, music, and entertainment. They are as common now as the Golden Arches. They are fast food for the digital millennium.

## ARE YOU A DIGITAL PIRATE?

In the final analysis, you must ask yourself: Am I, or is someone I know or love, a digital pirate? Are you, or they, okay with that? One thing is clear: It's a much more dangerous pursuit than it was a year or two ago, with real legal and financial consequences that far outweigh any cost savings or convenience if you get caught. If you're a black-market pirate, you're not only placing yourself at risk but you're undermining the economy of your country. Consider these industry loss estimates:

- The music industry estimates it loses at least over $4 billion a year—not counting Internet downloads—on revenues of $30 billion worldwide.[18]

- The movie industry estimates it lost $5 billion or more on revenues of $15 billion (box office and rentals) in 2002.[19]

- The PC software industry estimates it lost $29 billion in 2003.[20]

- The computer gaming industry estimates it lost $3 billion in 2001 (the latest figures available) on sales of $6.35 billion.[21]

Senator Everett M. Dirksen is reputed to have once said, "A billion here, a billion there, and pretty soon you're talking about real money."[22] That's money that could have gone to lower prices for media; money that could have gone for more jobs and better products; money that isn't lining the pockets of criminals and thieves. So read on. We'll lay out the playing fields, identify the players, and give you the information you need to be your own referee.

But understand what's happening. The way it's going now:

- The *war over intellectual property is corrupting youth*, turning them into scofflaws and criminals for sharing music with their friends, something that's always been a natural part of growing up. Both the music-loving public and the recording industry have legitimate rights, as well as issues.

---

18. Source: IFPI, the International Recording Industry Group, at www.ifpi.org. This is actually the street value of pirated disks. These revenues would represent at least $8 billion in list price revenues if sold legitimately.

19. Source: the Motion Picture Association of America, at www.mpaa.org and other media sources. This includes $3 billion in the U.S. and an IDC estimate of $2 billion outside the U.S.

20. Source: the Business Software Alliance, www.bsa.org.

21. Source: the Entertainment Software Association, www.theesa.org.

22. See www.bartleby.com/73/800.html.

- The challenges from those who dispute the legality and those who insist on protecting corporate profit margins at the expense of the public domain is assuredly *provoking governmental encroachment on our personal freedoms*, and as soon as Congress gets more involved in this dispute, you can be fairly well assured that we will have even fewer personal freedoms than we have now, just as we have fewer since Congress passed the Digital Millennium Copyright Act in 1998. Chapter 5, *Inside the Sausage,* is entirely devoted to understanding its meaning and ramifications.

- Digital piracy, whether it's an individual downloading tunes, movies, and software to their personal computer or the black-marketers who rage unchecked in countries such as China, Russia, Vietnam, or the Ukraine, are insidiously *damaging the world's economy* by forcing software and media companies to sustain high prices, depriving countries of a profound source of revenue and the government of legitimate business and consumer taxes, and perhaps most significantly, dispossessing individual nations and the world at large of meaningful employment.

The spectrum of digital pirates runs from Darren at one end, downloading his Coldplay tune from KaZaA, to Russian mobsters and former Colombian drug lords running CD duplicating plants because counterfeiting digital media is more profitable than running drugs. What change will they wreak upon industry, the arts, educational institutions, the economy, society, and their own souls? How do we counter nefarious behavior and yet encourage innovation and creation?

Read on. Let's see what can be done.

# 2

# IS IT COPYRIGHT
# OR THE RIGHT TO COPY?

Authors and creators deserve to receive the benefits of their creation. But when those benefits stop, what they create should fall into the public domain. It does not do so now. Every creative act reduced to a tangible medium is protected for upward of 150 years, whether or not the protection benefits the author. This work thus falls into a copyright black hole, unfree for over a century.[1]

**Stanford Law Professor Lawrence Lessig**

They're stealing all our content, sneaking it across the border at night and selling it in the streets at half the price...

The product is overpriced, inflated because the media have a government-sanctioned monopoly. We consumers shouldn't have to pay so much...

Think of the artists. This is piracy! You are depriving them of their livelihood...

Yeah, right, except the media companies have never cared about the artists. Most of them just get a flat fee and all the revenues go to the corporations...

It's absurd to think that just because you buy a copy of a work that that implies you have the right to make multiple copies of it...

But why not? Nothing was actually taken. The original (copy) still exists...

Piracy inhibits creation of new art. What's the incentive...

---

1.   Lawrence Lessig, *The Future of Ideas* (New York: Vintage Books, 2001–2002), p. 250. Lessig is a Stanford law professor and an active thinker and writer on copyright and intellectual property issues. His Web site is www.lessig.org.

No, artists will always create. Most of them realize they aren't in it for the money. The copyright system just creates inequity between those that are favored by the powerful publishers and the rest of them. In fact, it's copyright law that inhibits creation and keeps great work out of the public domain...

---

You probably imagine this is a conversation between kids down-loading Metallica songs from KaZaA, right? Or perhaps it's a graduate student at UC Berkeley justifying his pirated copy of Microsoft Office?

Nope. Actually it's paraphrased from a major court case in England, *Donaldson v. Beckett*, that took place in 1774—two years before the signing of the U.S. Declaration of Independence—and turned out to be a major milestone in copyright history. The debate centered on intellectual ownership of a now-forgotten book of poetry and the issue of whether there was a common-law precedent providing authors with a perpetual copyright on their works that they could in turn transfer to others, namely booksellers.[2]

In point of fact, as we will see later, there never was a common law relating to author's rights. It was simply a fiction created earlier by the English government to justify signing a treaty with

---

2.  The right to protect one's intellectual output is generally attributed to either of two sources: (1) the government, which will agree to enforce that protection in exchange for something (e.g., free access to libraries, creation of more work, etc.), or (2) natural law or God. The issue of whether there is a common-law right skirts the matter of the source of authority to protect intellectual output, but just assumes that somewhere along the way, it sprung up in practice. The discussion in *Donaldson v. Beckett* was all about the duration of a right to protection for a book of poetry—either for eternity or a time period set by the court. Many scholars agree there never was a common-law precedent for copyright protection (the U.S. courts affirmed this once again in 1834) and that the language was inserted into the governing copyright law at the time of *Donaldson v. Beckett* as a way to make the new law more palatable to the public.

Scotland that, in essence, stopped intellectual property piracy but also began limiting the power of the booksellers, who were getting too powerful for the Crown's taste.

While the argument in *Donaldson v. Beckett* seems to be about pirates versus authors, the outcome of the case favored neither. It favored the publishers. The judges *did* determine that an author had a perpetual copyright to a work he or she created—*but that right disappeared the minute the book was published!*

With this case, the notion that authors (and their publishers, their representatives in business) had any common-law right to their work was put to rest. Copyright emanated from the Crown, as codified in a law put into effect in 1710: the Statute of the Queen Anne, shown in Figure 2–1.[3] Here copyright remained limited to 14 years after first publication, unless the author was alive when it ran out; then another 14 years was granted.

As we shall demonstrate in this chapter, the lessons of history have taught us that copyright law is a legal sanction for a business or enterprise to make copies, usually for sale, of a work that belongs to someone—nominally the creative author or artist. It probably never was, nor ever will be, a form of legal protection for the creator, at least not in the fiduciary sense. Its true purpose is to protect the fiscal assets that accrue to the copier (publisher) of the work. Copyright law has, over its life, given ever more rights to the copier of the work without much demonstrable evidence that the artist has gained anywhere near as much, either creatively or financially. Nor does it seem that the diffusion of the ideas emanating from the work has been much enhanced. As in most aspects of creative life, the money has followed those who have figured out how to capitalize on the opportunity.

Given this circumstance, is it any wonder that intellectual property pirates have existed since the earliest civilizations? Let us tell the story of one.

---

3. Image and translation courtesy of http://www.copyrighthistory.com/anne.html.

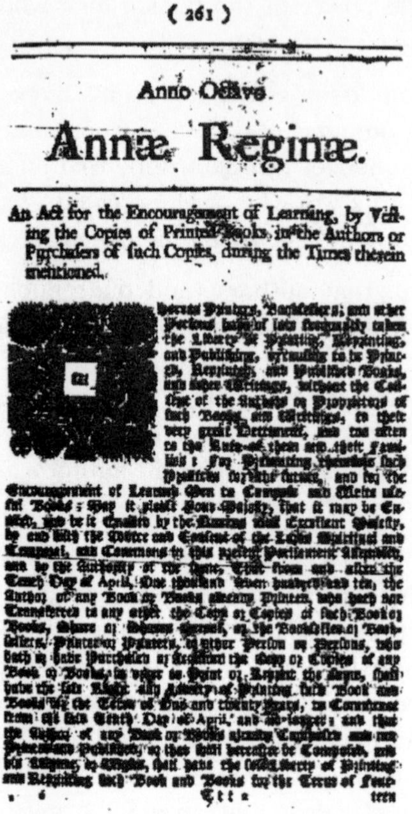

( 261 )

Anno Octavo

Annæ. Reginæ.

An Act for the Encouragement of Learning, by Vesting the Copies of Printed Books in the Authors or Purchasers of such Copies, during the Times therein mentioned.

**Anno Octavo**
**Annæ Reginæ.**

An Act for the Encouragement of Learning, by Vesting the Copies of Printed Books in the Authors or Purchasers of such Copies, during the Times therein mentioned. Whereas Printers, Booksellers, and other Persons, have of late frequently taken the Liberty of Printing, Reprinting, and Publishing, or causing to be Print-ed, Reprinted, and Published Books, and other Writings, without the Consent of the Authors or Proprietors of such Books and Writings, to their very great Detriment, and too often to the Ruin of them and their Families: For Preventing therefore such Practices for the future, and for the Encouragement of Learned Men to Compose and Write useful Books; May it please Your Majesty, that it may be Enacted, and be it Enacted by the Queens most Excellent Majesty, by and with the Advice and Consent of the Lords Spiritual and Temporal, and Commons in this present Parliament Assembled, and by the Authority of the same, That from and after the Tenth Day of April, One thousand seven hundred and ten, the Author of any Book or Books already Printed, who hath not Transferred to any other the Copy or Copies of such Book or Books, Share or Shares thereof, or the Bookseller or Booksellers, Printer or Printers, or other Person or Persons, who hath or have Purchased or Acquired the Copy or Copies of any Book or Books, in order to Print or Reprint the same, shall have the sole Right and Liberty of Printing such Book and Books for the Term of One and twenty Years, to Commence from the said Tenth Day of April, and no longer; and that the Author of any Book or Books already Composed and not Printed and Published, or that shall hereafter be Composed, and his Assignee, or Assigns, shall have the sole Liberty of Printing and Reprinting such Book and Books for the Term of fourteen…

**Figure 2–1**   The Statute of Anne, the first extant example of English-language copyright law.

# THE FIRST KNOWN COPY PIRATE

He was Irish, a monk. In 557 C.E. he traveled to a nearby monastery and copied, without permission, the Abbot's book of psalms, commonly called a Psalter (see Figure 2–2). It took him days. When the Abbot discovered a copy had been made, he demanded it back, but the monk refused. The Abbot appealed to the king, who ordered the monk to return the copy he had made. End of story.

Actually, it's not quite the end. Like all great copyright conflicts, this one is rich with intrigue. Our monk, named Columba (sometimes called Comcille), 36 at the time of the episode and an up-and-comer in Catholic Church circles and a future saint, had already established three of his own monasteries, which he was continually stocking with illuminated manuscripts and other works of religious literature. The Abbot's copy would have made a nice addition to his collection at the monastery at Durrow, about 100 miles southwest of what is now Dublin (and actually on the road to Tipperary).

The Abbot in question (Finnian of Moville, also a future saint), by the way, was one of Columba's former mentors and witness to one of the miracles by which Columba became a saint (a water-into-wine gimmick). Not only that, but there was already bad blood

**Figure 2–2** A page from a Psalter, or Psalm book, c. 1200. Copying a Psalter was the first recorded act of media piracy. Many books, especially secular ones, were illustrated and thus termed illuminated manuscripts. Source: Collection of the Cathedral Library, Esztergom, Hungary, courtesy of the Web Gallery of Art, http://gallery.euroweb.hu/html/zgothic/miniatur/1200-250/06e_1200.html.

between Columba and the king (Diarmait), since the latter had recently killed one of Columba's relatives while he had been under Columba's protection.

In his ruling against Columba, King Diarmait said: "Le gach bain a bainin, le gach leabhar a leabhrán," or "To every cow its calf, to every book, its copy."[4]

It gets better. After Diarmait's decree, Columba refused to return Finnian's book, and instead was part of a rebel uprising from the north. In the ensuing battle, Diarmait was ultimately killed, along with 3,000 others, in what is now known as The Battle of Cooldrumman. Shortly afterwards, Columba left Ireland—whether of his own volition or at the behest of the Church is not known—to build a monastery at Iona, Scotland, where he would try to covert at least 3,000 new souls to Christendom to replace the ones lost at Cooldrumman. He did. In fact, he blew well past the 3,000 mark and converted much of what is now northern Scotland to Catholicism.

Our first pirate, though, was also an author. Columba wrote over 300 books, at least a few of which survive to this day, before he died in Scotland in 597. And pirate though he was, Columba is nevertheless the patron saint of bookbinders. No surprise, he has his own postage stamp (see Figure 2–3). In his "Prayer for Ireland," he talks of respecting rights, especially those of the weak. Could he have been talking of artists and authors?

## A Prayer for Ireland, written by St. Columba

> May prosperity never cause Irish men and women
> to forget God or abandon their faith.
> Lord, help us to work together
> with a sense of Christian purpose
> and a common Christian goal.

---

4.   Mary L. Mulvihill, *Ingenious Ireland: A County-by-County Exploration of the Mysteries and Marvels of the Ingenious Irish* (London: Simon & Schuster UK, 2003), p. 150.

**Figure 2–3**    St. Columba commemorative postage stamp.

> Let us build a just, peaceful,
> and loving society where the rights of all,
> especially the weak, are respected.[5]

# THE FIRST COPYRIGHT

It was called a *copye*, created in 1476, the year that William Caxton first brought the moveable type printing press to England. That year the Crown, realizing the immense opportunity that the printing press gave authors wishing to publish tracts inimical to its interest, passed a law requiring all printers to inscribe their names and locations, and the titles of all works they wished to print in a government register. If approved, the printer received authorization to make a copye. Any rights that came with it, by the way, belonged to the printer, not the author. Copyright began as a method for the government to control content.

That's the way it remained for 80 years. In fact, during those years, the Crown issued successively stricter rules against "copying," or creating multiple copies of written work, in order to strengthen censorship.

---

5.    Image and poem courtesy www.augustinians.ie/orlagh, page St. Columba's Well.

In 1557, the next seminal date in our copyright saga, Queen Mary (Tudor) chartered the Royal Stationers Company of London, which gave a 150-year old guild of bookbinders, engravers, book sellers, and printers a government-sanctioned monopoly on publishing. All books had to be published by the Stationers, as the association of printers and booksellers came to be called, and the company set prices, determined which members could sell which kind of book to which market, and set up an exchange for trading "copyrights." (Typically authors sold their work to printers for a flat fee; any rights, royalties, or extra sales went to the latter.)

Queen Mary, of course, didn't set up the Royal Stationers Company to make printers rich. It was a horse trade that gave printers a monopoly, but gave the Queen the means to control what was published in England, which at the time was fending off the religious incursion of the Protestant reformation.

## THE SCOTTISH PIRATES

In 1695, the licensing acts that provided prepublication censorship to the government expired as Parliament, which had toppled James II in 1689 and taken over the business of governing, let older monarch-controlled monopolies lapse.

The Stationers cartel continued to divvy up markets and respect each other's copyrights, but once the licensing acts expired, piracy sprouted. Scotland, although ruled by the same monarch, had no copyright law. Therefore, books published in England would be copied in Scotland and resold in England at a fraction of the price charged by the Stationers. At the same time, independent authors could have their books printed in Scotland if they couldn't get them picked up by the Stationers. By targeting successful works, the bootleggers could avoid payments to editors and authors, marketing costs, and the risks of publishing unknown works. (Scotland, you might recall, was the final resting place of our first beloved book pirate, Columba!)

The chaos lasted 15 years, from 1695 to 1710, when England finally brokered a deal with Scotland over copyright protection.

As if in support of those who fight intellectual property piracy today, very few new works were published during the heyday of Scottish bootlegging.

England, at this time, wanted Scotland as a haven against potential attacks from the French and for support against uprisings from those endeavoring to put James Stuart, the Old Pretender and son of King James II, on the throne. For its part, Scotland wanted trade with England and a share of the book business. The result was a treaty and the previously mentioned Statute of Anne, which established a governmental copyright system. The public relations puff suggested that it was intended to eliminate the monopoly of the book trade (as well as the Royal Stationers Company), set up a copyright system that included Scotland, and encourage the production of new works.

But it was, at heart, a practical act. It grandfathered existing Stationers copyrights for 21 years and granted new works 14 years of protection, with an option to extend another 14 years. This was not a bad trade-off for the publishers in an environment where monopolies were increasingly under attack, and it was surely better than going out of business at the hands of the Scots. Yes, the statute recognized the author as holder of the initial copyright— one of the lobbying points the Royal Stationer's Company and the Queen had used to get support for the act—but in practice the copyright became that of the publisher upon first publication, a practice that continues to this day in many areas of publishing.

## COPYRIGHT AS POLITICS AND BUSINESS

Are you picking up on a theme here? From the first copyright act of 1476 to the ruling in *Donaldson v. Beckett* three centuries later, copyright was primarily about business, ownership of intellectual content, and political maneuvering. It never really concerned itself much with authors' rights to control the dissemination of their intellectual property or to benefit financially from their published work. Furthermore, since the passage of the Statute of Anne over two centuries ago, it's been more and more of the same.

You don't need to know all the gruesome details of the history of copyright in the Western World. But if you're going to make sense of today's controversies, it helps to see the progression and understand the distinction between copyright and the right to copy.

Is the Recording Industry Association of America (RIAA) *that* much different from yesteryear's Royal Stationers Company? Are the software counterfeiters of China much different from the Scottish book bootleggers of 1700? Are authors who received a flat fee from their printers in Shakespeare's time much different from today's musicians who get royalties on their music only after promotion costs, marketing costs, printing costs, and innumerable administrative fees are deducted from revenues? Table 2–1, at the end of the chapter, offers up a smorgasbord of political shenanigans behind the history of copyright law.

The progression is not pretty, nor is it pure. But it *is* a progression. After a millennium and a half, it is a little easier for those who create intellectual work to reap some financial rewards from that work. A *little*.

## 100 YEARS OF AMERICAN PIRACY

A year after the Constitution was penned, Congress exercised the authority it was given to "promote the progress of science and the useful arts" and created the Copyright Act of 1790.

Once that was in place, the new nation began immediately...pirating!

The Copyright Act of 1790 protected only U.S. citizens, not foreign authors or publishers. Since the Statute of Anne described earlier, England (or more accurately, Great Britain) had had reciprocal copyright agreements with other countries, and by the time of the Copyright Act of 1790, all the countries of the Western world with the exception of Russia, the Ottoman

Empire, and the United States respected the works of foreign authors and publishers.

In the early days of the new country, there was a lot more literature written in Britain than in the U.S., and the newly liberated American public still looked to Britain as the source of its culture. Without a reciprocal agreement with Great Britain, U.S. booksellers could obtain copies of popular works by authors like Sir Walter Scott, Charles Dickens, and Thomas Hardy, re-typeset them back in the U.S., and sell them for much less than the original, imported works. Moreover, they had neither the bother of sending money back to Britain to pay authors' royalties nor the risk of publishing books that weren't already bestsellers.

For example, in 1843 a copy of Charles Dickens' *A Christmas Carol,* which sold for $2.50 in London, could be purchased in the new world for six cents,[6] not a farthing of which went to Mr. Dickens.

British authors petitioned the U.S. Congress to change the laws, and no less a personage than statesman Henry Clay, known as "The Great Pacificator," argued on their behalf for decades, but to no avail. The printers and booksellers opposed such bills, citing potential loss of jobs, negative impact on the U.S. economy, and the impact higher prices would have on growing U.S. literacy.

U.S. authors were no happier than their British counterparts. Popular authors like Washington Irving, Mark Twain, Harriet Beecher Stowe, and James Russell Lowell found their books selling like hotcakes in Canada and Britain, without them ever seeing a penny's worth of royalties. They also found that their U.S. sales were compromised by the low price of pirated British books. Their pleadings with Congress had the same affect as had the British authors'—*nada*. The argument put forth by the publishers and the printers—that cheap books for the American public were worth more than protecting the income of a handful of American

6. Source: Harry Hillman Chartrand, writing for the *Journal of Arts Management, Law & Society*, Vol. 30, No. 3, Fall 2000 (www.culturaleconomics.atfree-web.com). Chartrand is an expert on copyright law, economics, and history, He is a publisher as well as lecturer at the University of Saskatchewan in Canada.

authors (or, even worse, *British* authors), many of whom seemed to be making a good enough living—held sway.

It wasn't until the industry began to change that publishers began to pressure Congress for international copyright protection. It happened like this. For the first 85 years after the Copyright Act of 1790, most books in the U.S. were published out of New York or Boston by publishers who had an informal agreement: Out of courtesy, none would publish books of the same British author as another. The publishers could thus sell the books cheaper than their British counterparts, but still buoy up prices enough to make a profit. Some even paid a little money to the British authors, but this was purely a gratuity.

In 1874, however, this pleasant "courtesy" system was rent asunder by a Chicago publishing firm with a new marketing idea: selling the great books of Europe in a set to U.S. households seeking a little intellectual or social status. The first set, the *Lakeside Library* (Chicago, remember?), was published by the firm of Donnelly, Gassett, and Lloyd. Bought as part of a set, a single book might cost 10 cents. Forget exclusivity. By 1880, there were 14 different "libraries," containing hundreds of book titles, available to Americans. The books were often printed on poor quality paper and with cheaper bindings than those sold in the East, but the words were the same.

Faced with competition from these upstarts, the Eastern publishers began supporting the idea of international copyright, since they would have a competitive edge over their enemies in Chicago through their established relations with English authors. They also started a price war amongst themselves, created their *own* libraries, and, in general, broke ranks at lightning speed.

Actual passage of an international copyright law couldn't take place until the big Eastern printers unions fell into line. For years they had lobbied Congress against an international copyright on the grounds that U.S. jobs in the printing industry would be lost. But the low-price publishers in the 1870s and 1880s had learned to cut costs by printing in cities with weak or nonexistent unions and by hiring women, who would work for a fraction of the wages paid to men. In other words, the jobs being protected by the lack of international copyright were no longer those of union members. By 1888, the printers, authors, and publishers were finally all aligned in favor of international copyright. The International Copyright Act, passed in 1891, offered copyright protection for books published outside the U.S. (although not books written by U.S. citizens and published outside the U.S.—a ruling that allowed the government to restrict imports of Henry Miller's notorious novels, *Tropic of Cancer* and *Tropic of Capricorn,* in the 1950s!).

Thus ended a century of government-sanctioned book piracy in the U.S. The new country's reign of book piracy lasted almost 10 times as long as the runner-up, Scotland.

## THE QUINTESSENTIAL AMERICAN PIRATE

With a lifespan that almost fit within the 100-year-span of American book piracy, Mark Twain (the *nom de plume* for Samuel Langhorne Clemens), embodied much of the conflict of the day over copyright and intellectual property rights.

Come to think of it, he embodied much of the *current* conflict.

As an author, Mark Twain saw firsthand the effects of a lack of reciprocal copyright protection with other countries. In 1876, *The Adventures of Tom Sawyer* sold for $2.75 by subscription in the U.S., but could be purchased in Canada for as low as 50 cents.[7] Yet a competing book from the U.K., Sir Walter Scott's *Ivanhoe,* could be had for 10 cents. When Twain went on his well-attended and profitable speaking tours abroad, he found fame and fans, but no book income. Twain understood firsthand the risks taken by printers and booksellers; he himself lost a small fortune

---

7.  Source material on Mark Twain is from Siva Vaidhyanathan's excellent book, *Copyrights and Copywrongs* (New York: New York University Press, 2001). The book discusses the history of copyright, especially in context of the three-way dynamics between publishers, writers and artists, and the public, and includes extensive discussion of Twain as a copyright advocate.

in 1891 investing in a new invention for automatic typesetting that didn't pan out (he eventually went bankrupt in 1894).

Early in his writing career, Twain was happy just to get books published and earn a little money from them. The existing system worked. But as he gained in popularity and an appreciation for the finer things of life, he became a more vocal proponent of expanding copyright laws. In 1875, Twain began writing articles in favor of international copyright for the *Atlantic Monthly* and gathering other authors to his side. He became a lifelong proponent of extending the length of copyright protection.

However, when the Eastern establishment's courtesy system collapsed and book prices fell through the floor, Twain took a hiatus from his position. In 1880, in a letter to William Dean Howells, his editor at the *Atlantic Monthly* magazine, Twain pointed out how cheaply he himself could now buy books: *Chambers Cyclopedia*, in 15 cloth-bound volumes, now cost $7.25, works for which he had previously paid $60. He saw value for the public in the availability of cheap, pirated books:

> I can buy a lot of the great copyright classics, in paper, at 3 cents to 30 cents apiece. These things must find their way into the very kitchens and hovels of the country. A generation of this sort of thing ought to make this the most intelligent and most best read nation in the world.[8]

He closed his letter saying he had decided he was now against any international copyright treaty.

> Morally this is all wrong—governmentally it is all right; for it is the *duty* of governments—and families—to be selfish and look out simply for their own. International copyright would benefit a few authors, and a lot of American publishers, and be a profound detriment to 20,000,000 Americans; it would

---

8.    Victor Doyno, *Writing Huck Finn: Mark Twain's Creative Process* (Philadelphia: University of Pennsylvania Press, 1991), as found in *Copyright and Copywrong*, Siva Vaidhyanathan, New York University Press, 2001.

benefit a dozen American authors a few dollars a year, & there an end.[9]

But Twain's 20,000,000 Americans let him down. Instead of buying the classics, the public bought what Twain thought were cheap and tawdry novels, most of which glorified the English way of life.

> They fill the imagination with an unhealthy fascination with foreign life, with its dukes and earls and kings, its fuss and feathers, its graceful immoralities, its sugar-coated injustices and oppressions.[10]

Twain soon realized those English potboilers competed with his books as well, and by 1886 he had reversed his position again. He was quite happy when an international copyright law was finally put into effect in 1891. From then on he remained a copyright advocate, chiefly in attempts to make the protection period longer.

Mark Twain was representative of another dilemma caused by copyright. Many of his stories and books borrowed from the oral tradition of slaves and other countrymen. In 1874, he published a story in *Atlantic Monthly* called "A True Story, Repeated Word for Word as I Heard It." It was the account of Mary Ann Cord, the cook at his family's Quarry Farm, and a former slave. Twain's rendering of dialect in this story became his hallmark, and the genesis of his later work, *The Adventures of Huckleberry Finn* (see Figure 2–4).

When Cord's tale was published in the *Atlantic Monthly*, it was already copyrighted in Mark Twain's name. But whose work was it, Twain's or Cord's? It was her story, in her own words. He had simply written it down.

According to copyright law at the time, it was Twain's. Since the Statute of Anne, copyright was always deemed to protect the

---

9. Vaidhyanathan, p. 60.
10. Ibid., p. 61.

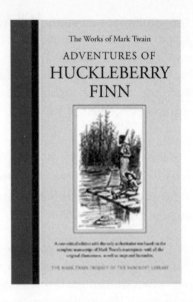

**Figure 2–4**   In 2003, the Mark Twain Project at the University of California, Berkeley, published the definitive edition of this classic book, with 665 pages from the original manuscript that had gone missing and were only discovered in 1990, as well as all the original illustrations by Edward Windsor Kemble. Twain's storytelling pulled from others before him. Was he a pirate? Source: www.ucpress.edu/books/pages/10015.html.

*expression* of ideas, not the ideas themselves. This tenet would later be challenged by new forms of media, especially movies, but it totally held sway at the time. To reward his accurate transcription, Twain was paid the highest amount the magazine had ever paid an author for a story.

It's unknown if he gave any of his earnings from the story to Cord.

## THE IDEA OF COPYRIGHTING IDEAS

Mark Twain's use of Mary Ann Cord's story, as well as other material he borrowed during his career, gets to two questions that have been part of the copyright saga since 557 C.E.:

■ Isn't all art derivative? Since Homer's time, haven't storytellers (and later, writers and artists, and for that matter, movie directors and computer game software developers) always built on one another's ideas? Didn't Monet learn from Cézanne? Hemingway from Turgenev? Quentin Tarantino from Godard?

▪ If it isn't all right to copy an entire work, how about a paragraph? Maybe just word or two? Sixteen bars...a few notes. The drum riff?

As a reflection of the first conundrum, copyright law, at least from 1710 to 1870, made a big distinction between *ideas* and *expressions*. You could protect the expression of an idea in a book, musical piece, engraving, or drawing, but you weren't permitted a monopoly on the idea itself.

Listen to the lawyer Sir John Dalrymple arguing for his client in *Donaldson v. Beckett* back in 1774:

> If I copy a manuscript and publish it, I am liable to civil action. If I steal a book, to a criminal one; the one is simply taking ideas, the other a chattel. But what property can a man have in ideas? Whilst he keeps them to himself they are his own, when he publishes them that are his no longer. If I take water from the ocean it is mine, if I pour it back it is mine no longer.[11]

In a letter to Helen Keller in 1903, Twain made it clear how often authors and creators took water from this common ocean:

> When a great orator makes a great speech you are listening to ten centuries and ten thousand men—but we call it his speech. It takes a thousand men to invent a telegraph, or a steam engine, or a phonograph, or a photograph, or a telephone, or any other important thing—and the last man gets the credit and we forget the others.[12]

---

11.  All quotes from *Donaldson v. Beckett* are excerpted from a transcript entitled "Proceedings in the Lords on the Question of Literary Property, February 4 through February 22, 1774" available on www.copyrighthistory.com, the Web site for an unpublished book, *The History of Copyright: A Critical Overview with Source Texts in Five Languages*, by Karl-Erik Tallmo.

12.  Vaidhyanathan, p. 65.

The separation of ideas from expression was affirmed in a lawsuit in 1853 involving Harriet Beecher Stowe's novel *Uncle Tom's Cabin*. A German publisher had translated the book into German and begun selling it in the States. The judge found against Stowe, arguing that the translated text was a significantly different expression of the ideas found in the English-language work, and therefore copyright protection didn't apply. The judge added an aside, "I have seen a literal translation of Burns' poems into French prose; but to call it a copy of the original would be as ridiculous as the translation itself.[13]

To us, in this day and age, when even genes and seeds can be patented and software or dance routines copyrighted, this idea may seem illogical. Yet any literary critic will tell you that foreign language translations differ—often greatly. Translators may translate the original author's words into images, ideas into facts, metaphors into images, and so on. Thus translations have their own copyright, distinct from the original work, as do new editions and versions of previously copyrighted work, *because the form of expression has changed*.

But is a copyrighted work property? And if so, whose? The elusiveness of the term *property* when applied to intellectual output has been debated for centuries, including by the country's founding fathers.[14] Thomas Jefferson himself, musing on the subject years after the Copyright Act of 1790, wrote in 1813:

> If nature has made any one thing less susceptible than all others of exclusive property, it is the action of a thinking power called an idea, which an individual may exclusively possess as

---

13. Ibid., p. 49.
14. Coupling the two words "intellectual" and "property" into one phrase, "intellectual property," however, was not common until the creation of the World Trade Organization and the World Intellectual Property Organization in the 1990s. Since then, it has come into common usage to the extent that it colors discussions of the nature of copyright and patents. The historical record and case law (see Table 2–1, The Political History of Copyright) would classify protections of intellectual output as a government-granted monopoly; the public to some extent, and publishers for sure, would now classify it as an inalienable human right.

long as he keeps it to himself; but the moment it is divulged, it forces itself into the possession of everyone, and the reader cannot dispose himself of it.[15]

Jefferson also pointed out one of the semantic difficulties in using the word *property* in conjunction with intellectual output by pointing out that, unlike with real property, taking an idea doesn't deprive the original owner of it. "He who receives an idea from me, receives instruction himself without lessening mine; as he who lights his taper at mine, receives light without darkening me."[16] Jefferson was always a little afraid that monopolists would extend or twist copyright to the protection of ideas, not just expressions.

Alas, this separation of church and state—between ideas and expressions—has muddied since *Stowe v. Thomas*. That case actually galvanized the growing cadre of American writers who were beginning to win international acclaim (including, of course, Twain) to start lobbying Congress for more copyright protection for themselves—especially since the courts weren't going to provide it. Less than 20 years later, in a revision to the copyright law in 1870, Congress added translations and dramatic adaptations to authors' copyright.

But what really breached the Chinese wall between idea and expression were motion pictures. Just 25 years after the 1870 law was enacted, Thomas Edison started selling what was called a *kinetoscope*, which strung a series of photographs together and allowed a single viewer to see a short movie. Within a year, European competitors had developed a projecting version of the kinetoscope. The movie business was up and running.

After years of debate about whether a movie should or could be copyrighted as a series of photographs, and if a movie could violate a book's copyright, in 1912 Congress amended the Copyright Act of 1909 to cover movies. In part, they were influenced by a

---

15. Vaidhyanathan, p. 23.
16. Ibid., p. 25.

1911 Supreme Court decision delivered by Oliver Wendell Holmes over the movie *Ben-Hur*.

The case centered on two versions of the movie—one written by a stage production firm that had acquired the dramatization rights from the author, General Lew Wallace, prior to his death, and the other a version by a company that had hired a screenwriter to read the book and write a treatment. Neither firm knew of the other at the time of the writing.

Justice Holmes opined that a movie could—and this one did—violate the original copyright owner's dramatization rights.

Since then, the erosion of that separation between ideas and expressions has become a full-fledged mudslide. The concept that a digital image of a book, song, picture, or movie could be copyrighted—like a reflection in a mirror—would surely have driven Jefferson nuts.

But then, our country's founders never anticipated the photocopier, the VCR, the computer, the CD burner, or the Internet, all of which give reality to Memorex's dream that you can't tell the digital reflection from the original. Even so, Jefferson's worst fears seem to have been realized by those who, in their capitalistic voraciousness, have sought ever wider interpretations of copyright law—or amendments to it when that failed. Even as *Donaldson v. Beckett* determined that an author lost the right to the expression of an idea once a work was published, so did authors in the 20th century relinquish their intellectual property claim to the publishing and media houses to whom they granted the publication or reproduction rights.

## A BORROWER BE: UNDERSTANDING FAIR USE

The other issue raised by Twain's retelling of Mary Ann Cord's story is the question of how much can be taken, borrowed, or lifted from a work before a violation of copyright takes place.

In the U.S., a key case, *Folsom v. Marsh*, took place in 1841. Folsom had published a multivolume collection of George Washington's letters; Marsh had republished 350 pages of them in an 866-page book.

The judge found for Folsom and against Marsh's prodigious excerption; thus began the concept of *fair use*. Through case law, then the Copyright Act of 1976, and once again through case law, the concept of fair use has been tested over and over. The Copyright Act of 1976 codified the concept, including the right to copy whole works for the purpose of criticism, comment, news reporting, teaching (making it possible for schools to copy copyrighted books and other published materials for class), scholarship, and research (see Chapter 1, *Are You a Digital Pirate?* for a discussion of fair use). Subsequent cases have ruled:

■ School districts cannot videotape entire educational programs shown on TV for reuse in the classroom (*Encyclopedia Britannica Educational Corp. v. Crooks*).

■ One author excerpting another's without permission can be fair use if it was not too egregious—in this particular case, it was 4.3 percent of the plaintiff author's work (*Maxtone-Graham v. Burtchaell*).

■ Quoting or paraphrasing from unpublished materials, in this case letters, in an unauthorized biography is not fair use (*Salinger v. Random House*).

■ Employees of a for-profit company copying whole articles out of scientific journals does not constitute fair use (*American Geophysical Union v. Texaco*).

■ It is fair use to copy a TV show onto a video tape for personal viewing (*Sony v. Universal Studios*).

■ It was fair use for Josiah Thompson to use a sketch of frame 237 of the Abraham Zapruder film of President Kennedy's assassination in his book *Six Seconds in Dallas*.

Fair use case law is constantly being reexamined. The bounds of fair use for parody have been tested by as varied a mix as Jack Benny, Groucho Marx, *Mad* Magazine, and 2 Live Crew. Music sampling—using bits and pieces from others' songs—violates copyright and has been challenged by the likes of George Harrison, Vanilla Ice, Yoko Ono, and about a million rappers. The singer John Fogerty was once sued for sampling his own music. He used some guitar chords on the song "The Old Man Down The Road," from the 1985 album *Centerfield*, that were similar to those he'd used in "Run Through the Jungle," which he recorded with Creedence Clearwater Revival in 1968—the rights to which belonged to a former publisher. After hearing hours of Fogerty singing and playing on the witness stand, a jury found in his favor.

More recently, humorist Al Franken was challenged in court by Fox News for using what Fox said was a trademarked term, "fair and balanced" (purportedly referring to the network's news coverage), as part of the title of his new book. On the heels of the lawsuit, Franken's book, *Lies and the Lying Liars Who Tell Them: A Fair and Balanced Look at the Right*, shot to number one on the bestseller list—even before it was published. U.S. District Judge Denny Chin, after listening to about half an hour of oral arguments, said the lawsuit was "wholly without merit, both factually and legally."[17]

In general, though, the rules seem to be getting tighter and the rulings more conservative. A case in 1991 featured a nearly forgotten rapper who had used eight bars of the Gilbert O'Sullivan song "Alone Again." After hearing the arguments, the courts took a practice that was common in the industry and descended from the time-honored musical tradition of building on another's work, and shot it down. The rapper, Biz Markie, had taken 20 seconds of music and looped it over and over again as background for his song—a song that clearly wasn't going to confuse listeners with the original or impinge on O'Sullivan's market for "Alone Again." The judge ruled against the rapper (his record company, Warner Brothers, chose to settle rather than appeal), saying in the process, "The defendants…would have us believe that stealing is rampant in the music business, and, for that reason, their conduct here should be excused. The conduct of the defendants herein, however, violates not only the Seventh Commandment

---

17. CNN, http://www.cnn.com/2003/LAW/08/22/fox.franken/.

(Thou Shalt Not Steal), but also the copyright laws of this country."[18]

## THE EXPANDING UNIVERSE

Since the Copyright Act of 1870, the courts and Congress have been steadily expanding the works that can be protected by copyright as well as the duration of copyright. When the Founding Fathers established the copyright laws in 1790, the principle was to afford the author copyright protection for a length of time, then let the work pass into the public domain. This, they felt, would serve to seed the creative landscape for newer creative works.

Copyright protection that once lasted 14 years and could be renewed for another 14 now lasts the author's lifetime—plus 70 years. Walt Disney's Mickey Mouse character will be 108 years old when the copyright runs out, unless Congress extends it again. Walt only lived 65 years. Works copyrighted today won't come into the public domain for four or five generations.

Where books were once protected, now movies, TV shows, recorded music, photographs, engravings, dramatic performances, unpublished material, dance choreographies, software, boat hull designs, Mickey Mouse telephones, and the trash basket on the Apple Mac desktop are protected. (For more details, see Table 2–1, The Political History of Copyright.)

This expansion has led to some weird situations—all proof that intellectual property protection is a seething cauldron, often sluiced with absurdity. Besides the time that John Fogerty was sued over the use of his own work, consider:

■ The cable TV companies in the 1980s that got to rebroadcast TV signals from the networks without paying royalties (because they didn't actually take possession of the content).

---

18. Vaidhyanathan, p. 142.

- The year (2000) that the Martha Graham Dance Company couldn't perform her works because the Martha Graham Trust wouldn't license the performances.

- Eugene O'Neill's daughter, Oona, disinherited by her father, who nevertheless gained control of the copyrights that came up for renewal after his death; the same for the children of William Saroyan, despite the fact that he willed his rights to a charitable foundation.

- The compulsory licensing laws for music that allowed the Beatles to sell more copies of "Twist and Shout" than the Isley Brothers without paying royalties, or Manfred Mann more than the Shirelles with "Sha-La-La."

- The rules that don't allow purchase and subsequent rental of music productions or computer software, but allow them for movies.

## THE MUSIC INDUSTRY'S WOES

It's the beginning of a new century. The music industry is in a panic! For years, it had been wildly profitable—some would say because of monopolistic practices and collusion. But a new technology has come along, pirates are using it to make songs available to the public for—pardon the expression—a song, and the public seems to have no compunction about bypassing legal channels. Legislators and law enforcement officials can't be bothered. The industry mounts a lobbying campaign trying to convince the public that pirating jeopardizes the livelihood of musicians and working class technicians, but the entreaties fall on deaf ears. The "man" is whining.

Does this sound familiar, like KaZaA, the music downloaders and the RIAA?

Nope, we're talking about London sheet music publishing a hundred years ago.

Adrian Johns, an associate professor of History at the University of Chicago, described the situation in an article in *Dædalus*.[19] A handful of sheet music publishers controlled the market at the time and were able to keep prices high by acting in concert. But along came a revolutionary technology—photolithography—that permitted the flawless copying of intricate sheet music scores. Simultaneously a hardware revolution took place: Pianos became cheap enough for the average middle-class homeowner to buy. A social phenomenon ensued. Everyone wanted a little culture near the hearth; piano sales soared. And they all needed music.

The first sheet music pirates set up operations in homes and warehouses, and sold their music on the streets or through word-of-mouth marketing channels. The public snapped up the cheaper copies.

The industry responded first by lobbying the government for more laws and then hounding the police for protection. But in early 20th century England, a man's home was still his castle, and the authorities balked at chasing pirates back into their living rooms on behalf of an unlikable set of music publishers. Eventually, the music publishers took matters into their own hands and established squads—often composed of ex-police—to conduct unofficial raids on the pirates. Rough tactics prevailed.

Eventually the industry was heard in the courts—some of the pirates had been flagrant—but in the meantime the business had changed. The publishers had to lower prices, open up markets, and welcome some of their former pirating competitors into the business when they went legit.

At first, the entrenched publishers hadn't understood the new phenomenon. Then, they fought it in the courts and lobbied their position with the government, and when stymied, took more direct action

---

19.  Adrian Johns, "Pop Music Pirate Hunters," *Dædalus*, Spring 2002, published by the American Academy of Arts and Sciences.

on their own. Finally, they adjusted their business model, lowered prices, and suffered themselves to compete in a new market with new competitors. The public shed nary a tear.

---

# WHERE ARE WE TODAY?

Without a doubt, copyright and copyright laws are difficult to understand and probably even more difficult to interpret. Yet the clear trend throughout the recorded history we have presented in this chapter has been to move away from protecting the creators' rights to their own intellectual property and toward granting more rights to the property owners.

Some say that, given the progression of 20<sup>th</sup>-century copyright legislation, we are really right back where we started with *Donaldson v. Beckett*. To a vast majority of music-loving, Internet-savvy citizens, the RIAA, whose six members control 70 percent of the music business, or the MPAA (Motion Picture Association of America), or the BSA (Business Software Alliance, backed in large part by Microsoft) are the evil equivalent of The Royal Stationers Company, and the U.S. Congress is as politically culpable and commercially corruptible as the Crown in the 1700s. Moreover, for all the talk of the creator's right to protection for his or her works, most copyrights are held by publishers still, just as they have been for some 400 years.

Are writers, musicians, artists, dancers, photographers, and even boat hull designers better off than they were 400 years ago? Surely. Just ask the writers, musicians, artists, dancers, photographers, and boat hull designers in places like Malaysia, Taiwan, and China—where bootlegging movies, music, and software is a way of life—whether they would like more or less copyright protection.

But the one group from which we hear the least is the public, a constituency whose rights and privileges received much forethought by the founding fathers of the U.S. Indeed, it was for the public that the Constitution gave Congress the right to grant copyrights. The founding fathers' concerns were about encouraging the creation and dissemination of knowledge, not about creating a system that would make a megastar out of a Britney Spears, an Arnold Schwarzenegger, or a John Grisham, and a megacorporation out of a Disney, an America Online (AOL/Time Warner), or a Bertelsmann.

Take a moment to carefully consider the monumental dynamic tension that the clash between intellectual property and digital piracy has engendered between:

■ The public's right to access knowledge and art, and the artists' and publishers' right to rewards from the time and money they have invested.

■ The pace of technology and the pace of legislative change.

■ The technology vendors (who make, for instance, DVD or MP3 players) and the media content owners.

■ The established players and newcomers, whether recording companies or artists.

This dynamic tension has swung back and forth over the center of gravity for intellectual property like a pendulum for the last 400 years. In many ways, the tautness between these conflicting and competing forces has become more like playing the electronic game Pong than a swinging pendulum. The Newtonian principle of gravity states that the pendulum, when stilled, rests dead center, yet from the current perspective, it seems there is a permanent and increasing tilt in the direction of those who own, but have not created, copyrighted intellectual property.

Everyone will agree in principle that change is good—for people, for institutions, for life. But even so, it is humankind's nature that in the face of inevitable change, we find it difficult. Often we absolutely resist, even when we know change is good for us. Consider this: At one swing of the pendulum, the citizenry wants the music industry to change, to embrace the new venue for acquiring tunes. Another swing and the citizenry is asked to pay a small fee for downloading songs, at which it balks. Another swing is toward the music industry, swearing that every downloader is a thief and ought to be punished by fines, jail, or both. Swing the pendulum again and once the 99 cents a tune is rolling in, all illegalities are forgotten.

It's a new millennium. Things *have* changed. Professor Lessig says in his book *The Future of Ideas* that technology is moving so rapidly that business methods and models, as well as policy, simply have to move more rapidly as well. Those things need to change. Lessig also wants to see that "the space for innovation remains open and that the resources for innovation remain free." [20] That's something that shouldn't change. It's important to understand the concept of copyright and its application to intellectual property, because it has a powerful and direct bearing on many aspects of your increasingly technology-driven life. Suddenly, in this new digital millennium, it has become possible to commit serious, punishable offenses with what was once viewed as an innocuous, personal, and pleasurable experience with various forms of published media. Should this trend continue and spill over into other aspects of our rights of personal expression and freedom, it is likely we will lose more of both. [21]

As we follow our digital pirates forward in the chapters to come, let's welcome change and keep this truth from the philosopher George Santayana in mind: "Those who cannot remember the past are condemned to repeat it." [22]

---

20. Lessig, p. 261.
21. See *Lost Liberties: Ashcroft and the Assault on Personal Freedom*, Cynthia Rosen ed. (New York: The New Press, 2004).
22. *The Columbia World of Quotations* (New York: Columbia University Press, 1996). See http://www.bartleby.com/66/29/48129.html.

**TABLE 2–1**  The Political History of Copyright

| Date | Event | Outcome | Political or Business Motivation |
|------|-------|---------|--------------------------------|
| 557 | Columba copies Finnian's Psalter to use in his own monastery. | King Diarmait orders him to return the copy to Finnian. | There was previous bad blood between Columba and Diarmait; after the ruling, Columba supports an uprising in which Diarmait is killed. |
| 1456 | Gutenberg invents the printing press. | Control of content moves from religious houses and individual authors or their patrons to owners of printing presses (which were scarce and expensive). | The printing press creates a radical change in the price of making copies and in their quality, and shifts financial rewards from publishing to printers from authors (such as there were). |
| 1476 | First English copyright law | Printers have to register what books or pamphlets they produce. | The Crown wants to prevent the distribution of information unfavorable to the government and to obtain revenues from selling licenses. |
| 1557 | Company of Stationers of London incorporated under Queen Mary | A long-time printer's guild gets royal sanction for an official monopoly on printing and begins controlling prices and distribution via a system of Stationers' Copyrights that could be bought, sold, or traded. Copyrights were perpetual (lasting for eternity). | A Catholic monarchy gains additional control of content through prior censorship (the register) from a guild/company headed by a Roman Catholic. |
| 1624 | Statute of Monopolies | Parliament abolishes guilds and assumes the responsibility of regulation in their market areas—the Stationers Company excepted. | The Statute helps erode the power of the Crown (and increases that of Parliament) as the Crown makes money selling monopoly rights; now Parliament assumes the mantle of censor. |

**TABLE 2–1**    The Political History of Copyright  (Continued)

| Date | Event | Outcome | Political or Business Motivation |
|---|---|---|---|
| 1695 | Lapse of the licensing acts | Parliament lets the last of the licensing acts which governed the rights of publication lapse, essentially abolishing prepublication censorship. However, under no copyright constraint, booksellers and printers in Scotland retypeset popular books from England and resell them at a lower price. | Under pressure from vocal intellectuals such as John Milton and John Locke, Parliament lets the licensing acts lapse, but in practice nothing changes. The Stationers Company becomes a cartel, copyrights remain with publishers, and authors sell their material to the Stationers Company members for a flat fee. The increasing piracy from Scotland seems to be an unintended consequence. |
| 1710 | Statute of Queen Anne | A new copyright law is created to prevent future bookseller monopolies, granting some rights to authors, and encouraging production of more work. | The Queen brokers the treaty with Scotland, giving them some of the book trade in return for coming under the copyright law, and to ensure support against potential invasions from France or an uprising of Jacobites; the Stationers Company trades some market control for the ability to continue as a monopoly. |
| 1769 | Millar v. Taylor | In a challenge to the Statute of Queen Anne, Taylor reprints a book published by Millar after the copyright runs out. Millar sues, claiming a perpetual copyright under common law. | The court finds for Millar and for the first time asserts copyright under common law, clearly a promonopoly, probusiness, pro-Stationers' Company ruling. |

**TABLE 2–1** The Political History of Copyright (Continued)

| Date | Event | Outcome | Political or Business Motivation |
|------|-------|---------|----------------------------------|
| 1774 | Donaldson v. Beckett | A Scottish printer republishes the same book involved in Millar v. Taylor, challenging the ruling of Millar v. Taylor. | This case goes to the full House of Lords, which is less inclined to support the Stationers Company monopoly and more inclined to assert the power of government. Donaldson wins, and copyright is determined to be a state-granted right or license, not a right given to authors by God. |
| 1787 | U.S. Constitution | Article 1, Section 8 gives Congress the power to promote "science and the useful arts" through laws protecting intellectual property, but for limited time only. | This is a compromise between promoting business (the exclusive rights), a position favored by James Madison, and guarding against the power of monopolies, a position favored by Thomas Jefferson. |
| 1790 | U.S. Copyright Act | Act puts into law the intent of the Constitution and extends copyright to maps and charts. The term length is 14 years, renewable for another 14, for a total of 28. | As a descendent of the Statute of Anne, U.S. copyright still favors publishers over authors. |
| 1802 | Extension to the Copyright Act | Adds designs, engravings, etchings, and prints to copyright protection. | Allows U.S. artists and engravers to make prints of classic works of art and resell them in the U.S. under copyright protection; encourages the distribution of cheaper European art in the States. |

**TABLE 2–1** The Political History of Copyright (Continued)

| Date | Event | Outcome | Political or Business Motivation |
|---|---|---|---|
| 1804 | Napoleonic Code | Codifies post-French Revolution rule for business, including copyright. Introduces the concept of "moral rights" for authors. | Splits author's rights into (1) economic rights and (2) moral rights. The former could be sold, licensed, etc. while the latter gives the author rights beyond the sale of economic rights in how the work can be displayed, edited, resold, etc. |
| 1831 | Extension to the Copyright Act | Coverage for sheet music is added and the copyright period extended another 14 years (total of 42). | Longer period of copyright favors owners (mostly publishers). |
| 1834 | Wheaton v. Peters | Peters wants to publish a condensed version of his predecessor's reports, recordings, and notes of court proceedings, Wheaton sues. The court finds for Peters because Wheaton hadn't filed the right paperwork. | In this decision the court establishes that the U.S. recognizes no "common law" rights for authors and that copyright is a monopoly granted by the state. |
| 1841 | Folsom v. Marsh | Marsh republishes as excerpts 350 pages of a collection of George Washington's letters first published by Folsom; the courts find for Folsom. | Establishes that there is a right to "fair use" of another's work—but that taking 350 pages verbatim is not fair use. |
| 1853 | Stowe v. Thomas | A German publisher translates Harriet Beecher Stowe's *Uncle Tom's Cabin* into German and sells it in the U.S.; Stowe sues, but the courts find for Thomas. | Although this keeps intact the idea that you can copyright expressions of ideas, but not the ideas themselves, it galvanizes American authors into pressuring Congress to add foreign translation to the copyright laws in 1870. |
| 1856 | Extension to the Copyright Act | Right of performance of dramatic works. | |

**TABLE 2–1**  The Political History of Copyright  (Continued)

| Date | Event | Outcome | Political or Business Motivation |
|------|-------|---------|-------------------------------|
| 1865 | Extension to the Copyright Act | Photographs. | |
| 1870 | Copyright Act of 1870 | Paintings, statues, fine arts, and translations are included. Codifies that U.S. copyright is a right granted by the state, not a right by natural law. | Puts into law the concept established in Wheaton that no common law right to copyright exists. |
| 1886 | Berne Convention | Extends copyright to authors outside the country of origin. Eventually offers protection of life plus 75 years, but also promotes concept of author's "moral rights." | U.S. doesn't sign, preferring the shorter copyright span of the Copyright Act because of the freedom from author control of derivative or follow-on works. |
| 1891 | International Copyright Act (Chace Act) | Copyright granted to non-U.S. citizens if reciprocated. | Eastern publishers and printers finally support authors with Congress to protect business from lower-price Midwestern publishers. |
| 1909 | Copyright Act of 1909 | First time all copyright laws are put into one bill. First sale doctrine codified. Also allows corporate copyright and work for hire. Extends copyright to 28 years, renewable for another 28, for a total of 56. | Helps newspapers and later motion picture companies to get copyright protection, giving them the rights of persons. Also establishes rules for when authors are "work for hire" employees. This is the first time companies get the same rights as people. |
| 1912 | Extension of Copyright Act | Gives copyright coverage to motion pictures after years of lawsuits under the 1870 Act. | Blurs the separation of copyright protection for "expression" not "ideas." Even a "treatment" could be copyrighted. Screenwriters become employees and contract workers. |

**TABLE 2–1** The Political History of Copyright (Continued)

| Date | Event | Outcome | Political or Business Motivation |
|---|---|---|---|
| 1955 | Universal Copyright Convention | Substitutes for signing the Berne Convention and covers only 28 years of protection (for foreign authors selling books in the U.S.). | Enables the U.S. to offer minimal protection of foreign works without signing onto all the conditions of the Berne Convention. |
| 1976 | Copyright Act of 1976 | Extends copyright to life of author plus 50 years; for anonymous works for hire, 75 years from publication, 100 years from year of creation. | Sets the stage for signing the Berne Convention later and makes it easier for the U.S. to have reciprocal copyright agreements—important since the U.S. is not a net exporter of content. |
| 1984 | Betamax case | Universal Studios and Disney sue Sony, maker of the Betamax video tape recorder. The case begins in 1979 with a ruling that home taping was "fair use," then is reversed on appeal in 1981 and reversed again in 1984 by a 5–4 majority of the Supreme Court. | Public opinion was largely against the concept (jokes about "video police"), and experts thought enforcement would be difficult. Many countries, however, impose a tax on VCRs and blank tapes and pay the proceeds to the movie industry. |
| 1988 | U.S. signs Berne Convention. | Extends U.S. copyright to life plus 50 years. | U.S. signs in order to extend international copyright to life plus 70 years without major debate. Mickey Mouse is 60 years old at the time. |

**TABLE 2–1** The Political History of Copyright (Continued)

| Date | Event | Outcome | Political or Business Motivation |
|------|-------|---------|-------------------------------|
| 1998 | Sonny Bono Copyright Term Extension Act | Extends the copyright coverage to life plus 70 years, mirroring many countries that are signatories to the Berne Convention. | Gives U.S. publishers and authors reciprocal rights for those countries that also have 70-year copyrights; the Disney Corporation, whose copyright on Mickey Mouse in the cartoon Steamboat Willy is set to expire in 2003, spearheads lobbying Congress. |
| 1998 | Digital Millennium Copyright Act | The DMCA amends the Copyright Act by outlawing the use of techniques to prevent unauthorized copying and penalties for circumventing those techniques. | The law mandates that hardware manufacturers build machines capable of recognizing copyright protection systems and sets the content industry against the MP3, VCR, CDR, and DVR industries. |

# US AGAINST THEM?

We're dealing with an industry where an unspoken strategy
is that the killer app (software application) is piracy.[1]

**Michael Eisner, CEO and former chairman of Disney**

Were the manufacturers of the printing press forced to protect the monks?[2]

**Andy Grove, CEO and founder of Intel**

The fundamental hypocrisy of the music industry (and of some artists) in the current
debate over the MP3 4mat, Napster and other 4ms of online xchange of music is that
they're talking about copyright, intellectual property and other such noble concepts
when the only thing that they're actually trying to protect is the commercial value of
their musical "product."[3]

**Prince, the artist**

Overhead, picture-perfect cumulus puffs float in the light breeze. The mother
of the bride lays to rest one of 756 worries about the day: the weather has
cooperated. The bridal party leaves the bower and steps out into the dappled
sunlight. Guests commence circulating around the hors d'oeuvres and

---

1. Quoted in Devin Leonard, "This Is War," *Fortune*, May 27, 2002. Eisner was testifying in support of a bill introduced by Sen. Fritz Hollings that would have the
government require technology companies to build protection against piracy into
their equipment.
2. Ibid. Grove was replying to the same issue as was Eisner.
3. Prince, "4 The Love of Music," posted on his Web site in 2000 after he changed
his name back to Prince (from the unpronounceable symbol he had used since
1993). He wrote in defense of the music-sharing service Napster.

sipping glasses of Mondavi Reserve. A deejay has set up his equipment in the party tent, and half a dozen large loudspeakers are blowing happy tunes all over the place. You wander over and take a look at his gear; wow, there's hardly anything here! You recall wedding deejays of a few years ago who lugged big trunks full of turntables, CD players, and hundreds of vinyl and plastic platters to play. This guy has a laptop computer, a mixer board and an amplifier. That's it. When you ask him about it, he tells you he has about 3,000 MP3s on the laptop and a cool software program that lets him arrange them into a playlist. If a wedding guest asks him to play something, he searches for it and can slip it right in to play next.

As you're marveling at this robust and compact technological development, you hear a loud, sudden commotion, followed by a collective gasp from nearby guests.

It's *Them*!

You crane your neck and see four men in black jackets racing toward the party tent. One stops to say something to a man in a tux whom you recognize as the father of the bride. The man in the black jacket hands him a piece of paper, and as he does so, you see the back of his jacket. There are four large white letters: RIAA. The other three men have surrounded the deejay; one is reading him his rights, and the others are confiscating his computer. It's the Men in Black—but not the Will Smith and Tommy Lee Jones kind.

---

Far-fetched? Well, technologically this vignette is au courant and, given the current state of downloaders-versus-the-music-industry, such black-jacketed enforcement is not beyond the bounds of credulity. Nor would it be out of step with history, as we saw in our last chapter.

But the scenario is too simplistic, too *Us* versus *Them*. Read further and you'll see that sometimes we are them, while at other times, they are us. To make matters even harder to understand, the factions in this war over intellectual property often come at one another from the flanks as well as from the front. You need a scorecard to keep track of the players and some color commentary to describe their strategies and positions. It's game time. Let's get to it.

This deejay, by the way, has broken two laws: one, downloading copyrighted music he did not pay for, and two, using that music in public performance without paying royalties for the right to do so.

And of course the Recording Industry Association of America (RIAA) doesn't really run around in flak jackets confiscating computers and interrupting weddings, but it has taken a tough stance against those it perceives have violated the copyrights of its members. The subpoenas the RIAA began issuing in the fall of 2003 were the most public manifestations of the war between the music industry and its customers.

This spectacularly well-covered confrontation—it was practically a media event—painted the music industry as *Them* with a capital "T." The single most covered subpoena was that issued to 12-year-old Brianna LaHara, a Manhattan honor student who would have had to scratch up $150,000 for each of the 1,000+ songs she'd downloaded if the RIAA hadn't been willing to settle with her Mom for $2,000. (For more on this, see Chapter 8, *Eliot Ness or Keystone Kops?*.)

But the music industry has looked out for itself on other intellectual property fronts for years. Consider:

■ Two men entered the Wilde-Meyer art gallery in Scottsdale, Arizona, and told the owner that she would have to stop playing the radio for background music.[4]

■ Restaurant waitstaffs are breaking the law if they sing "Happy Birthday" to customers. The song is under copyright, and singing it in a public venue such as a restaurant is technically a public performance, meaning a royalty should be paid to ASCAP.[5] The tune was written in 1893, and the lyrics first

---

4. Personal interview with author Rochester, 2002.
5. The American Society of Composers, Authors, and Performers.

appeared in print in 1924 and were first copyrighted in 1934. The copyright, now owned by Time Warner, brings in $2 million a year. As of now, the song won't enter the public domain until 2030.

- College radio stations, once the greatest U.S. venue for introducing new groups (and where we first heard Smashing Pumpkins), have been told they must pay play fees, just as their commercial counterparts do. In most cases the funds aren't there, and the stations have resorted to playing "independent" local groups—perhaps not an entirely bad thing (think of the indie movement in the film industry) but the stifling of a legitimate venue for listening to new music nevertheless. Consider: Has *this* had an impact on CD sales?

- In 1996, ASCAP informed summer camps in the U.S. that many songs commonly sung around the campfire—songs like Woody Guthrie's "This Land Is Your Land," Bob Dylan's "Blowin' in the Wind," and Irving Berlin's "God Bless America"—were copyrighted material for which royalties should be paid. Although ASCAP was willing to settle for a blanket royalty fee as low as $257 for some camps (and as high as $1,500), the society backed off after a summer of bad press, saying such "public performances" were okay if they weren't for commercial gain.

While the music industry starred in our little wedding vignette, it's not the only content industry confronting its own customers over copyrights. The computer software industry disrupts business for the companies for whom it obtains court authorization to audit. Customers at preview screenings of blockbuster movies aren't happy about having their pockets emptied in search of little camcorders.

## IF WE ARE US, WHO IS THEM?

Upon the bounding main in the 1700s, it wasn't always easy to tell the pirates from the good guys. The pirates didn't always fly the Jolly Roger, and the King's navy might plunder just as much as those they brought to justice. To the English, Sir Francis Drake was a gentleman and commissioned "privateer," but to the Spanish, he was a ruthless pirate. Jean Lafitte ran a 10-boat pirating concession out of Louisiana and sold his stolen goods to the upper crust of New Orleans. William Dampier augmented his pirate booty with fees for speaking and writing in London. Henry Morgan, the "King of Pirates," operated out of Jamaica for years until he was finally caught and thrown into a British jail—then he was released by Charles II, knighted, and made governor of Jamaica.

Who is *Us* and who is *Them*?

Upon the bounding *digital* main, the question still applies. Are we the public? Are we the same public that America's founding fathers felt so strongly needed easy, inexpensive access to knowledge? Are we the content creators for whom intellectual property laws offer the opportunity for recompense for our work? Are we the customers who pay the cost of the monopoly granted by the government to copyright and patent holders? Are we the 45 million investors in the companies being ripped off by downloaders?

Just exactly who is *Us* and who is *Them*? Was Pogo right when he said, "We have met the enemy... and he is us"?[6]

At least we can tell you who some of the players are. Let's assume for the sake of argument that the *Us* in our equation includes (intentional or not) unauthorized music, movie, game, and software downloaders, copiers of CDs, corporate misusers of software licenses, software and content counterfeiters, distributors and resellers of material obtained in violation of intellectual property laws, and probably everybody who uses KaZaA to download.[7]

Now we need a *Them*. There are several camps. In fact, there are as many camps as parties in an Italian election. Those with the

6.  The quote comes from Walt Kelly's immortal comic strip, *Pogo*. See http://
www.igopogo.com/we_have_met.htm, for full details of the quote's exact origin.
7.  It's usually more accurate to use the term *file-sharing* than *downloading*, since
services such as KaZaA are designed so that you can partake of files from other
computers, while other users of the service can partake of files from yours. We're
all sharing files. We use both terms in this book, although not interchangeably.

highest degree of "themness" would probably be the trade associations and lobbying groups that, through powers of attorney granted by their members, actually go after "us." Call them Camp A. They include:

- The RIAA, which lists 1,000 labels as backers but whose top five members—BMG, EMI, Sony, Universal Music, and Warner Brothers—make up 75 percent of the recorded music industry. They all now have their own music downloading sites, use KaZaA themselves to track downloaders (and for that effort are under suit for violating KaZaA's licensing agreements), and use statistics on music downloading over KaZaA to fine-tune their marketing strategies.

- The Motion Picture Association of America (MPAA), run until spring 2004 by former studio head Jack Valenti, a one-time bomber pilot and aide to President Johnson, which represents all the major studios. The MPAA is a lobbying group as well as a support group for law enforcement.

- The BSA, an association of companies from Adobe Systems to Symantec, which makes its money from member donations, software license-infraction fines, and court awards from successful lawsuits. The BSA is as concerned about software licensing violations as it is about outright piracy.

Camp B might be considered the content vendors, chief among them Disney, Sony, and Microsoft, which have the lobbying and business clout to drive their respective trade associations as well as their own lobbying and enforcement divisions. Disney, you will remember, made over $600 million in 2003 with its tribute-to-piracy film, *Pirates of the Caribbean,* starring the roguish and lovable Johnny Depp. Sony once got busted for making up reviews for its movies from a fake reviewer at a real newspaper (does that violate intellectual property rights?) and makes more money selling audio equipment (like MP3 Players) than it does selling recorded music. Microsoft is constantly embroiled in lawsuits brought by companies like Apple Computer and Sun Microsystems alleging copyright and patent infringement.

Of course, as we know from childhood, not all campers get along. In 2003 the British Broadcasting Company (BBC) announced it planned to put all—that's right, all—of its archived TV shows and movies online for free downloading as a service to the public (which, in Britain, is also its owners). This sent shockwaves through the other major worldwide TV networks, none of whom want to compete with free BBC stuff. Most network executives are hoping the BBC conversion of film and broadcast video will go slowly enough that they will be retired by the time all this content hits the beach.

Then there's Camp C. Let's call them the technology providers, both hardware and software. These include all those makers of MP3 players, media playing software, CD burners, memory sticks, wireless networks, broadband Internet systems, cable descramblers, satellite dishes, home networks, peer-to-peer file-sharing software, video cards, PC speakers, and CD label-making software. Camp C includes Microsoft, Apple, AOL, and Sony, who are members of Camps A and B as well. See? Many of them are both *Them* and the *Enemies of Them* at the same time.

The Camp D slot we might as well give to the Internet Service Providers (ISPs) who play a middleman role for Camps A through C and the pirates. They sell Internet access and services, which means they covet subscribers and are loath to irritate them. They have therefore fought to keep errant subscribers' names out of the hands of Camps A and B, but the courts and Congress have pushed them into becoming snitches—although case law swings back and forth on how assiduously they have to comply with Camp A and B subpoenas (more on how this works in Chapter 8, *Eliot Ness or Keystone Kops?*). These are reluctant *Thems*.

Are we done, you ask? Oh, no. Camp E we will assign to the politicians and courts—those arbiters of modern life who always seem to find the messiest ways to deal with any rapid technological change. Congress, you may remember, actually named a major extension to the Copyright Act of 1976 after Sonny Bono, the guy who's only claim to fame was that he sang "I Got You, Babe," with Cher back in the 1960s (see Chapter 5, *Inside the*

| Camp | Who | What |
|------|-----|------|
| **A** | Media trade associations and lobbyists such as BSA, MPAA, RIAA | Influencing legislation and enforcing copyright laws; represent Camp B |
| **B** | Bertelsmann, Disney, Sony, Microsoft | Create media content; hires Camp A; often at odds with Camp C |
| **C** | AOL, Apple, Microsoft, Pioneer, Sony | Provide the hardware and software to play the media; often the same players as Camp B |
| **D** | Internet Service Providers, college networks | The connectivity between pirates and media; often persecuted by Camps A and B for providing essentially a passive service |
| **E** | Government and courts | Role is to be fair and balanced, but almost always tips toward more powerful and moneyed interests of Camp A |
| **F** | Critics | Earnest complainers and freedom fighters for the interests of free or unfettered media rights for Camp G |
| **G** | Us | The intended beneficiaries of intellectual property, over whose rights to use the battle is being fought |

**Figure 3–1**   A schematic of the camps.

*Sausage: The Making of the Digital Millennium Copyright Act).* They are supposed to be an *Us*, but seem to be a *Them* more often than not. Many feel this is because the government is inordinately influenced by the media companies, which also control the newspapers and TV stations, but it would be cynical of us to agree with this view. We simply think individual legislators have sold out to their various vested-interest constituencies.

Which brings us to the cynics who populate Camp F: the critics. These are the academics, pundits, gadflies, and anticopyright Web site purveyors, and the inevitable gaggle of journalists, bloggers, and adze-grinding attorneys and consultants, each of whom is more than able to find fault with the current trend toward increasing intellectual property protections. Their solutions, when prescribed, are often impractical and lopsided to the point of ludicrousness. But then, in a way, that's the job of the gadfly. You got *Us's* and *Thems* all over the place here.

The last camp is Camp G, specifically mentioned in the United States Constitution as the intended beneficiary of what intellectual property protections the government offers: us, the American public. Our only voice in the matter may be our elected representatives or the dollars we vote with in the market—unless you consider illegally downloading media an act of civil disobedience. We may not know for certain how assiduously the former are looking out for us, but what else is new?

There are other players as well, from the customs officials who bust counterfeiters to the venture capitalists who bankrolled Napster and KaZaA, from the hackers who find ways around software protection algorithms to the software developers who sweat for years to produce a single feature in a software application only to see it sell for pennies in the piracy bazaars. It includes musicians who deplore illegal downloading, and it includes musicians who perceive it as one of the finest marketing mechanisms. It includes the widows and orphans who own shares in the funds that own Disney and Microsoft and the widows and orphans who are downloaders.

So, have you got the message? We are *Us*, but we are also *Them*.

## WHAT'S A LITTLE RIP, MIX, BURN AMONG FRIENDS?

Although Camps A through C represent the strongest coalition against the pirating *"Us,"* they sometimes exhibit the internal strife of a coalition of Afghan warlords. One small example: In May 2003, the BSA, the Computer Systems Policy Project, and the RIAA made a joint statement against forcing the consumer electronics industry to bake anticopyright into computer and entertainment hardware. This was a way to show solidarity with the camp selling the technology that makes their customers want more music and software (but also makes it easier to pirate—go figure).

The MPAA, however, just couldn't go along. Its client, the motion picture industry, preferred to lobby for just that—protection mandated in hardware to prevent DVD copying—first before Congress and then, when that failed, to the Federal Communication Commission (FCC). Without that protection, the industry was cool to the idea of committing high-definition content to either broadcast or optical media—they felt it was just too easy to pirate. This created a chicken-and-egg situation for the adoption of high-definition television (HDTV) in the U.S., which the FCC is trying to promote. No high-definition content, no HDTVs sold. No HDTVs, no reason for high-definition content.[8]

But this little difference of opinion between members of Camp A is nothing compared to the apple fights, night raids, and outhouse tippings between the entertainment companies in Camp B and the technology companies in Camp C.

Both camps have the same customers: us, the consumers. Both want us to buy—the key word here being *buy*—their products. But the most sought-after features in Camp C products are the ones that allow customers to *avoid* buying Camp B's products. Conversely, if Camp C's hardware products don't find a market, who needs Camp B's media? So they need each other. They're wedded to each other. But it's a fractious, squabbling, dish-throwing marriage.

Napster provided a sense of urgency—and hearings before Congress on the broadcast flag issue the forum—but the lightning rod for the conflict might have been Apple Computer's 2001 ad campaign around the slogan, "rip, mix, burn."

The ad (see Figure 3–2) was created by Chiat-Day, the same agency that created Apple's famous Orwellian TV commercial broadcast during the 1984 Super Bowl to introduce the Macintosh personal computer. The "rip, mix, burn" slogan instantly hit an entertainment industry hot spot. Although the term "rip"

---

8.  In this case, the industry prevailed. In November, 2003, the FCC mandated a "broadcast flag" be built into HDTV tuners as of July 2005. See Table 10–1, Knights on White Horses, in Chapter 10, *Through the Fog: The Future of Intellectual Property.*

Rip. Mix. Burn.
The new iMac.
With iTunes + CD-RW drive.

**Figure 3–2** Innocence or intemperance? For a while, Apple marketing encouraged people to use the Mac's software and CD-making capabilities to personalize their music collections. It did not make the music industry happy, and the campaign was withdrawn, domestically at least.

technically means convert from another medium,[9] the entertainment industry interpreted it as an invitation to "rip off" the music industry. In testifying before Congress in the winter of 2002, Michael Eisner, former CEO of Disney, used the phrase as an example of how the technology industry is deliberately aiding and abetting piracy.

As much as Steven Jobs fumed later that Eisner didn't know what the term meant, it *is* true that a lot more music was being downloaded illegally than legally.

But the technology industry, Camp B, didn't like being portrayed as the arms merchants of the copyright wars and countered. Andy Grove, CEO and founder of Intel, has pointed out that the entertainment industry fought video rentals tooth and nail and now gets

9. The term was first used in image processing, when designers used raster image processing (RIP) to create digital bitmaps of images. The processing smoothed low-resolution images, and such images were said to be "ripped." This technique was called ripping. The term now generally refers to the process of reading analog CD (such as .wav or .cda) files and converting to digital (.mp3) files.

50 percent of its revenues from them. This chapter's opening quotes give the flavor of the discourse in 2002 about the subject.

Camp C thinks Camp B is a bunch of dinosaurs, Camp B thinks Camp C is a bunch of flesh-eating raptors.

To get a feeling for the nature of this *interfamilia* fisticuffs, just follow what's happened to copy protection on DVDs.

- When DVD players first came out in 1997, they had "region" codes on them that prevented DVDs from other regions from playing on them. This was to help prevent piracy. Users quickly discovered ways around the codes.

- In 1999, the new Region Code Enhancement came out. This offered tighter protection, but it also prevented some legitimate disks from playing. The technically adept once again figured a way around the codes, and eventually the full decryption algorithm was put onto the Net by a teenager.

- In 2000, a new rule put the onus for checking on region codes on the hardware, not the software. Hackers couldn't get at them. But a hardware company came out with a Chinese-made DVD player that let users turn off copy protection.

- The industry pressured the hardware company to drop the line, but in November 2002 a company called 321 Studios offered a program that bypasses regional lockouts and piracy protection. 321 Studios boldly sued nine entertainment companies for the right to distribute the software before they could retaliate. At the end of 2003, the case was still in the courts and had metastasized to other countries amid a blizzard of countersuits.

And so it goes. As we saw, the entertainment industry got its broadcast flag, and Camps B and C are once again playing nice with one another. But will it last? The continual advance of broadband communications, PC-based media centers, and wireless in the home would make us think not. There will always be some of *Them* willing to help *Us* against other *Thems*.

# MUSIC IS THE SOUL...OF PIRACY

If you go by the numbers and continue with our classification of the Camps and of the pirating public as *Us*, then there are more of *Us* than *Them*. This is why the issue of music "sharing" has become so interesting—sharing over peer-to-peer networks went from a few thousand hackers sharing software and PC games over obscure Internet bulletin boards and chat rooms to over 60,000,000 people worldwide in a matter of two years. Thank you, Napster; thank you, MP3. A background geek activity became a social movement, a mass movement, a society-altering movement.

Scott Dinsdale, an executive vice president of the MPAA, summed up the entertainment industry's prevailing view of public media-sharing at the Consumer Electronics Show in 2002 when he said, "The ability to share programming was one thing when it was limited to two or three friends, but now it's a million friends."[10]

Ah, but is "one thing" a legal thing, an ethical thing, or a business thing? Was it okay for a few people to share a song but not a million? As we saw in Chapter 1, *Are You a Digital Pirate?*, copying and sharing are as old as humankind; it's just that our ways of doing these things have evolved with time and technology. The Internet has stretched our concept of the meaning of "fair use," which was designed for less ubiquitous and greatly more controllable media, beyond recognition. And since we're asking you that question, what are your thoughts on these three scenarios?

1. If a little bit of copying and sharing is legal, but a lot isn't, doesn't that agree with the downloaders? Isn't it just the definition of "a lot" that's in question? And are we also making a clear distinction between an act that is *illegal* and an act that's just *unethical*?
2. One of the foundations of case law is intent; is it the file-sharer's first and true *intention* to distribute a file to millions of friends, or is that simply a by-product of downloading a copy for their own personal use?

---

10. See http://www.contentworld.com/newsdigest/061103_feature_article2_2.html.

3.  What would happen if a national resolution were put on the ballot for the voting public to decide whether or not downloading media from the Internet for personal use was legal?[11]

Unfortunately, unless it is modified subsequent to this writing, the DMCA precludes such sharing and even gives media companies the right to hunt down copyright violators. As we'll see in Chapter 5, *Inside the Sausage: The Making of the Digital Millennium Copyright Act,* the DMCA and its enforcement has helped exacerbate a me-versus-them antagonism in this country. Europe and the Far East, on the other hand, have yet to take the matter as seriously as the U.S. The European Union has expressed distaste for the U.S.'s legislate-and-prosecute-first-and-ask-questions-later mentality.

The antagonism has been particularly strong with music file-sharing. Software we need to do our work. Movies we usually only watch once or, at best, a few times. But music is a highly personal experience. We can listen to the same song a dozen or a thousand times in the course of our lives. Music crosses every boundary known to people. It is one of the most available and expressive art forms. Lester Thurow, the world-renowned economist, even refers to it as the world's oldest profession—claiming roaming musicians were paid for their work in times more ancient than those in which sex for hire appeared.[12]

Ever since the days of underground FM rock and the advent of the compact cassette, music-lovers have been putting their favorite songs together into a unique personal concert. When that personal concert is shared with others, it becomes a form of communication—indeed, communion. Many feel this kind of communication has been taken away from us by those who

---

11.  In fact, we know the answer to that. In the fall of 2003, IDC conducted a survey for us of over 900 respondents from over 30 countries, and we asked just that question: Who felt that downloading music over the Internet ought to be legal? The answer was pretty clear: everybody. The data are shown in Figure 9–3 in Chapter 9, *Angel on My Shoulder: What's in It for Me?* Survey respondents, by the way, were predominately adult and college graduates, not just teens.

12.  Interview with author Gantz, September 2003.

regard music as a business—the record labels and increasingly monopolistic radio networks.

It's inconceivable that the music industry will ever be able to stop the illegal downloading of music files on the Internet. The music industry executives and their lobbyist, the RIAA, know this. In a ludicrous reversal of the Biblical story, Goliath is flinging pebbles at 60 million or more Davids, hoping to instill enough fear to curtail their downloading. But it won't work, especially with youth. Isn't it their sacred duty, practically a biological imperative, to thwart the restrictions placed on them by adults? To stir up the pot, make messes? Did Shawn Fanning, creator of Napster, set out to create an environment in which 3 billion songs are downloaded a month, or was he just trying to find a new way to share music with his dorm mates? And will a generation with the most permissive parents in history stop downloading because a bunch of media fat cats say they shouldn't?

In a sense, the massification of digital media downloading is delivering on the promise of the Founding Fathers' copyright legislation to return media to the *public domain*. Think about it: The Internet is causing widespread massification of *everything* informational, from telephone numbers to jokes to news and entertainment and, yes, even porn. Sometimes the course of events has its own impetus. As the entertainment industry strives to extend the length of copyright ownership and tighten its grip on fair use, the public retaliates by taking back the digital night.

## A PIRATE'S ARGUMENT

In the summer and fall of 2003, starting before the RIAA launched its infamous first wave of 261 copyright-violation lawsuits, we conducted focus groups with graduating high school seniors and college students. (See Chapter 7, *Dude, Where's My MP3?*, for more information on this particular age group of digital pirates.) We polled on attitudes and behavior regarding music, movie, game, and software downloading.

The polls were illuminating, since they mirrored arguments we'd seen in trade journals, Electronic Frontier Foundation (EFF) positions, and academic papers on piracy—just phrased them in teen lingo.

But to tell the truth, in subsequent discussions with older people—parents, colleagues, and business people—we heard the same prodownloading arguments.

They go like this:

*Pirating isn't so bad.* In the focus groups, we asked about the connotation of the word pirate and learned that for many of the kids the picaresque image of Johnny Depp in Disney's *Pirates of the Caribbean* came to mind. Pirates don't really steal, and digital piracy is more like "obtaining" than stealing.

At the same time, in our discussions at IDC with BSA marketing types, we learned that there are similar attitudes in some countries among adults that make using the term "piracy" to mean unauthorized use of software problematic. Pirating is more roguish than evil. Pirating is a lesser form of stealing. This is not a view shared by the BSA, of course.

*The album is an outmoded form factor.* In the focus groups, the kids told us that the real beauty of burning CDs or listening to music on their PC is that they can personalize their listening experience, creating a mix like radio stations or jukeboxes, but with their own song choices. The ease of creating personalized mixes with the new technology just diminishes the value proposition of the CD album. Tough luck, RIAA. For young people, the days of buying CDs are pretty much over. As one of the kids said, "We missed the CD generation. By the time we had our licenses and were driving around, spending our money on things like gas and cheeseburgers, Napster had been invented and we all had MP3 players."

Many of those running record stores agree. Mike Dreese, co-owner of the fabulously successful Newbury Comics chain of New England media stores, has been convinced of this fact for several years. He's branched out into DVDs and a range of other media-related paraphernalia and says, "In five years, you'll be very hard pressed to find an environment that looks like a Strawberries or a Tower [Records] or a Newbury Comics." Dreese says we will get music by "burning it onto your TiVo, through your satellite radio, or through a wireless hand-held device."[13]

He may be right. Tower Records, the company that invented the mega record store, went bankrupt in early 2004. It had launched a $110 million expansion drive in 1998, but started declining from its peak of 200 stores in 2001. But Tower is in good company. HMV shuttered stores in New York and Boston in 2003, as did Sam Goody's, and Best Buy gave away its Musicland subsidiary in 2003 to a buyer that would pick up the costs of its leases and debt. The record store is another endangered form factor, along with the CD.

*Products are overpriced and sold by greedy megacorporations.* The focus group students felt that the price of a CD—most cost $14–$17—is just too high when they only want to listen to a few of the songs on it. Instead of buying it, you ask around, find a friend who has it, borrow it, and copy the songs you want onto your computer. Or, even easier, download it. The cool thing is to burn your mixes on a CD to play in the car or on a Walkman. The cost differential of 50:1 is nice, too. A blank CD only costs about 30 cents. Added value stuff, like liner notes and cover art, isn't worth the difference.

So kids know the economics as well as adults. What they may not know is that over the last half decade, the music industry has actually produced fewer CDs, while at the same time raising prices. Even before Napster's debut in 1999, the music industry was raising prices (about $2 a CD from 1997 to 2000), and since then it has been releasing fewer CDs (down 14 percent from 1999 to 2002). This is grist for the mill of those who blame the record industry, not pirates, for falling CD sales.

Yes, in 2003 the music industry began lowering prices—Universal went first—but even a 30 percent discount, which some of the

---

13. "Encounter: Mike Dreese," *The Boston Sunday Globe Magazine*, February 23, 2003, p. 4.

new prices represented, didn't hack it for a public that thinks if it's on the Internet, it's free, and if you buy a CD, you still pay for a lot of cuts you don't care for.

*Downloading isn't the problem.* There are plenty of articles on the self-inflicted nature of the record industry slump. Indeed, in a study in 2002, Forrester Research proclaimed that "contrary to protests from record labels, piracy is not responsible for the 15 percent drop in music sales in the past two years,"[14] although in its 2003 update Forrester pointed out that in part to combat piracy, "music and movie companies will embrace legitimate downloading and streaming services."[15]

Large industries are slow to embrace change; the telephone companies let the Internet get away, the post office is *not* your email provider, and Polaroid missed out on digital photography. As Michael Wolff, author of *Autumn of the Moguls*, a book about the men who created today's media giants, says in a column written in the fall of 2003, "All industries instinctively try to defend themselves from obsolescence—usually at the point when they are already obsolete."[16]

But even if the record industry slump is *entirely* self-inflicted, does that really change the ethics of downloading copyrighted material?

Jonathan Zittrain, professor of Internet law at Harvard, is one who questions suing individual downloaders. He sees the music industry behaving with mercenary instincts, while the downloaders seem to revel in the illicit act of downloading. (See the complete interview with Professor Zittrain in Chapter 7, *Dude, Where's My MP3?*). If no one stands up to the media moguls, we will never know the merits or strengths of their stand. The RIAA continues to sue downloaders, and some of their targets are going

---

14. Forrester Research press release, August 13, 2002, "Downloads Did Not Cause the Music Slump, but They Can Cure It."
15. Forrester Research press release, September 2, 2003, "CDs and DVDs to Go the Way of the LP."
16. In *Newyorkmetro.com*, October 13, 2003.

to court. The outcomes of these cases should prove interesting over the next few years.

*Record companies rip off the artists.* This one we heard from both kids and adults, and from artists and nonartists. Most would be more willing to spend on CDs if they thought the money would get to the artists. (See sidebar, *Music CD Sales: Courtney Love's View of Where the Money Goes.*)

Consider what Joni Mitchell said to David Wild in a 2002 *Rolling Stone* interview:

"I've never really had a good deal in the business," Mitchell said. She contemplated never recording again, or perhaps selling her music on the Internet. The music business, she said, is top-heavy and wasteful, the music it puts out is calculated for sales, and that she is ashamed to be part of it. "You know, I think it's just a cess-pool."[17]

*On the Internet I'm pretty much anonymous.* Some people think they're electronically invisible on the Internet. Nothing could be farther from the truth. Your computer broadcasts a digital signa-ture, called an IP address, whenever you're on the Internet; indeed, how could email messages and information requests be served to you if nobody knew where you were?[18]

*I'm not of the age of majority, so I can't get in trouble with the law.* Federal copyright law does not distinguish between minors and adults. That's why the RIAA can threaten to sue a twelve-year old.

*But I didn't do it.* Some people didn't and have been wrongfully accused. But if it happens to you, it will still cost you some bucks to get out of trouble. Sixty-six-year-old Sarah Ward was charged by the RIAA in 2003 with downloading over 2,000 songs, among them "I'm a Thug" by Trick Daddy, using KaZaA. Mrs. Ward, a sculptor, owns a Mac (which doesn't run KaZaA) and doesn't even know how to download. She had to hire an attorney to get the charges dropped. The attorney representing the record labels

17. "Women in Rock," *Rolling Stone*, October 10, 2002.
18. Learn your IP address at this Web site: http://www.whatismyip.com/.

(Sony Music, BMG, Virgin, Interscope, Atlantic, Warner Brothers and Arista, by name) wrote her attorney to say, "We will continue our review of the issues you raised and we reserve the right to refile the complaint against Mrs. Ward if and when circumstances warrant."[19]

*If they don't want me to download, then why do I have the software and hardware with which to do it?* Coming out of the mouths of teens, this reasoning seems specious. One college networking specialist we spoke with responded thus: "You have a knife. Does that mean you have to use it to kill someone?" But in truth, the software, hardware, and media industries are at cross-purposes—in those different camps we talked about. They all want you to buy their products, even when one product violates the law and rights of another product. The flames are fanned by academics, musicians, and outspoken critics of the media conglomerates, and by governments that wink at or even encourage illegal software and media downloading. At heart, the entertainment industry would probably tolerate a little illegal downloading, like inventory shrinkage in the warehouse or breakage on the factory floor, but in dribbles and drips, not oceans and waves. It really all boils down to money: The music industry is losing it, and someone has to pony up.

Denial extends to both sides of this issue: Downloaders know that the availability of MP3 players doesn't make violating copyright protection any less illegal. But there is irrationality on the other side as well. Companies or industries rarely attack, arrest, or fine their own customers for alleged theft or misuse of their product. The entertainment industry had years to head Napster off at the pass by building its own online offerings, but instead (out of fear? anger? resistance to change? not realizing how popular online downloading could become?) cut back music development production and raised prices. Gunning down teenagers for their love of music—the industry's product—belies a need to look at more fundamental business issues concerning cost of goods, distribu-

---

19. Chris Gaither, "Recording Industry Withdraws Suit," *The Boston Globe*, September 24, 2003, pp. C1–C2.

tion channels, profit margins, and delivering product that consumers actually want to buy.

*I only download a little bit. They're after the big uploaders, not me.* Not so. The RIAA believes that everyone should be scared, so they go after the big fishies and the little fishies, the fishies that move music upstream and the fishies that move it downstream. Rippers need to back away from the belief that media file-sharing is a matter of degree. It isn't. The judge is unlikely to rule you less a shoplifter if you steal a candy bar than if you steal a handful of candy bars. Likewise, you only need to be convicted of stealing one copyrighted song, even if you downloaded or distributed a thousand. At fines up to $150,000 a tune, who wants to be caught, fined, or convicted?

You can also say that you're careful when you download; you only peer with other KaZaA members. But you know what? Anybody can join KaZaA, including the RIAA, which has set up dummy servers with music on them in order to identify and ensnare offending downloaders. Do you think you can you tell the difference between a friendly peer computer and the RIAA's dummy?

*Bands don't really make any money on their CDs; they earn their living on touring, so it doesn't really matter that much if I download their tunes.* If bands want you to download their music for free, they'll put it on their Web site for you. Even if they don't make much (or any) money on their CDs, that's none of your business and not an excuse for them to make even *less* money. Let's put the shoe on the other foot: It's *your* band, or movie, or novel, and someone has put a copy of it on *their* computer, without your knowledge or approval, and is offering it for download on KaZaA. *Now* how do you feel about it? Or try this on for size: Your favorite band can't tour because the label says their CD doesn't sell well enough to sponsor them.

*It's mine. I bought it, and I can make copies for myself if I want to.* That's right, you can. If you own a record, tape, or CD and want to make a copy of it on your computer, you're entitled to do that. You can probably even give a friend a song or two—maybe

even a CD—and no one will mind. Just don't go into mass distribution, either on the Internet or anywhere else.

What if it's *not* your property and you distribute it? Would you
feel that's either morally wrong or illegal? Kerry Gonzalez found
out that it was both. In the summer of 2003, he obtained a prerelease copy of the movie *The Hulk* from a friend and uploaded it to
an Internet Relay Chat (IRC) site. In so doing, Gonzalez
attempted to disable the tape's security code, but that very code
was his undoing, making it easier to trace it back to him. He pled
guilty to copyright infringement in court and apologized: "I was
not allowed to have this copy of a tape. I took it home. I captured
it onto my personal computer," he told the judge. Gonzalez was
fined $2,000, made to pay $5,000 in restitution to Universal, and
sentenced to six months' probation.[20]

---

## MUSIC CD SALES: AN INDUSTRY VIEW OF WHERE THE MONEY GOES

Realistically, a record company may not even pay 25 cents for a
blank CD, but it's a mistake to think that's how much it costs to produce an album. According to ASCAP, the American Society of Composers, Artists and Publishers, it's a lot more complicated than that.
Figure 3–3 shows the typical recording artist royalty breakdown.

---

20.  The movie industry routinely sends thousands of DVD and VHS copies of prere-
     lease films, called "screeners," to the people who vote for film awards—e.g.,
     Cannes, Sundance, Montreal, etc. According to Jack Valenti, retired head of the
     MPAA, of the 68 titles sent out in 2002, 34 were pirated and found on the black
     market, mostly in Asia and Russia. The industry promptly voted a ban on screen-
     ers, but then relented in 2003 for those involved in choosing films for the Acad-
     emy Awards (Oscars). But those receiving screeners must sign a document
     agreeing that, among other things, any pirated screener traced back to them
     (through a digital signature) would result in their immediate and unequivocal
     expulsion from the Academy of Motion Picture Arts and Sciences. Source: Jack
     Valenti, "In War Against Film Piracy, Some Must Pay a (Small) Price," *The Wall
     Street Journal*, October 29, 2003, p. D10.

| | |
|---|---|
| $17.00 | CD retail price |
| -25% | Packaging deduction |
| $12.75 | Royalty base |
| x 16% | Royalty rate |
| $2.04 | Artist royalty |
| x 1,000,000 | Album sales |
| **$2,040,000** | Artist royalties |

**Figure 3–3**   ASCAP breakdown of CD costs. Source: www.ascap.com/musicbiz/money-recording.html.

It's difficult to make much money on album sales. The $4.25 packaging charge is basically materials and manufacturing, which the label deducts right off the top. A 16 percent royalty is average.

This artist or group is earning a 16 percent royalty; generally, artists get somewhere between 10–25 percent of the list price of their CD, after the packaging charge ($4.25) has been deducted.

There are many people who get a remunerative slice of an artist's CD. In many cases, the artist or group gets an advance against royalties, a sum paid up front by the label and repaid out of royalties as the album sells. Usually, the owner of the copyright is someone other than the artist. There are also loads of production costs, from the cover artist to the producer, sound engineers, and technical experts, to the time paid for the recording studio, all of which are negotiated to some extent between the label and the artist. Most labels pay the lion's share of support costs: publicity, promotional gimmicks in music stores, touring, and a host of other sales, marketing, and distribution costs. To put the artist's earnings in perspective, ASCAP says an artist earns about eight cents per song. Based on a sales figure of one million single-plays, (which might be a combination of CD purchases and various media airplays, including radio, television and satellite broadcasts) the artist will earn about $80,000, compared to earning about $600,000 from touring.

All this when only 10 percent of all CDs are financially successful.

---

## MUSIC CD SALES: COURTNEY LOVE'S VIEW OF WHERE THE MONEY GOES

In a speech at the Digital Hollywood online entertainment conference in New York, May 16, 2002,[21] recording artist Courtney Love gave her own view of the economics of CDs.

"Today I want to talk about piracy and music," she began. "What is piracy? Piracy is the act of stealing an artist's work without any intention of paying for it. I'm not talking about Napster-type software. I'm talking about major label recording companies."

In her example, she takes a mythical four-person up-and-coming rock band that signs with a record label and gets a 20 pecent royalty rate and $1,000,000 advance (which she also claims is mythical, but which allows for a best-case estimate). Figure 3–4 shows her cost breakdowns.

She then shows how much gets charged against the band: commissions, business expenses, tour support, independent promotion, a portion of video production costs, etc., as shown below.

As she puts it, while the band is waiting the year for the release of the record, each member has $45,000 to live on after taxes. Once the record sales begin, the label begins recouping its advance. By

---

21. Source: www.cdbaby.net/articles/courtney_love.html.

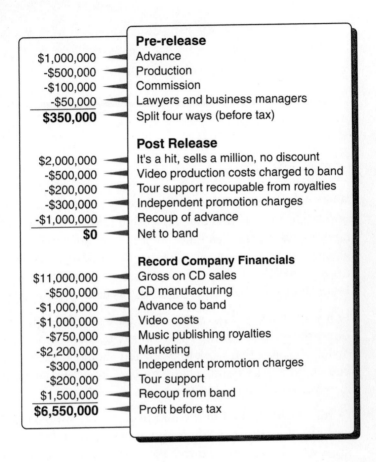

**Figure 3–4** Courtney's calculations.

the time record sales and the band tour concludes, the label has made $6.6 million, the band zero.

"Of course, they (the band) had fun. Hearing yourself on the radio, selling records, getting new fans, and being on TV is great, but now the band doesn't have enough money to pay the rent and nobody has any credit."

Worse, she asserts, the band owns none of its work: the label does. "When the contract runs out, writers get their books back. But record companies own our copyrights forever."

---

## WHICH CAMP ARE YOU IN?

What did you think about downloading copyrighted media when you began reading this chapter? What knowledge did you possess *before* you began reading? What new information have you gleaned from reading it? Chapter 2, *Copyright or the Right to Copy?*, explained copyright law; has your understanding of the issue changed? Have your thoughts or feelings changed?

In a way, what we are trying to do here is a little like sex education—make sure you have the information and tools you need to make decisions that work for you. You should at least know where you stand on the issue. Then you can go off and make decisions for yourself when the lights are out.

Gordon Gekko said it in the film *Wall Street*: "Greed is good." You can say that the recording and movie industry executives are greedy, but aren't the downloaders greedy, too? Greed means to want or desire something to excess, which implies ownership. Most of the world's great wars have been fought over property—from women (Helen) to gold (the Aztecs) to land (Genghis Khan). So here we are at the new millennium, the record business and its consumers squabbling like two barbaric warlords over something that neither can truly possess: the spirit of artistic creation. Whether it is music, video, art, poetry, computer games, or software, it can only be the genuine "property" of the individual who created it, but it may be more valuable as it is shared with others. Anything else is a legal subtlety.

Both sides need to chill out.

Think about a future scenario, say like the one William Gibson envisioned in *Johnny Mnemonic*, where you can upload digital data right into your brain (or *wetware*, as Gibson called it). Who can own that data? Who even knows if you have it?

If there is one thing the *Us's* and the *Thems* can agree on it's probably this: In this information-rich, entertainment-oriented, digital age, it's time for a new vision of what it means to protect—and share—intellectual property. Ah, but what is that vision? Read on.

# 4

# INSIDE THE CORPORATE INTELLECT: A DAY AT MICROSOFT

Great. I'm glad someone is telling this story. We worked our hearts and souls out designing this software. I hate to see it ripped off.[1]

**Kevin Schofield, Microsoft researcher**

What do you do when your local retailer is selling Windows 2000 for a fourth of the original price? How about when you suspect one of your competitors to be distributing illegitimate software? Or when you see a Web site offering Certificate of Authenticity (COA) labels without software? The answer is easy—you contact Microsoft's Anti-Piracy Hotline at (800) RU-LEGIT (785-3448). [2]

**Microsoft invitation to report piracy**

In the plaza between Buildings 16 and 17 on Microsoft's Redmond, Washington, campus are small metal plaques set into concrete tiles in geometric patterns. They look like they might be weathered brass or tarnished pewter, perhaps stainless steel with a coating. The one furthest from the building, the first one, is worn, the word "Basic" barely visible. On it is the date: 1975. Next to it is the plaque for 1976: Basic 4K, Basic 8K, Basic Disk. Next to that, 1977: Fortran compiler for CPM. 1978: Cobol 80, Edit 80, Macro Assembler for the 8080. Each year seems to have a few more lines on

---

1. Interview with Kevin Schofield, General Manager, Strategy and Communications, for Microsoft Research, September 24, 2003.
2. From the Microsoft piracy hotline Web site: http://www.microsoft.com/piracy/reporting/piracy_in_us.asp.

it, a few more product titles. By the time you get to 1990, there are 20 products listed. From there on, one plaque is no longer enough, and each plaque then represents one product. So you get multiple plaques per year.

On and on they go, marching toward the cafeteria between the two buildings: Microsoft Basic, Microsoft Cobol, Microsoft DOS, Microsoft Access, Microsoft Windows, Microsoft Money, Microsoft NFL Fever, Microsoft Expedia, Microsoft Encarta, Microsoft Outlook, Microsoft Visual Basic, Microsoft PowerPoint, Microsoft Transaction Server, Microsoft Back Office, Microsoft Investor, Microsoft Baseball 3D, Microsoft Media Player, Microsoft Bookshelf 99, Microsoft Moto-cross Madness, Microsoft Window NT, Microsoft Golf, and so on.

All told, there are 425 plaques, fanning out like a tree of regimented, stylistic branches, and ending with The Magic School Bus Explores Bugs, Version 1.0, shipped February 2, 2000. The names on these plaques are the legions of Microsoft product history, the corporate equivalent of initials carved into the trunk of a giant oak.

These modern-day petroglyphs describe the rise of Microsoft and, in so doing, tell the story of the personal software industry. They chronicle the waves of technology that have brought us the Internet, the MP3 player, camera–cell phones, Blaster worms, spam, video games, warez groups, digital sampling, offshore software development, flash mobs, instant messaging, smart bombs, and the concept of the nerd as master of the universe.

Were you to levitate from, say, the 1993 plaque for Microsoft Flight Simulator (Version 5.0, shipped September 17 that year), up a half mile or so, to where you could see all of Redmond and adjacent Bellevue, only then would you begin to get a sense for the size and scope of the enterprise that has grown out of the efforts of a teenaged Harvard dropout. The East Campus, as it is now called, consists of scores of mostly nondescript two- and three-story office buildings mingled in and around residential and light commercial areas.

Here in King County, Microsoft lays claim to 9 million square feet of facilities. The corporate campus, as it called, accounts for two-thirds of that. Actually, it looks less like a campus than an encampment: buildings strung out with no real master plan, just a big sprawl that grew as the organization grew and new office spaces were required. No architectural grandeur, like a Middlebury College, Harvard Yard, or University of Washington central campus. No gleaming corporate headquarters, like IBM's Somers, NY, facilities designed by I.M. Pei, or Oracle's gleaming glass towers 839 miles to the south in Belmont, California. Just a lot of nondescript buildings, mostly tan or sandstone colors, with garden apartment landscaping and no external signs to indicate the disciplines of those toiling inside.

Nevertheless, here we are, within the matrix that represents the heart of one of the biggest intellectual property factories in the world—the factory that built all the products described on the plaques in the plaza, the factory that built the software running on over 500 million computers, the factory that built a $30 billion corporation, the factory that created 10,000 employee stock-option millionaires, the factory that employs enough software developers to populate a major state university, the factory that inspires awe, enmity, and antitrust suits the world 'round, and, of course, the factory that produces the software most pirated on earth.

## WHY MICROSOFT?

Okay, we've described Microsoft. But why delve into the inner workings of the company for a book on digital piracy? Is this to be an apologia for Microsoft? Is it to defend a company the government sued as a monopolist? To defend the price of software for a company that has some of the highest gross margins on earth?

No. This is less about Microsoft than about the effort that goes into creating the content that we, if we follow our us-versus-them theme from the last chapter, might choose to copy, pirate, or otherwise illegally use. It's to show us why the media, software, and entertainment companies feel so proprietary about their products and so combative when protecting them as intellectual property.

It's hard to think of software as something tangible. We pirates, if you will go along with our convention from the previous chapter, pretty much know what goes into making a CD: studio time, musicians, editing, marketing, and distribution, right? We saw the breakdown in the last chapter. We've also seen enough movies about making movies, not to mention DVD trailers, to more-or-less get the concept, although we may not have a clear picture of a movie's theater/video rental/DVD/foreign distribution/syndication path to market nor why the average movie costs $82 million to make.

Software is more mysterious. Programmers type into their computers strange agglomerations of words and symbols, which eventually get rendered into strings of ones and zeroes that the computer understands. These agglomerations allow you to spell check a document, play a game, or hear music. If you took all the computer commands that make up a modern software program and printed them out, you might have 10 million lines in your printout. If you printed it in a book, it would have 312,000 pages, which, if stacked on your desk, would be about 100 feet high. Even worse, the paragraphs (subroutines) in this book would connect not just to the paragraphs before and after, but to hundreds or thousands of other paragraphs in complex and ever-changing ways. Think of a Web page with gazillions of hyperlinks and you begin to get the idea. This is why it takes geeks to write software. And sometimes, only software can write software.

What we hope to present in this chapter is the intellectual component of intellectual property. What goes into the software burned onto the CDs that get sold for a few bucks in the open air markets of Beijing, Bangalore, Moscow, and Jakarta? If we're going to understand piracy, we might as well know what we're *really* pirating, because it's a heck of a lot more than a five-inch disc made of plastic and aluminum. By way of illustration, we offer the story of the development of Microsoft Office 2003.

# THE BIRTH OF MICROSOFT OFFICE 2003

On October 21, 2003, Microsoft officially launched Office 2003, a suite of products that includes Word, for word processing; the Excel spreadsheet; Access, the database manager; Outlook, an email, address book, and calendar program; PowerPoint, for presentations; Publisher, for desktop publishing; and a variety of accompanying tools and utilities. List price for the standard edition is $399, but because of upgrade pricing, academic discounts, and volume pricing, almost no one will pay that. A more realistic price is $239, what you would pay to upgrade to the standard edition. Upon publication, Office 2003 was available in seven languages and released in over 20 countries. Eventually it was available from Microsoft in 39 languages and from business partners in 60 more.

Creating Office 2003 took two and a half years—unless you count the previous 10 years of Office products from Microsoft (and you should), which contributed to the product's DNA. Over its 30-month gestation period, over 2,000 software engineers worked on Office 2003. Over *two thousand*.

In a small office in Building 17, Eric LeVine, Group Program Manager, Microsoft Office, lays out the process for us. It's like this, he says: "We work in a cycle that starts with planning, goes through coding and then test, field trials, and then launch. After launch, in fact, throughout development, we have a customer feedback process, too."

Eric's an animated speaker, and while talking, he's been drawing on a white board. His diagram looks something like Figure 4–1.

In his role as program manager for Office 2003, LeVine is in charge of the back end of the process, gathering the customer feedback that gets folded back into the planning and design process. The other "Softie" in the room is Mike Angiulo, Group Product Planner, Microsoft Office, who manages the planning process for Office. It is his office we are using, and on the wall is a picture

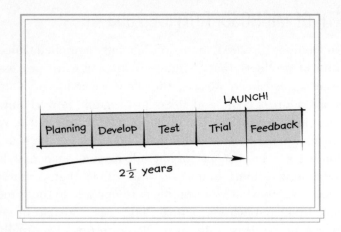

**Figure 4–1**  The Microsoft planning process.

of him as he flies a biplane in air races. It's something he does to relax from the stress of developing software at Microsoft. LeVine and Angiulo—young, well-spoken, and with demeanors that belie their heavy responsibilities—are the bookends of the process of getting a major piece of software out the door. They are the wranglers of the cash cow for the biggest software company on earth.

## PLAN, WRITE CODE, TEST; PLAN, WRITE CODE, TEST

As LeVine continues his explanation of the product cycle, he points out that the functions he's listed aren't really linear—one doesn't end before the next starts. They often occur simultaneously, with the intensity of the effort ebbing and flowing depending on the relationship of each to the launch date.

Inspired, he draws more lines showing how this works, pointing out that by the time of the Office 2003 launch, planning has already peaked for the *next* version of the product—Office 2006 or 2007 or whatever name Microsoft chooses. By now the diagram looks more like Figure 4–2.

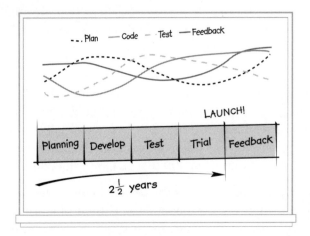

**Figure 4–2**   Constant reinvention may be the best way to characterize how Microsoft revises its software products.

So, how would you plan for the writing of a book 100 feet high?

The process starts with a *vision document*, which basically lays out the objectives for the new product. It can be as short as a page or, as is the case with Office 2003, about 40–50 pages long. The vision document becomes the touchstone or reference point for all decisions made during the two-and-a-half-year journey down the developmental birth canal. It allows managers to keep a rein on programmers, whose natural penchant is to incessantly add clever little features and modifications to their work for the beauty of it—and end up totally missing the launch date. If a feature or proposed modification doesn't conform to the vision document, it gets scrapped or tabled until the next version.

After that, a more detailed roadmap is built—now we are into many, many pages of detail about the product—and later, a more detailed, piece-by-piece, feature-by-feature product specification. Angiulo points out that for Office 2003 there were thousands of detailed software specs produced.

"We do a lot of work inside here to manage how this team of more than 2,000 will be broken into smaller teams," adds LeVine. "We need to control the chaos, create groups that are small enough to have ownership of their part of the process and make the investments they need to do their job."

This is one of the reasons there are so many planners among the developers and testers on each development team—about one in five in the effort are planners. Do the math: If the actual number of people working on Office 2003 was, say, 2,400, and the average team size was 6 people, we're talking about coordinating the schedule and output of 400 teams. Quite the choreography!

From the roadmap comes the detailed plans—technical recipes, if you will—that the developers use as their blueprints for the code that will become the software program. Every few days, they produce enough software to be tested. It's the tests that determine how and whether all the different moving parts of the larger programs will work, and under which conditions they won't. Office 2003 will be a product with more moving parts than a Boeing 757, which is why at least half of the 2,000 people on the project are testers. In fact, hundreds of other developers at Microsoft have the task of developing the software that will be used to test the software and, yes, the software to write software that will test software.

Thus does Office 2003 gets shepherded along. Code, test, integrate, test, recode, adjust, test, finalize, test, get feedback, retest, and so on. Each day, programmers turn in completed code by 4:00 p.m., and overnight it is blended with the code from other teams into a skeleton version of the product, called a "build." This allows for testing the interplay between the software written by the different teams. When the skeleton is fully fleshed out, the product is done.

## KNOWING WHEN TO QUIT

The months go by. A year prior to launch, the planning and product management teams have pretty much decided what features and enhancements will be in Office 2003—from new and better versions of stuff that was put into Office 2000 to new features requested by customers to features that just didn't make it into Office 2000. The process of baking these features into software code is in full swing.

The key to getting a software product out on time is to limit its features and functions and to "freeze" the design well enough in advance that the product can be fully tested before launch. This is a lesson learned the hard way at Microsoft, which was once known for releasing "buggy" software and fixing it when customers complained.

But releasing bug-free, perfectly performing software is not so simple. The market for software products moves swiftly, and totally freezing a product design an entire year before launch isn't always feasible. Case in point: By the fall of 2002, it was clear that spam was becoming a scourge for email users. A spam filter is a program that can separate emails that users want to read from those of Viagra peddlers, fly-by-night mortgage brokers, or Kira-a-college-girl-gone-bad. Yet there were no plans to put a spam filter into Outlook, the email component in Microsoft Office 2003.

At a critical product development meeting, Microsoft's first and most famous software developer, Bill Gates,[3] weighs in with a suggestion that it should be included. Instantly, spam filtering jumps 1,000 slots on the priority list. The Office 2003 team will have to change the design of Office 2003—in effect adding a new moving part to our software Boeing 757 while the test pilots are flying it.

More on the spam filter itself later, but the process of adding it to the Outlook component of Office 2003 takes deadline-driven teamwork between the Outlook development subteam, the team in the R&D lab that developed the spam filter itself, the software testers, and even the managers of Microsoft's own email systems.

This is far from routine, adding last-minute features to the product in reaction to conditions that change faster than a major

---

3.   When Gates moved up to chairman and gave the day-to-day reins of CEO to
     Steve Ballmer, he added "chief software architect" to his title. See
     www.microsoft.com/billgates/bio.asp.

application software product cycle. But actually, it *is* routine. There is always *something*.

Fast forward to six months before launch. It's time for the ultimate smoke test (turn on the engine and see what smokes) for Office 2003, what the industry calls "beta testing." (Yes, there is "alpha testing," but you never hear much about it.)

Beta testing for Office 2003 means Microsoft issues a prelaunch trial release of the product to some of its best customers, to let them find out what works and what doesn't. In this case, it's the biggest beta test in the history of the world: 600,000 customers. By now, LeVine's team is working full-tilt boogie, taking automated feedback in real time about bugs, problems, performance choke points, mysterious behaviors, glitches, and holes. From this input, his team generates a punch list for final fixes before launch. The problems get sorted into those that must be fixed before launch, those that will be attended to in later releases, and those that must be put off until the next release of Office (Office 2006, 2007, 2008, or whatever).

Over 2,000 people labored for over two years on Office 2003. All for $239, list price. The development costs work out to about three person-months for each penny you or I pay for the product.

No wonder Microsoft ranked intellectual property protection as its number one concern in a 2003 survey of software executives conducted by the Business Software Alliance. No wonder over 500 Microsoft lawyers and other staffers worldwide chase down software pirates, support law enforcement in over 100 countries, and lobby governments around the globe on behalf of tougher laws and better enforcement.

## MICROSOFT AS MICROCOSM

Big and (in)famous as Microsoft is, it still represents less than 15 percent of the total packaged software industry. In 2003, the industry brought in over $150 billion in worldwide revenues, through the sales efforts of over 50,000 companies. As you'll see in Chapter 6, *Global Fallout*, software piracy takes a big chunk out of the revenue these firms *could* make, affecting jobs, tax collection, and the various companies that supply the blank CDs, cardboard boxes, printed matter, and holographic security stickers, the air freight and trucking companies, the distributors, and the retailers. In countries where software piracy is high, artificially low market prices for pirated software (practically free, right?) inhibit sales of indigenously developed software. It is pretty much the way it was when pirated books written by English authors depressed the prices for Mark Twain's books, as we pointed out in Chapter 2, *Is It Copyright or the Right to Copy?*.

Almost all software publishers suffer from piracy, companies as diverse as:

- Autodesk, which makes software used by civil engineers and industrial designers to create everything from buildings to cars to movie animation.
- Adobe, which makes the ubiquitous Photoshop, Acrobat Reader, and other Web tools.
- Symantec, which makes antivirus, security and system maintenance software.
- IBM, which makes large database management software, email systems, and development tools.
- Oracle, which makes large database management systems.
- Macromedia, which makes software for Web and multimedia designers and animators.

But Microsoft is the juiciest target for pirates. This is a function of demographics (Microsoft has more kinds of software that run on more computers than any other company), expediency (you can't run 90 percent of the computers in the world without Microsoft's operating system software), culture (these are American monopolists, right?), and envy (Bill Gates won't miss my hundred and fifty bucks).

# THE LEGAL BEAGLES

As a result, Microsoft works on multiple fronts to protect its software. These include:

- Enforcement support and lobbying by its legal team and marketing folks. Brad Smith, Senior Vice President and General Counsel, heads the legal team, while Nancy Anderson, who works for him as Deputy General Counsel, handles global antipiracy efforts. At Microsoft, fighting piracy is a cabinet-level position.

- Support and funding for the BSA, the lobbying and antipiracy trade association that is the most visible and active antipiracy interest group in the world.

- Education efforts with resellers and customers on the impact of piracy and the prevention of abuse of legitimate software licenses.

- Notification, under the "notice and takedown" provisions of the Digital Millennium Copyright Act (see Chapter 5, *Inside the Sausage: The Making of the Digital Millennium Copyright Act*), which allows Microsoft to shut down Internet pirates through their Internet service providers (ISPs).

- Technology such as product initiation, which requires customers to "activate" their software before they can get a code that will let it work.

- Other tools for software licensing and management that make it easy for conscientious customers to "do the right thing."

The Microsoft antipiracy team includes lawyers, government lobbyists, paralegals, investigators, liaisons with law enforcement, education specialists, and public relations and communications specialists. Although the Department of Law and Corporate Affairs houses most of them, fighting piracy is a task that's really dispersed throughout the company. There is no way to tell what percent of Microsoft's resources is spent fighting piracy, but as Brad Smith puts it, "It's in the hundreds of millions of dollars, if not more than that. It might be that no company on the planet spends more trying to promote respect for its intellectual property rights."[4]

Enforcement through the Microsoft teams works as you might expect. First, a tip or lead comes in, perhaps from a consumer who has been defrauded or an employee who has been laid off. So a case starts with a piece of information, and then the investigators go to work, perhaps visiting a store that is suspected of selling pirated software. They might even buy a computer to see if it has unlicensed software installed. If it looks like the case might involve criminal activity, special investigators, usually with a background in law enforcement, get involved. If the investigation pans out, the lawyers get involved. Is the case worth pursuing? Should it be turned over to the police? If it's a civil case, the lawyers, usually working with outside law firms by now, file papers. If it's a criminal case, they work with the enforcement agencies to lend support.

The scope of these efforts is staggering. At any one time, there are probably over 1,000 cases pending in as many as 90 countries. The general outcome is a settlement rather than a trial, except for hardcore criminal cases. "Our general approach," says Smith, "is that if it's possible to reach an agreement and resolve things quickly, that's better than having things drag out for years and years."

Is it working? Yes and no. As Smith suggests, fighting piracy is a journey, not a destination. Robert Holleyman, CEO of the Business Software Alliance, looks back on the BSA's 13-year history and sees real progress. "Since we started tracking software piracy, it has dropped ten points, and in some countries as much as 40 points. In the beginning, only a minority of countries had intellectual property protections in place. Now most do. And there is much more legal software in use."[5]

Enforcement is often accompanied by lobbying and, in some cases, strategic investment. A cover story in Forbes[6] revealed

---

4. Interview with author Gantz, September 2003.

5. Interview with author Gantz, September 2003.

6. Robyn Meredith, "Microsoft's Long March," *Forbes*, February 17, 2003, pp. 78–86.

how Microsoft is investing nearly a billion dollars in China alone, funneled through the government, to help develop a local software industry, support basic research at Chinese universities, and train others in its software development practices—all in hopes of obtaining government support to combat piracy through education and enforcement. Microsoft is in it for the long haul, not expecting any sea changes for at least 10 years.

In the field, fighting piracy takes place one lead, one lawsuit, one investigation, one educational white paper, one customer visit, and one plea at a time. "My goal," said Eugene Danilov, the Anti-Piracy Unit Manager of Microsoft Moscow, in an interview in Moscow in March of 2003, "is to get each small business to buy just one legitimate software package. That would be a big step."[7]

## FIGHTING SPAM

Let's get back to Office 2003. Remember that spam-filtering feature that got shoved into Office 2003 at the last minute? (Thank you, Bill!)

Let's think about that. None of us much likes spam. IDC statistics find that spam is growing at least twice as fast as legitimate person-to-person email, and if you believe other experts, from 50–85 percent of email is spam. We're talking about 4.7 trillion—TRILLION—spam messages a year worldwide.[8]

Wouldn't it be nice to have a little "bot" in your computer to delete all those unwanted emails? You could put them into a special spam basket and then delete 'em all with a satisfying click of the mouse. (Some sound effects would be nice, too; maybe a garbage disposal?)

Sounds good, right? The trick is making sure that the emails from your spouse or boss don't get tossed into the spam bucket. And spammers get smarter and smarter about how to defeat simple filtering tests, such as siphoning off emails containing the word Via-

---

7.   Interview with author Gantz, March 2003.
8.   "Worldwide Email Usage Forecast," IDC, October 2003.

gra in the subject line. Ideally, a filtering program would be able to adapt to conditions over time, learning from experience which emails are spam and can be chucked versus which should be passed through to be personally reviewed.

At Microsoft, according to Robert Rounthwaite, Chief Architect, Anti-Spam Technology & Strategy, work on this capability began at Microsoft as far back as 1997, with a core team of five Ph.D.s in the R&D organization studying how machines could be taught to learn. In an email context, such a computer system might use information based on the words in an email, the length of the email, time of day of the message, sender address, background colors, fonts, and so on to look for relationships that might be used to classify that email. "Of course," says Rounthwaite, "the system looks at a hundred thousand things, which is why we have to use a system." Over time the system would learn which of the characteristics were the most likely to predict that an email was, in fact, spam.

"Funny," says Rounthwaite parenthetically, "when I first heard you were doing a book on digital piracy, I assumed you wanted to talk about spam. Spammers are actually stealing something, aren't they? From the bandwidth and resources to ship and store their emails to the lost resources used to block spam. Hotmail (now MSN Mail) is a free service offered by Microsoft, and a substantial portion of the budget is for blocking spam or, if the blocking is unsuccessful, sending to people who don't want it."[9]

Pirates are plundering bandwidth and siphoning off corporate budget dollars. It's an interesting thought, but for now, let's stick to the product development trail.

From 1997 on, Microsoft's R&D team continued to work on the technique, along the way realizing it might work as a spam filter. They built a prototype. They also built a test database of emails from Microsoft's own email database. The messages in the database were preclassified as to whether they are spam or not. The R&D team began to test their prototype with this real email

---

9.   Interview with author Gantz, September 2003.

data—terabytes of it. It seemed to work. The computer-learning algorithm seemingly was able to identify spam, and to get better the more messages it scanned. In the technological old days—in other words, 20 years ago—we might have called this "artificial intelligence," but today that term is now out of vogue. "Spam filtering" will suffice.

By the early 2000s, the R&D team believed it had a program that would work. But the Office product teams declined to take it on, tabling it for the version of Outlook that will come after the Office 2003 launch. Then, as we have said, Bill Gates made his wishes known in that meeting in the fall of 2002: He would like spam filtering in Office 2003.

Thus began the delicate process of merging this R&D capability into a nearly final Office 2003. R&D scientists worked with key software coders and testers to develop the feature. The code written by the R&D people needed to be rewritten to follow the development rules used by the Office 2003 Outlook team. New tests had to be designed to test that code. Other teams had to be alerted that this new feature was coming. In turn, hundreds of other software programs had to be modified to work with this new feature. Versions for 39 languages had to be developed. The task was immense.

Eventually, the spam filter made it into the October 2003 release as just one more feature of Outlook, which is but one application in the Office 2003 suite. Scientists worked for half a decade on abstruse mathematical algorithms, while others developed the prototype and email database, and developers, coders, and testers throughout the Outlook team made last-minute adjustments—thousands of man-hours, or genius-hours, just to contribute one new feature for only one of a many applications.

All there for the pirates to take.

# THE TESTS OF TIME

Any similarity between writing a 312,000-page book and a 12-million-lines-of-code software program breaks down when you get to the editing phase. In the case of a book, you do a little fixing and editing as you go, but most is done at the end. Correcting mistakes is a relatively straightforward part of the process.

Not so with software. At Microsoft, there is a software tester for every software developer. Testers work in teams with the developers, they work in their own special department, and they work in the R&D labs on new ways to test. Parts and pieces of Office 2003 get tested every day, along with their integration with major components—those are tested in the daily "builds" of the program.

Microsoft didn't always do it this way. In the early days, testing was done by development teams at the end of program development. But programs were often buggy when shipped or delayed from late-in-the-cycle testing. For example, in the 1981 version of the Basic programming language for the IBM PC, when the user divided by 0.1 the program gave a wrong answer—a highly embarrassing bug! There was a bit of a *laissez-faire* attitude: Let the customers tell us what's broken, and we'll fix it. Problem was, customers didn't like this idea—not at all.

In 1984, Microsoft established a test division separate from its development division, but that didn't work so well either. Integrating components and testing took place late in the development process, leading to product delays. Developers would write code and throw it over the wall to the testers, who were left to clean up the mess.

One product, Word 3.0 for Macintosh, released in February 1987, was seven months late and shipped with 700 bugs.[10] Microsoft had to ship a free update to customers two months later at a cost

---

10.  Michael A. Cusumano and Richard W. Selby, *Microsoft Secrets* (New York: Touchstone Books, 1998). This is an excellent review of Microsoft's development and testing history recommended to us by some of the people we interviewed at Microsoft.

of $1 million. A version of Word was being developed for Windows at the same time, and its problems were even worse. Testers coming late to the product cycle would find bugs; developers would have to write fixes, which would then have to be tested again. The fixes themselves often would result in additional bugs. At times, bugs were discovered faster than developers could fix them.

But nothing defines Microsoft as much as the way it learns from mistakes. Hence the chopping up of big development groups into teams and products into smaller components. Hence the rigorous testing throughout the development process. Hence the long and extensive field trials.

"We are always looking at ways to improve the process," Kevin Schofield, General Manager, Strategy and Communications for Microsoft Research, told us. "For instance, when a bug goes into the bug database for a product, we will write a test for it and include it in our test suite so we will find it if it occurs again. We put this into the regression test suite, which is used to test for bugs."

For the Windows operating system, Schofield points out, the regression tests take eight weeks to run from beginning to end, on an enormous farm of computers. There is even a science to knowing which test to run early in the regression suite and which later; you want to test early the stuff that will take longest to fix. It takes yet other testing software to determine which code is affected by which tests—and thus to prioritize the testing.

Then come the field trials. In the old days, software beta tests usually involved only a few dozen customers, who would take the prerelease software and put it through its paces. With Windows 95, however, Microsoft broke the mold, sending out multiple preview versions of the product in successive waves, each bigger than the last. The final wave went to 400,000 customers. Office 2003 beat that figure by almost a quarter of a million users, and was the biggest beta test for any software product—probably *any* product—ever.

Microsoft doesn't perform its extensive testing and debugging simply out of the goodness of its heart. It does it because it makes good business sense. A product that doesn't have to be recalled and a customer who's satisfied the first time are of far greater benefit than the cost of better and earlier testing. Even if you're the biggest, and in some respects only, game in town, fixing a bug once a product is in the field is many times more costly than fixing it early in the development process. Quality control can even contribute to lowering prices.

## GETTING HELP FROM WATSON

"We have been working for years," says LeVine, "on learning how to incorporate feedback from customers before and after the product ships. We have been especially aggressive in Office." What he describes here is dubbed "Watson," referring to any portion of a process that includes this kind of continuous feedback loop.[11] Although Microsoft has used versions of Watson for years, this iteration is a new way to obtain continuous feedback from customers—feedback that goes not just to product support, but directly to the front-line development teams as well.

It began in the late 1990s, when Microsoft developers realized they could use the fact that most of their customers were on the Internet or had email. Each time they had a problem, the details could be collected automatically. Now, if you have a crash in just about any Microsoft product, you will get a dialog box that asks if you want to send information about the event to Microsoft. If you click yes, the details are sent automatically to Microsoft and are put into the product problem database. The product planners decide whether the problem gets fixed with a patch, a service release, or an update, or simply waits for the next version of the product.

Concomitantly, patches, service releases, and updates can be downloaded directly to registered users, where they can be

---

11.  Repeated inquiries at Microsoft yielded no one who actually knew why Watson is named Watson.

quickly installed to correct the problems. Not only is this expedient, but it's less costly for Microsoft than the old method of mailing everyone a replacement CD. It's much easier for the customer as well.

Take the online help function on Microsoft's support Web site. Whenever you access it, you have the opportunity to give feedback to Microsoft. The Content Watson, as it is called, collects this live customer feedback, which is then used to update the online help information on a daily basis.

LeVine's team also uses more proactive ways to obtain feedback from customers, querying them on the ways they use the various applications and asking for their experience with certain product features after release. In fact, they will go to some customers and train them on the feature just to get earlier feedback. After all, by the time a major customer acquires the new version of Office, deploys it, trains employees on it, and then is in a position to provide feedback, the vision document for the next version of Office has already been completed; even the detailed specs could have already been written.

"By getting continuous feedback," notes LeVine, "we should be able to increase reliability of our products by a whole order of magnitude."

Alas, that baked-in reliability becomes just another reason Microsoft Office is such a juicy target for pirates.

## HARNESSING GENIUS

As you saw with the spam-filtering example, Microsoft Research, or "The Labs," as it is known—the division that conducts basic or "pure" research—can play a direct role in product creation.

Formed in 1991, Microsoft Research employs 700 scientists, mostly Ph.D.s, in five labs on three continents. Most work in Redmond, but 100 or so work in Cambridge, England, another 100 in Beijing, and the rest in San Francisco and Silicon Valley. At any one time, they will be organized in 50 or so teams, working on upwards of 500 different research projects. They study every-thing from adaptive systems, astronomical mapping, and cryptog-raphy to, as we saw, machine learning, natural language computing, visual computing, and wireless networking. A typical publication has a title such as "Customizable Segmentation of Morphologically Derived Words in Chinese" (Andi Wu) or "Improved Left-Corner Chart Parsing for Large Context-Free Grammars" (Robert C. Moore).[12]

Research direction is set by the team leaders, rather than being dictated by the product groups or even Bill Gates. As Kevin Schofield, puts it, "these researchers could work in any computer science lab in the world, but one of the reasons they come here is so they can see their stuff end up in customers' hands."

Schofield, in a third-story office in Building 112, one of two hous-ing Microsoft Research in Redmond, is laying out the way the lab works and how research is pumped into product teams. In fact, it is his area that is the liaison between R&D and the product groups. "Some companies try and do technology transfer with process, but we believe the best way is through relationship."

He goes on to explain that Microsoft doesn't force the product groups to use the output of the labs, and the product groups don't tell the labs what to research. The two groups come together out of free will. Funding is centralized—both Bill Gates and Steve Ballmer are big fans of research—so the lab researcher doesn't have to continually beg for money from the product groups.

The researchers are an eclectic mix. "Let's say you are research-ing user interface design," says Schofield. "You quickly discover that is it is more than software design. You need to know how real people use the software. So our researchers will include sociolo-gists, anthropologists, ethnologists, cognitive psychologists, and so on. You need to know how users, sitting at screens looking at a software program, actually see it, what order they will press the keys, how do they think about the task they are trying to accom-plish, what's going on in their mind? Does the software let them

---

12. See http://research.microsoft.com/research/pubs/.

attack the steps or task in the order they want, or is it forcing them to do it one particular way?"

He points out that Microsoft is probably the world leader in software usability research, and describes how Microsoft usability labs evolved from focus group settings based on precepts of experimental psychology. Not only can they observe test subjects at work on individual software programs behind one-way mirrors, but now they even have an entire mock office set up so that they can test teamwork and collaboration.

The research can include everything from truly abstruse concepts like Bayesian equation theory, statistical physics, and abstract state machine language to field trials with actual customers. One of these field trials from Microsoft Labs is the reason you now see so many people at Microsoft using two monitors on a single computer. "We have discovered that, because of the rich visual system we use to perceive things, adding an extra monitor can create an immediate increase in productivity of 10–15 percent for computers users. Monitors are so cheap now that the investment is worth it."

Deep inside products like Windows XP, Office 2003, and the Microsoft XBox are DNA strands from the Labs. This DNA, too, is some of what the pirates are getting when they counterfeit software CDs, load illegal copies of Windows onto computers at the distribution points, or add unlicensed seats on their corporate networks. They're not just stealing digital zeroes and ones on a plastic disc. They're stealing *mindware*.

## PIRACY'S LONG SHADOW

Half the people at Microsoft are software developers. They don't dwell on software piracy, and guaranteed, some of them download MP3s from KaZaA. They really just want to develop and ship good software.

"I feel proud," said Mike Angiulo, "when I go to a computer store and see Microsoft Office sitting on the shelves. Of course, by then I've moved on to the next version."

And Microsoft, one of the most profitable companies on earth, can surely weather the revenue losses from piracy and afford the overhead of combating it. But as you'll see in Chapter 6, *Global Fallout*, piracy affects not only the companies whose software is pirated but also other companies in the software food chain, governments, and even end users. It profoundly affects people, from the beginning of the chain to its end.

Brad Smith puts it this way: "Yes, we suffer the most losses from piracy because we are the biggest software company and make a good target, but people miss the fact that those hurt even worse than us are the small start-up developers, especially in other countries. For them, combating piracy is a matter of economic life or death, determining whether they can continue to work, to develop software in their own country. One of the reasons there are so many talented Russian software developers working in the United States is because they weren't able to be successful in Russia, with one of the highest piracy rates in the world."

There is no message here for counterfeiters and criminal enterprises, as Smith calls them, who steal other goods besides software. They worry only about getting caught.

But there is a message for the rest of us, we pirates who operate in the gray areas where ignorance, inattention, insensitivity, or momentary convenience consign us to the ranks of brigands. The message is this: Piracy poses a risk beyond simply getting caught. Think of toxic waste dumping: There is a financial risk, yes, of getting caught in the act and fined, but the greater and more devastating risk is harm to the environment. Piracy degrades the software environment, making the strong companies stronger and the weak ones weaker, as Brad Smith points out and as the data in Chapter 6, *Global Fallout*, will show.

The irony for those who see Microsoft as a target, or who justify piracy to themselves on the grounds that Microsoft is already rich enough, is that pirating Microsoft software creates the old ripple effect throughout the entire software market, making Microsoft push for even more stringent protection and forcing competitors to compete against artificially low prices of pirated Microsoft software.

You may believe that piracy is the wrong word for liberating knowledge, or that intellectual output can't really be property, but by now you must realize that years of effort and millions of dollars are required for its creation. Bill Gates started his business by writing a program. He struggled for several years, living in a ratty motel room in Albuquerque, New Mexico, to grow Microsoft. Walk in his shoes—*really* walk in them—and see how it would feel to have your work pirated.

We conclude with the words of the poet James Russell Lowell, who penned the motto of the American Copyright League in 1885:

> In vain we call old notions fudge,
> And bend our conscience to our dealing;
> The Ten Commandments will not budge,
> And stealing will continue stealing.[13]

---

13. James Russell Lowell, November 20, 1885, for the American Copyright League, founded in 1883. Bartlett, John, comp. *Familiar Quotations*, 10th ed, rev. and enl. by Nathan Haskell Dole (Boston: Little, Brown, 1919). Source: Bartleby.com, www.bartleby.com/100/501.78.html.

# 5

# INSIDE THE SAUSAGE: THE MAKING OF THE DIGITAL MILLENNIUM COPYRIGHT ACT

> The Congress shall have Power...To promote the Progress of Science and useful Arts, by securing for limited Times to Authors and Inventors the exclusive Right to their respective Writings and Discoveries.
>
> **United States Constitution, Article I, Section 8**

The fountainhead of copyright law in the United States is this statement. It comes early in the Constitution and stands in august company along with other declarations relating to levying taxes, coining money, building roads, and waging war. Before penning this statement, the founding fathers debated long and hard over what "exclusive rights to writings and discoveries" should cover and how long those rights should last. The debate revolved around the balance between public good and the promotion of progress. The decision came down on the side of the public good.

From this simple declaration came the Copyright Act of 1790, and from that came a chain of extensions, amendments, replacements, and updates over the last 200 plus years. The end of that progression is the subject of this chapter, the Digital Millennium Copyright Act of 1998 (DMCA). It is thoroughly modern. Its language is peppered with technological terms from the modern age: words like encryption, digital media, and Internet. It targets modern behavior: software "cracking," digital file copying, and Internet file access. It answers to modern politics: lobbying by powerful entrenched interests with today's media-sensitive politicians.

It would be nice to think that those who govern today are still concerned about that balance that Washington, Jefferson, Madison, Adams, Franklin, and others fretted over. Yet it is increasingly evident that in today's world, Libra's scales are tipped in favor of promoting progress rather than insuring the public good.

The DMCA and its cousin, the Sonny Bono Copyright Extension Act, provide a case in point. These two pieces of legislation, passed by Congress within a week of each other, stretched U.S. copyright law into a new shape and shifted the balance between public good and business interests in the direction of a small group of wealthy, powerful copyright holders.

The government *could* use its powers and negotiating skills to mediate between the often conflicting interests of business and consumers— between the makers of CDs and the buyers of CD burners; between software publishers and dirt-poor graduate students; between Sony Pictures and the buyers of Sony DVD burners; between the music industry and the online downloaders.

But as you saw in Chapter 2, *Is It Copyright or the Right to Copy?*, you can go all the way back to England at the turn of the 18<sup>th</sup> century and find government swayed by political expediency and business interests in matters copyright. You also saw how it has become easier over the past 200 years to be remunerated for intellectual effort through copyright protection laws. Of course, few of those who actually *create* the work are reaping those rewards, since a concurrent trend has been to move copyright ownership from the hands of the artist or creator into those of the business entity that produces, manufactures, and markets the work. There are plenty of media and software millionaires and even billionaires. Those business entities, whether we're talking about music, movies, computer games, or computer software (or books for that matter), are well-heeled and powerful. Like any other life-form, they will go to nearly any length to protect their lifeblood assets. It's their duty to the species—er, stockholders.

Some argue that in the age of the Information Society, we need more protections for business, since information can be viewed as a corporate or economic asset. But others see in these laws unintended consequences that put the concept of intellectual property and the individual's rights to fair use of copyrighted media at risk.

Germany's chancellor Otto von Bismarck (1815–1898) is reputed to have quipped that making laws is like making sausages: The less one knows about the process, the more respect one has for the outcome. This particular sausage, the Digital Millennium Copyright Act, while tasty to the industry that lobbied for it, gives plenty of others indigestion.

## ANTECEDENTS TO THE DMCA

The U.S. Copyright Act is officially termed Title 17, United States Code,[1] and was enacted in 1790 by Congress as provided for in the Constitution (see Chapter 2, *Is It Copyright or the Right to Copy?*). Copyright law has been subject to a number of amendments since its inception. A major overhaul resulted in the Copyright Act of 1976, which established the basis for modern copyright law. Since 1976 Title 17 has had 49 amendments, or "statutory enactments." Some are simply administrative, while others are significant, dealing with various forms of intellectual property protection for semiconductors, home satellite television, architectural works, computer software, and unpublished work, as well as criminal penalties for copyright infringement, special copyright for works published for the blind and disabled, and work made for hire.

Each of these amendments has lagged a social or technological trend. It takes time to recognize the trend, define the issue, mobilize the interested parties, and pass a law. When technology is driving the changes that need to be accommodated, that lag can become a yawning gulf.

---

1.   The Code and all its amendments can be found at www.copyright.gov/title17/92preface.html.

In the 1980s, people in the computer industry were screaming for laws to protect against hackers. Computer stuff is generally difficult for people outside the profession to figure out, and the legal and judicial systems were certainly no exception. It took the lawyers and courts years to catch on and pass the reasonably tough laws we have today protecting computer systems against unwanted intrusion.

As the 1990s dawned, consumer audio electronics were at a technological peak. Audiophiles had several types of high-quality recording devices, and computers were beginning to ship with recordable CD drives. Stimulated by the imprecations of corporate music copyright holders, Congress passed the Audio Home Recording Act (AHRA) in 1992, an amendment to the 1976 Copyright Act.

The AHRA is a remarkable document in several ways: one, as laws go, its brevity (only ten pages); two, the fact that about a third of it involves definitions of digital media, digital devices, digital recording, and other digital details; and three, it actually grants John Q. and Jane Public a number of rights for making their own personal-use copies of digitized audio media. Specifically, Section 1008, "Prohibition on certain infringement actions," reads:

> No action may be brought under this title alleging infringement of copyright based on the manufacture, importation, or distribution of a digital audio recording device, a digital audio recording medium, an analog recording device, or an analog recording medium, or based on the noncommercial use by a consumer of such a device or medium for making digital musical recordings or analog musical recordings.[2]

This was the good part, the part that supported the public's right to make *personal copies for noncommercial use*. But then there was the other part, the one that gave an override royalty for multiple copies to the copyright holders. It wasn't enough that they had gotten the basic copyright royalty fees when they sold the

2.    See www.loc.gov/copyright/title17/chapter10.pdf.

recorded album. Now that it was possible to make digital copies, they felt entitled to an additional fee, or two or three, when we made our personal copy of the original recording.

The really devious (or clever, if you were a music industry executive) aspect of this was that the copyright owners got to collect the digital copy fee *up front*. The AHRA, in attempting to define a variety of digital recording devices and their nuances, was in effect facilitating a legal mechanism that would allow media copyright holders to collect royalties from the *manufacturers* of digital recording devices. This was called the Serial Copy Management System, or SCMS, and its design was to allow you and me to record a copy of our (audio) media for our own use.

The system also set up the U.S. Register of Copyrights as the banker, collecting from $1–$8 for each device sold and 3 percent of the wholesale cost of recording media, and dispersing it to various named federations of musicians and composers.[3] There is no actual determination of whether you or I actually copy music or not, nor can the music companies come after us if we do.

But Congress and the music industry lobbyists were not very prescient with their technology forecasting. The digital recorders— digital audio tape (DAT) and minidisks (MD) for which the AHRA was written—never really took off as consumer items. It's unknown how many people used digital recorders to make copies of their copyrighted music. Never mind: They paid the royalty fee nonetheless. For a brief moment, the music industry thought it had the solution to digital copying: The AHRA paid them something for their copyrights, with the added benefit of being largely invisible to consumers.

But remember what we said about the lag between technology and the law? The lawmakers who wrote the AHRA didn't take into consideration the personal computer and its newest innovation, the recordable CD drive—far more popular and pervasive than DATs and MDs. PCs sporting the new CD burner/player drives took off big time.

---

3.  Similar systems exist in other countries, although not uniformly and with varying definitions and royalty rates.

# THE PIECES START TO FALL INTO PLACE

In 1994, seeing technology advances eroding commercial media interests, the Working Group on Intellectual Property Rights in the U.S. Patent and Trademark Office prepared a white paper entitled "Intellectual Property and the National Information Infrastructure" recommending new legislation. In essence, the paper put forth the argument that

> Creators, publishers and distributors of works will be wary of the electronic marketplace unless the law provides them the tools to protect their property against unauthorized use. Advances in digital technology and the rapid development of electronic networks and other communications technologies dramatically increases: the ease and speed with which a work can be reproduced, the quality of the copies, the ability to manipulate or change the work, and the speed with which copies can be delivered to the public. The establishment of high speed, high-capacity information systems makes it possible for one individual, with a few key strokes, to deliver perfect copies of digitized works to scores of others—or to upload a copy to a bulletin board or other service where thousands can download it or print unlimited "hard" copies. Just one unauthorized uploading could have devastating effects on the market for the work.

> Thus, the full potential of the NII (National Information Infrastructure) will not be realized if the legal protections that extend to education, information and entertainment products and their use in the physical environment are not available when those works are disseminated via the NII.[4]

The Digital Future Coalition (DFC), a confederation of concerned public interest organizations ranging from the American Library Association and the Computer and Communications Industry Association to the National Council of Teachers of English and

---

4.  See www.uspto.gov/web/offices/com/doc/ipnii/.

the United States Catholic Conference,[5] was concerned about the proposed legislation:

> Members of the DFC recognized that if the policy proposals delineated in the White Paper were implemented, educators, businesses, libraries, consumers and others would be severely restricted in their efforts to take advantage of the benefits of digital networks.

> In 1995–96, Congress debated (the proposed) legislation, the NII Copyright Protection Act, to implement the changes listed in the White Paper. This legislation ultimately stalled as the 104th Congress closed in the fall of 1996, in part because the DFC and other concerned parties helped to demonstrate that the bill did not provide for adequate balance between ownership and access rights, and a domestic consensus did not yet exist on how to update copyright law.[6]

The effort to provide greater copyright protection for commercial interests was revived during the following Congressional session, now disguised in an act intended to conform to legislation that had been enacted in Europe.

## THE DMCA IS BORN

In 1996, the World Intellectual Property Organization (WIPO) adopted a new worldwide Copyright Treaty. WIPO was formed in 1974 under the auspices of the United Nations to ensure intellectual property laws were uniformly administered. It is a powerful organization whose impact affects everything from belles lettres to pharmaceuticals—and now digital intellectual property, such as software. The WIPO superceded a similar organization that was

5. For a list of DFC members, go to www.dfc.org/dfc1/Learning_Center/members.html.
6. See www.dfc.org/dfc1/Learning_Center/about.html.

created to enforce the Berne Convention[7] treaties and laws, and moved its headquarters the 150 kilometers from Berne to Geneva.

The WIPO Copyright Treaty of 1996 added a number of significant protections covering:

- Computer software, regarding programs as literary works (Article 4).

- Control for authors over the rental and distribution of their works (Articles 6 through 8).

- The design and organization of information in database files created by database management systems (Article 5).

- Modification of digital rights management information contained in works without permission (Article 12).

- Prohibition of circumventing copy protection with hardware or software technology (Article 11).

Given its lack of foresight in computer hardware, software, and associated digital rights management trends in the 1992 AHRA, the United States Congress had little choice but to adopt the WIPO Copyright Treaty, essentially *in toto*. It was passed into law as the Digital Millennium Copyright Act in 1998, just days after the Sonny Bono Copyright Act (more on this later). Both laws were passed by a voice vote—the old "aye" or "nay" method—making it virtually impossible to know who voted for or who voted against its passage.

It was almost as sneaky as the way Congress votes itself pay raises.

The DMCA, which also implemented new copyright protections not part of the WIPO treaty, got lots of support from the entertainment industry and practically no coverage in the news media—President Bill Clinton's highly publicized affair with Monica Lewinsky was grabbing all the news headlines. The lobbyists who were instrumental in getting the WIPO Treaty adopted in 1996 were the

---

7.  The Berne Convention took place in 1886 and codified the European view of copyright—including longer protections for copyrights and more powers for creators over derivative works. It also set standards for reciprocity in copyright protection between countries.

same lobbyists who shoveled the DMCA through Congress. In retrospect, many scholars and legislators believe there should have been more floor debate and discussion, and possibly revisions, before the DMCA was passed. Unfortunately, this did not occur and now it's the law, part and parcel of Title 17, United State Code.

## THE DMCA DISSECTED

From a corporate copyright holder's perspective, the good news in the DMCA's passage is that it put a finger in the dike of digital anarchy. It gave business the legal leverage to prosecute copyright infringers. But was that good news for the rest of us?

Let's see for ourselves, as we examine the different elements of the DMCA.

*Title I, Chapter 12 – Copyright Protection and Management Systems.* From a digital rights perspective, the corporate copyright holder constituency fared quite well: The DMCA opened the doors for them to prosecute acts of *digital* copyright infringement, something unanticipated in 1992's AHRA. In the main, the DMCA states that John Q. or Jane Public can be prosecuted for using a circumvention tool or technique that allows access to a copyrighted work. An example is a software program that decodes DVDs,[8] allowing

---

8. The first software to remove DVD encryption was DeCSS, released to the Internet in 1999 by Jon Johansen, a teenager from Norway who simply wanted to be able to watch DVDs on his personal computer, which used the Linux operating system. He was charged with copyright violation but was acquitted, the Norwegian court determining that once someone buys a DVD, they have the right to use it as they see fit—in this case, playing it on a Linux-based PC (www.globetechnology.com/servlet/ArticleNews/tech/RTGAM/20030109/gtnor/Technology/techBN/). Another decryption software program, Qrpff, was developed by Keith Winstein and Marc Horowitz at the Massachusetts Institute of Technology the following year. Weinstein says the main reason they created Qrpff was to show that constitutional law cannot impede what one considers an act of free speech—in this instance, the creation of technological solutions to problems. Indeed, many legal scholars challenge the constitutionality of the DMCA on the grounds of First Amendment rights (www.pcworld.com/news/article/0,aid,43943,00.asp).

you to make copies or cripple the copy-protection to suit your own purposes.

Say there are 10 minutes of commercial content on the DVD prior to the beginning of the movie that are encrypted to force you to watch them every time you play the DVD. The DMCA states you cannot remove that encryption to excise or skip over the commercials. You not only cannot perform acts of circumvention, but you may not possess the tools or techniques with which to do so. For example, you cannot use 321 Studios DVDX software to burn copies of DVDs or a software program that removes the encryption from the DVD.[9]

Movie studios were quick to take advantage of DVD encryption technology, creating eight different regions, or "standards," for worldwide distribution of incompatible formats that would enable them to control product distribution. For example, in North America, where movies are first released on DVD, the standard is Region 1. Other parts of the world do not get the DVD movies for another six to 12 months, and then only in their own specific encoded format (Region 2, 3, 4, etc.). DVD players sold in each respective region only play DVDs with corresponding region-encoding. It was a precedent-setting use of technology—intentionally creating incompatibily when hardware, software, and media manufacturers had for years struggled, as with the compact cassette, to agree on formats, standards, and compatibilities. There was a kind of reverse-compatibility issue as well: DVDs in most overseas markets sell for less than they do in the United States, so delaying publication and using incompatible formats helped protect the profit margins for the ever-gluttonous domestic U.S. market as well.[10]

---

9.    If the letter of the law were upheld, then you could be arrested and charged for owning a felt tip pen or Magic Marker, both of which can be used to paint over the encryption in the outer edge of many DVDs and certain copy-protected CDs as well. One of the major reasons for the new Super Audio and DataPlay CD formats is copy-protection.

10.   It's possible to buy a "zone-free" DVD player that will play a DVD from any region. You can also install software on your computer to do the same thing. In a countermove, the MPAA incorporated Regional Code Enhancing, or RCE, to befoul Region 1 DVDs when played on zone-free players. The battle goes on, and on, and on....

*Title II – Online Copyright Infringement Liability Limitation.* Perhaps the most pervasive (perverse?) use of the DMCA has been in the realm of the online world: the broadside launched against peer-to-peer (P2P) file sharing. Although the Act does not specifically address the P2P phenomenon, it does give copyright holders recourse and holds ISPs accountable for the acts of their customer/subscribers. Specifically:

- An ISP cannot be held liable for copyright infringement if, when properly notified by the copyright holder, it in turn notifies the subscriber of the alleged abrogation and institutes a "takedown," in essence removing the offending subscriber and/ or copyrighted content from service.

- The copyright holder is granted the legal right to issue subpoenas to copyright infringers located and identified through their ISPs.

The DMCA provides a "safe harbor" for ISPs whose customers might be breaking copyright laws. The *quid pro quo* is that the ISPs must actually take the customers' offending content off any Web sites they are hosting. For example, if you have a Web site on Mindspring and are allowing others to download copyrighted files, the ISP would be exempt from litigation if it acted swiftly to remove the copyrighted materials and/or deny you an Internet connection.

This provision led to legal wrangles over whether ISPs must also furnish the names and addresses of the *alleged* pirates. (We emphasize alleged, because the copyright holder need only demonstrate the most rudimentary just cause to issue a subpoena.) Court cases have been going back and forth on the issue of "naming names" since 2002, involving not just traditional ISPs but also universities, some of which resisted providing names of file-sharing students and some of which didn't.

The attitude of the ISPs over this portion of the DMCA may be seen in testimony by Verizon General Counsel William P. Barr before Congress in September, 2003, when he referred to the subpoena powers granted by the DMCA as "sweeping, invasive, unsupervised." He testified that what he called a "broad and promiscuous subpoena procedure" grants "truly breathtaking powers to anyone who can claim to be or represent a copyright owner; powers that Congress has not even bestowed on law enforcement and national security personnel."[11]

## THE STRANGE CASE OF ROSS PLANK

Ross Plank owns a small Web site maintenance company called Site Nurturing that he runs from a home office in Southern California. He's worked with companies large and small, including Warner Brothers and Paramount TV. Plank is a busy guy who takes his computers seriously and has never gotten into media downloading; he doesn't even have KaZaA installed on his computer. That's why he was a little surprised when Comcast, his Internet Service Provider, sent him a letter from the RIAA charging him with downloading hundreds of Spanish-language songs under the alias *mario@kazaa.com*.

An IP address is a unique identifier for your computer, and when Plank read complaint he found that the IP address for "Mario" was not the same as his. "I tossed it and forgot about it," Plank says, "until I got a call from a reporter at the *Washington Post* asking me for a comment on having been sued by the music industry."

Plank was one of the 261 individuals the RIAA sued in August 2003, using powers granted under the Digital Millennium Copyright Act.

---

11.  Testimony of William Barr, executive vice president and general counsel, Verizon Communications, before the Senate Committee on Commerce, Science & Technology, September 17, 2003, available at http://commerce.senate.gov/hearings/index.cfm.

Plank was frightened and stressed out. "I haven't downloaded any-thing, and I don't have any of the software on my machine. They're suing me for $150,000 a song, which adds up to several million dollars. I don't have that kind of money. I didn't even have enough money to hire an attorney to fight them. I saw most people paying (the RIAA) off because they didn't have the money to fight them."

But Plank was fortunate. The Electronic Frontier Foundation[12] learned of his case and stepped up to the plate with legal services. EFF attorneys filed an "Answer of Ross Plank to Complaint" in U.S. District Court[13] and, at this writing, are hoping the RIAA will drop its suit.

"It's a giant intimidation machine," Plank says, "They want to scare everyone into not downloading, but what bothers me is they're suing everyone, not using the law to compensate the artists for the royalties lost from downloading their song."

In point of fact, the settlement fees go back into funding more complaints.

"I tell you, this is enough to scare anybody out of downloading, but basically I'm guilty until proven innocent. I don't think that's the way the law should work. What's more, they haven't done their due diligence. They're suing an address, and it's not even mine. It's like suing a car in an accident, not the driver."

Since the suit was filed against him, Plank has changed his atti-tude toward the music industry.

"We were big buyers, we have over 500 CDs, but I've stopped buying them. I just won't support the industry in any way. I mean,

---

12.  See www.eff.org. The Electronic Frontier Foundation, an organization started in 1990 to defend constitutionally guaranteed (digital and online) rights, was co-founded by John Perry Barlow, a lyricist and member of the Grateful Dead.

13.  See www.eff.org/IP/P2P/plank_answer.pdf.

just a few years ago, the record companies were convicted of price-fixing![14]

"We (at Site Nurturing) do a lot of software and Internet development, and to me that's intellectual capital. I believe it's legitimate for someone who creates something, such as artists or computer programmers, to have rights to their work. They should be compensated. But I think the challenge here is dealing with an industry that is so set in its ways that it hasn't figured out a way to deal with this other than litigation and trying to take down their consumers!"

Plank didn't have a firm position on downloading songs from the Internet before all this happened. "I really felt that people would download something to check it out before buying it. I know a lot of people feel like that, who don't realize it's an issue. I heard about someone who upgraded to the $29.95 version of KaZaA and was convinced she was getting a service, pretty much felt she was paying for the songs. This is one of the growing pains of a new technology. Sometimes, what they think is going to kill an industry ends up making more money for it. The challenge is for companies to stay on a competing level. When companies start to sit back and resist changing the business model they lose sight of what doing business really is."

What does Plank tell his friends now? "Download at your own risk. It's dangerous, you can be sued for it. Your chances may be low,

---

14. In September, 2002, Universal Music, Sony Music, Warner Music, Bertelsmann's BMG Music, and EMI Group, plus retailers Musicland Stores, Trans World Entertainment, and Tower Records, agreed to a settlement paying $67.4 million in cash and $75.7 million worth of CDs to be distributed to public and nonprofit groups. Attorneys-General in New York and Florida (on behalf of all 50 states) charged price-fixing between 1995 and 2000 to keep CD prices artificially high, a practice termed "minimum-advertised pricing" (MAP). At settlement, the companies agreed to refrain from MAP for seven years. Consumers were overcharged to the tune of $480 million. CD prices were supposed to drop by up to $5, but did not. The attorneys took home $12.5 million; the distribution to consumers was only a few dollars per person; author Rochester received a check for $13.86.

but I couldn't believe that out of all the millions of downloaders, they came after me."

"There's one other thing," Plank adds. "I don't listen to that (Spanish) kind of music at all. One of the songs I'm accused of downloading is "El Bastardo" the bastard or something like that. I thought that was kind of ironic."

---

There are a few other things the DMCA permits. For example, copying for the sake of backing up a computer requiring maintenance, is acceptable under the law. Gee, thanks! Then there's something called "ephemeral recordings," which refers to copies made for the convenience of evaluation in distance education, libraries, for certain types of archives, and for broadcast purposes, when it is more convenient to put a digital copy on a server (including the new digital satellite "radio" services).

*Title V – Protection of Certain Original Designs.* Oh, did we mention that DMCA protection includes copyrighting boat hull design? Yep. You might snicker at this, since it smells like a pork barrel, but in its implications, Title V opens the legal door to the distinct possibility of *copyrighting an idea.* If ideas were copyrightable, and if Xerox had been able to copyright some of the research it was doing into computers in the late 1970s and early 1980s, we might not have the Macintosh, Windows, computer networking, the graphical display, or the mouse. Xerox might be the sole copyright owner, with complete control over five of the major technologies essential in our daily computing lives.

# I GOT 20 MORE YEARS, BABE

Working its way through the U.S. Congress at the same time as the DMCA—it passed just two days earlier, also by voice vote—

was another milestone change in copyright law. It was initiated by Salvatore Bono, an entertainer popular in the 1960s as the male half of the husband and wife duo Sonny and Cher. They had a several hits, the biggest of which was their signature song, "I Got You, Babe." They split in the 1970s, and Sonny faded from the scene as an entertainer, only to emerge in the 1980s as a politician. Stymied by the local government when he tried to open a restaurant in Palm Springs, he ran for mayor of the town in 1988 and was elected. He ran for the U.S. Senate in 1992 and lost, but was elected to the U.S. House of Representatives in 1994.

Now he had power. In 1996, Sonny Bono sponsored a bill to change the term length of copyright. According to his widow, Mary Whitaker Bono, "Sonny wanted the term of copyright protection to last forever."[15] Fortunately, wiser heads prevailed in Congress, and copyright was extended for only (*only?*) 20 years when the bill passed. An individual author's work is now copyrighted for 70 years after his or her death, and corporate copyrights have been extended to 95 years.[16]

The bill was tested in the courts almost immediately. This was the eleventh time Congress had extended the length of copyright in the past 40 years, and Eric Eldred was having none of it. Publisher of Eldritch Press, an online book publishing concern devoted to providing online versions of out-of-copyright books, Eldred and others, supported by Harvard University Law School's Berkman Center for Internet and Society Openlaw group, challenged the Sonny Bono Copyright Extension Act all the way to the Supreme Court. In 2003, the Court voted 7–2 in favor of the law. In a masterfully

---

15. Some members of Congress counseled Sonny's widow, Mary Whitaker Bono, who had taken his seat in Congress, that a copyright lasting forever would likely be unconstitutional. Jack Valenti, president of the Motion Picture Association of America, proposed an alternative: that copyright last forever, less one day. See http://cyber.law.harvard.edu/cc/evrmootcourt/.

16. Sonny Bono did not live to see his act pass into law; in January, 1998, he died in a skiing accident at Lake Tahoe.

written dissent of the Court's ruling, Justice Stephen Breyer said in part:[17]

> The Constitution's Copyright Clause grants Congress the power to "promote the Progress of Science... by securing for limited Times to Authors... the exclusive Right to their respective Writings." The statute before us, the 1998 Sonny Bono Copyright Term Extension Act, extends the term of most existing copyrights to 95 years and that of many new copyrights to 70 years after the author's death. The economic effect of this 20-year extension—the longest blanket extension since the Nation's founding—is to make the copyright term not limited, but virtually perpetual. Its primary legal effect is to grant the extended term not to authors, but to their heirs, estates, or corporate successors. And most importantly, its practical effect is not to promote, but to inhibit, the progress of "Science"—by which word the Framers meant learning or knowledge.
>
> The "monopoly privileges" that the Copyright Clause confers "are neither unlimited nor primarily designed to provide a special private benefit." ... The Copyright Clause and the First Amendment seek related objectives—the cre-

---

17. Eldred, a resident of Derry, New Hampshire, had originally become interested in online "eBooks" for his children. While some titles had to be removed as a result of the Supreme Court decision, a significant number of books, in extraordinarily handsome HTML format, remain in the public domain for public enjoyment. Incredibly, a pamphlet entitled *A Bridge to the Past: A Teacher's Guide to the North Bridge and Battle Road Units of Minute Man National Historical Park*, which is described as a "printed booklet" for sale at the Minute Man National Historical Park bookstore, was at issue in the case. It is copied onto unbound three-hole-punched, 8.5x11-inch paper, double-sided, black-and-white. The booklet bears neither date nor copyright, but a company named Eastern National claimed to have copyrighted it and asked Eldred to remove it from his public domain site. The Minute Man National Historical Park is a national park located in Concord, Massachusetts, whose purpose is to "interpret the colonial struggle for natural rights and freedoms" during the American Revolution of 1775. Eastern National is a private publishing company that has an exclusive contract with the government to publish and sell its works at 130 U.S. National Parks.

ation and dissemination of information. When working in tandem, these provisions mutually reinforce each other ... At the same time, a particular statute that exceeds proper Copyright Clause bounds may set Clause and Amendment at cross-purposes, thereby depriving the public of the speech-related benefits that the Founders, through both, have promised. [Legal citations deleted for clarity.][18]

Copyright holders lobbying Congress for an extension felt their arguments emboldened by the fact that during the period 1993–1996, the European Union had lengthened its term of copyright laws. The feeling was that U.S. copyright law should be consistent with that of the EU. This reciprocity in honoring international copyright began in the late 1800s under an agreement known as the Berne Convention for the Protection of Literary and Artistic Works, to which the U.S. finally signed on in 1988. Victor Hugo (1802–85), author of *Les Miserables*, played the Sonny Bono role[19] at the meeting in Switzerland, clearly concerned about English-language publications of his works without due royalty. Great Britain's Arthur Conan Doyle, creator of the legendary master detective Sherlock Holmes of Baker Street, was probably just as concerned about the French doing the same with his creations.

So, in 1996, there were some social as well as legal precedents for the United States and its European friends to remain on the same copyright page, so to speak. The EU 1993 Directive on harmonizing the term of copyright protection was their equivalent of the Sonny Bono Copyright Term Extension Act of 1998.

## WHAT HATH THE DMCA WROUGHT?

Laws change, mutating to fit the times to which they apply. Laws impact other laws by virtue of precedents—a lawyer cites a case where a law was previously applied and says it applies in another,

---

18. *Eldred et al v. Ashcroft*, No. 01–618, 537 U.S. Supreme Court, 2003. See www.copyright.gov/docs/eldredd1.pdf.
19. Curiously, like Sonny Bono, Victor Hugo died before the Berne Convention laws were enacted.

somewhat different case. Now the law has been reinterpreted and can go in an entirely new direction—maybe good, maybe bad. There are some directions the DMCA (and the Sonny Bono Copyright Extension Act) are taking us that we, as citizens, need to be concerned about.

Consider:

*Anticircumvention could lead to an abolition of copying in any form.* You have a legal right to make copies of media you buy, for whatever purpose you choose. The music and movie industries are attempting to deny you that right with various encryption and anticopying technologies. The DMCA supports that denial—it nearly makes *thinking* about making a copy illegal. Anticircumvention will permeate other forms of innovation and creative endeavor, such as reverse engineering, which makes it possible to develop better products, and testing various technologies and systems to assure their integrity or to find weaknesses.

In 2001, Edward Felten, Professor of Computer Science at Princeton, was contacted by the Secure Digital Music Initiative (SDMI) organization, writing on RIAA letterhead,[20] advising him that his intention to reveal the technology underlying certain "digital watermarks" used to encrypt digital media would be met with stern resistance. Felton had participated in a challenge contest sponsored by the SDMI, called "Hack SDMI," and had, in fact, broken the encryption. When the RIAA and SDMI learned that he and his colleagues from Princeton, Rice, and Xerox intended to present a paper on the subject at a forum of technologists, they sent Felten a letter invoking the nondisclosure agreement on which the $10,000 prize was contingent (and which Felten hadn't signed):

> We recognize and appreciate your position, made clear throughout this process, that it is not your intention to engage in any illegal behavior or to otherwise jeopardize the legitimate commercial interests of others. We are concerned that your actions are outside the peer review pro-

---

20. See www.cs.princeton.edu/sip/sdmi/riaaletter.html.

cess established by the Public Challenge and set up by engineers and other experts to ensure the academic integrity of this project. With these facts in mind, we invite you to work with the SDMI Foundation to find a way for you to share the academic components of your research while remaining true to your intention not to violate the law or the Agreement. In the meantime, we urge your [sic] to withdraw the paper submitted for the upcoming International Information Hiding Workshop, assure that it is removed from the Workshop distribution materials and destroyed, and avoid a public discussion of confidential information.[21]

Fearing a lawsuit from the RIAA, Felten opted not to present the paper but then, with the support of the EFF, sued the SDMI to determine that he could, in fact, present scientific results without violating the DMCA. A judge dismissed the case and Felten didn't appeal; no ruling was ever made regarding the DMCA's applicability to scientific research. Felten later presented his paper at another conference.[22]

What did Felten want to demonstrate with his research? That the digital watermarking technology, intended to make digital works more secure, was not as secure as thought. What could have been the SDMI's opportunity to take advantage of Dr. Felten's work instead devolved into acrimony and a senseless lawsuit.

Another landmark case involving copy protection was *U.S. v. Elcomsoft*, in which Dmitry Skylarov, a Russian programmer, was arrested in the summer of 2001 while attending a computer conference in Las Vegas. His crime under the DMCA was the creation of a software program for his company, Elcomsoft, that by circumventing encryption, permitted owners of electronic eBooks to translate their book from the Adobe eBook format to the more popular Adobe PDF. The program only worked on legitimately purchased eBooks, but could be used to put eBook content onto

---

21.   Ibid.
22.   The paper is available at www.usenix.org/events/sec01/craver.pdf.

other computers. The mild-mannered Skylarov was jailed for three weeks and then detained in the U.S. for six months before being allowed to return to his wife and two small children. The case, also defended by the EFF, went to jury trial in December 2002, and, 18 months after Skylarov's arrest, ended in acquittal. The jury felt that Elcomsoft's product may have violated the law, but the DMCA itself was confusing, so if the company and Sklyarov *had* broken the law, they had done so unintentionally.

*What has happened to "fair use"?* The DMCA says that nothing in the Act "shall affect rights, remedies, limitations, or defenses to copyright infringement, including fair use, under this title." Problem is, the Copyright Act of 1976 pretty much rendered fair use subject to individual interpretation, which suggests there is little in the way of governance that can be applied. If the music industry deems that fair use of a song is 30 seconds, not one entire song, then downloading that song constitutes copyright violation. Many argue that sampling a CD leads to a purchase; others (including the music industry) do not.

The DMCA was put to the test in a fair use case in the fall of 2003 when two students at Swarthmore College, Nelson Pavlovsky and Luke Smith, posted on a school Web site documents owned by Diebold, a company that makes voting booth technology (as well as ATMs), in order to prompt public discussion concerning electronic voting. Diebold issued a DMCA-inspired cease-and-desist order, and the college pulled the suspect material. Derek Slater, a student at Harvard, posted the documents on a Harvard site in support of the Swarthmore students. Harvard, too, got a cease-and-desist notice and pulled the documents off the Web. Harvard's legal counsel soon determined that it was indeed fair use; Diebold backed down and the documents went back up. Then the Swarthmore students and a nonprofit ISP sued Diebold for copyright protection abuse.

There is a more subtle inhibitor to fair use embedded in the DMCA, and it has to do with copy protection and encryption. Even when fair use of content is allowed by law, actually extracting that content from encrypted or protected media can be technically difficult. You may be able to retype text, if that's the material, but what if it's a song or video? If you want to embed a bit of the original into your own content—say a parody or review—you simply won't be able to get your hands on it. Well, you can if you ask the copyright holder, but then your ability to get access to it may depend on *how* you want to use it. For instance, will this be a positive review? Fine, here's the material. However, if your review is unfavorable....

The upshot is that we really don't have the entitlement of fair use any longer. The old sensibility was that allowing a small portion of a work to be used in another work was a spur to new ideas and works, or at least a form of publicity or marketing, have been subsumed by the sense of intellectual property ownership. This is especially true when the property in question is owned by a business or corporate entity. If copyright owners were the artists themselves, who generally enjoy sharing ideas and their interpretations, it is likely there would be much less stringent controls over fair use.

*The DMCA may threaten the promulgation of ideas.* Proponents of the DMCA say stricter protection of intellectual property fosters innovation—but you can just as well argue the other side. The world thrives on new ideas, but if engineers, designers, and artistic creators fear copyright infringement and lawsuits, fewer will be willing to innovate. Add to this digital intimidation, if you will: the seemingly benign provisions regarding reverse engineering and the Act's open invitation to find more ways to apply the provisions of the DMCA to a wide array of Internet and related technologies.

The DMCA states in Section 104, "Evaluation of Impact of Copyright Law and Amendments on Electronic Commerce and Technological Development," that a report would be issued to Congress within 24 months of the Act's passage, and it was. Public comment was permitted, and the few members of the public who commented said that provisions of the DMCA were at odds with the doctrine of first sale. You remember that, right? It says that you have the right to buy copies of a copyrighted work and then resell, rent, or lend that copy to others. You buy a book at Barnes & Noble and sell it back to Annie's Book Stop. Legal. You buy a CD or DVD at Best Buy and sell it back to the local used-media shop. Legal. But now, thanks to the DMCA, it is possible to encrypt media to only play on certain devices. Music, for example, plays in your home CD player, but not your car or your computer. Alas, media cannot be copied in any legal manner (we're back to the anti-encryption argument again). But read what the Register of Copyrights said in the 2001 report:

> The Effect of Section 1201 [of the DMCA] on the Operation of the First Sale Doctrine.
>
> Several commenters argued that section 1201's protection of CSS for DVDs against circumvention affects consumers' exercise of the first sale doctrine by enforcing technological limitations on the way DVDs can be used. These commenters asserted that because CSS is proprietary technology that is licensed to device manufacturers under restrictive terms, the use of CSS limits the potential playback devices for DVDs, which, in turn, limits the potential market for resale of DVDs. Second, they argued that because licensed playback devices enforce region codes, DVDs purchased in one region of the world cannot be as easily resold in other regions, again limiting the potential resale market.
>
> This argument is without merit. The first sale doctrine codified in section 109[23] limits an author's distribution right so that subsequent disposition of a particular copy by its owner is not an infringement of copyright. The first sale doctrine does not guarantee the existence of a secondary market or a certain price for copies of copyrighted works. If fewer people may wish to purchase a used DVD, or if they would pay less for it due to CSS, that

---

23. Section 109 of U.S. Copyright law, Title 17, deals with the right to make copies of "phonorecords."

would not equate to interference with the operation of section 109. Many circumstances in the marketplace may affect the resale market for copies of works—improvements in technology, introduction of new formats, and the quality and cultural durability of the content of the work. None of these factors can properly be said to interfere with the operation of section 109, even though they could reduce the resale market for a work or even render it nonexistent.

Perhaps the Register is correct. Maybe buying a DVD in the U.S. and trying to sell it in Asia is like buying a book written in English and selling it in China. But maybe it's also like buying a book written in disappearing ink: You can read it once, but not twice. Either way, the Register's words show a bias toward the protection of the copyright holder's rights, not those of the owner—which was what the first sale doctrine was all about, giving the owner certain inalienable rights to sell, trade, or share with others what he or she has purchased. Indeed, one can see the argument against peer-to-peer file-sharing being set up in this opinion: publisher's rights first, then owner's rights; possession of copyright superceding possession of property. If, indeed, that is the case, can a file-sharer be said to be in possession of either? In all likelihood, the answer is no.

This becomes an exercise in circular logic. The proponents are right from their side, while the protesters believe they are right from theirs. Maybe it's all the public's fault; only 47 people took the time to comment.

*The DMCA undermines the Constitutional intent of copyright law.* As we discussed in the beginning of this chapter, the founding fathers of the U.S. wanted copyright law to respect a balance between the interests of copyright holders and the rights of everyone else. But ownership of copyright has turned artistic expression into a commodity, just another "product" that can be bought and sold. Michael Jackson owns the copyright to many of the Beatles' songs, which he bought for $47 million in 1985. He, in turn, sold his catalog of music copyrights to Sony in 1993 for $110 million.[24]

Given that the DMCA makes copyright ownership so much more lucrative, we likely will see it become an even more desirable commodity, and corporate copyright owners will likely lobby Congress for even more stringent copyright protection and longer copyright terms in the future.

An interesting case is unfolding in the software industry. SCO, a Utah-based software company, has sued IBM and others alleging that various versions of the Linux operating system use programming code from SCO's copyrighted UNIX operating system. But Linux is not your everyday operating system: It was created by the unremunerated volunteer efforts of thousands of programmers under the rule that anyone can use Linux or write additional software for it, provided they share those enhancements. SCO claims that bits and pieces of Linux were taken from SCO software. Ironically, UNIX was created by Bell Labs and given to the world as free, open-source software. SCO's UNIX is a variant of that. SCO claims that the DMCA favors its position, in the same way it ruled against Eric Eldred (mentioned earlier). In an open letter on the SCO Web site,[25] Darl McBride, SCO Group President & CEO wrote:

> SCO argues that the authority of Congress under the U.S. Constitution to "promote the Progress of Science and the useful arts..." inherently includes a profit motive, and that protection for this profit motive includes a Constitutional dimension. We believe that the "progress of science" is best advanced by vigorously protecting the right of authors and inventors to earn a profit from their work.

This is a radical definition of the United States Constitution and copyright laws. Nowhere will you find mention of the protection of the profit motive, even though this is to some extent implicit in affording copyright protection. Yet who among us knows of a

---

24. The joke goes, if you hear a Beatles song in a commercial, Michael Jackson owns it.
25. See www.caldera.com/copyright.

painter, author, musician, or scientist who embarks upon their chosen form of creative expression with the sole intent of making a profit? Is that not the stated intent of business, not art? Should SCO win its case, slated to go to trial in 2005, it will be a setback for the "progress of science and useful arts" inasmuch as it will cause a pall to settle on the whole open source movement.

---

## SIX QUESTIONS ON COPYRIGHT FOR JONATHAN ZITTRAIN

We spoke with Jonathan Zittrain, assistant professor for Entrepreneurial Legal Studies at Harvard University and faculty co-director of the Berkman Center for Internet and Society.[26]

Q: Is downloading copyright infringement and stealing, or is it fair use? Can you legally download a digital version of a song you bought on a record?

A: Fair use is much more narrow than most people think. Fair use is a standard, not a rule, and it often requires a lawsuit to decide it. Many people honestly don't see downloading as stealing, since it doesn't deprive anyone else of the song itself—only a chance to profit from its sale. They might say, "it's not a pie, it's just sniffing the aroma." Still, I think it is generally an infringement to download large amounts of copyrighted material without permission. Even if you already own the corresponding CD, the case could be made that a network-derived copy is infringing.

Q: How come it was okay to swap music on tape but now, as music industry executives state, since it's digital and perfect, it isn't? Further, they say it was okay when only a few did it, but now that we have millions to share with it's not okay.

A: Copyright law has always been complicated, and now that it routinely impinges on individual behavior, it's all the more a big mess.

---

26. See http://cyber.law.harvard.edu/home/.

Conscience and convenience have governed individual behavior in the past; for example, many people feel socially awkward ordering up, say, a descrambler to steal cable TV service. Now copying has become quite convenient. The real objection the music industry has to services like KaZaA and Grokster is that they are thought to seriously dampen profits. So long as the industry frames its pricing around the scarcity of its product, there probably indeed is such an impact.

Q: Why do you think so many young (and older) people feel it's OK to download?

A: First, because the "stealing," if such it is, is indirect: it's taking money out of the pocket of someone who might otherwise be able to charge for the music. That's a harm, but a distinct one from the harm of, say, having one's car stolen. Second, there is a lasting impression of the American music industry as often being at odds with the creative artists it enlists. People may feel it's OK to copy music if it's "merely" hurting a company that in turn was giving a bad deal to an artist anyway. Finally, consumers want convenience, and the industry has been slow to offer equally convenient legal alternatives.

Q: You say copyright law is a big mess. What is your legal opinion of the Digital Millennium Copyright Act?

The DMCA is a big mess, too. It has reinforced the mercenary instincts of the copyright holders, who now want to see every possible profit from a work go to them and who think that the way to reconcile old business models with new technologies is to alter the technology to suit the business model—which then cuts off a range of other innovation wholly unrelated to intellectual property.

Q: You've called the Internet "an instrument of anarchy." Is there any way to plug up the increasingly free flow of information, as the RIAA has attempted to do?

A: The record companies are acting like pit bulls. There's a "take no prisoners" attitude on both sides of the issue. It may take the form of a new Internet which uses its own technologies to control copyrighted media.

Q: What are the most appropriate solutions to digital piracy, ones that will make all parties satisfied?

A: I credit that if copyrights were to be rendered inconsequential by technology, then creators will create less—and many will cease to create at all. There are a number of good alternatives; for example, the iTunes model or Harvard Law professor Terry Fisher's proposal for an alternative compensation system based on compulsory licensing. We need to focus our thinking away from income structures that ossified in the early 20$^{th}$ century and toward a combination of technological advances and rewards for innovation that will enhance rather than stanch the flow of ideas, which is fundamental to a free society.

## THE BELL TOLLS, BUT FOR WHOM?

Many see the DMCA is a carelessly concocted law, pieced together in haste by interest groups and from WIPO materials (did we mention the protection of boat hull design tacked on the end?), the implications of which we of the digital millennium are only beginning to realize. Congress has eroded the rights of *both* copyright holders and those who use copyrighted media by losing sight of the balance we talked about in Chapter 2, *Is it Copyright of the Right to Copy?*, and earlier in this chapter.

We need rights to use digital media ethically and legally no less than we need rights to use analog or print media; yet those rights are slowly eroding as copyright ownership becomes big business. Read the Book! See the Movie! Buy the DVD! Buy the Soundtrack

CD! Watch the Television Series! Buy the Stuffed Animal at Wal-Mart! But don't expect to own or share any of these forms of media with others unless you pay us once again for the rights to do so. And if you show any ingenuity, such as figuring out how to override our technological protection, we'll sue you, throw you in jail, and transform you from a talented computer hacker-college student into a convicted felon!

Hyperbole? Perhaps, but it was no less than General Counsel and Executive Vice President of Verizon, William F. Barr, who referred to the RIAA lawsuits against file-sharers, in testimony before Congress, as "jihad against 12-year-old girls."[27]

Maybe the DMCA is not *that* bad for the citizenry, but as DMCA case law evolves and lawsuits test its boundaries, there are plenty of reasons to be wary.

One is the impact on citizen privacy. Verizon's Barr, in his testimony before Congress over a district court ruling that his company would have to turn the names of file sharers over to the record companies, said, "The District Court has created a Frankenstein monster that Congress never contemplated and that has the potential to cause irreparable harm to public confidence in the privacy of Internet communications."

He added later that the DMCA "threatens to turn our Federal courts into free-floating subpoena mills, unhinged from any pending case or controversy, capable of destroying anonymous Internet communication, and threatening privacy and due process rights as well as public safety."

In his testimony, Barr pointed out that the generation of subpoenas as authorized by the DMCA has little or no oversight, and that not just media companies but private citizens can issue takedown notices to ISPs. He named two pornographic publishers that have already issued subpoenas for names in the same manner as the

27. Testimony as part of a panel discussion before the U.S. Senate Committee on Commerce, Science & Transportation, on September 17, 2003, as reported by David McGuire, staff writer for *The Washington Post*. See www.washingtonpost.com (registration required).

RIAA subpoenas. He also talked of the growing industry of "bounty hunters" who search the Internet for transgressors. In this Wild West atmosphere, mistakes happen. In 2001, Warner Brothers sent a letter to UUNet demanding it terminate the account of someone who was sharing Harry Potter videos over the net. UUNet investigated and found that the offending material was a one-page book report written by a child. How many other mistakes go unnoticed?

Companies are already stretching the DMCA beyond the uses Congress envisioned in 1998. Besides the Diebold case, in 2002 Wal-Mart used the DCMA to attempt to get FatWallet, a company that runs a price comparison Web site, to disclose the name of the individual, probably a Wal-Mart employee, who had revealed prices for an upcoming Thanksgiving Day sale (if the prices had been published there would be no copyright violation). In January of 2003, Lexmark International sent a cease and desist notice to Static Controls, Inc., which made a chip that allowed third parties to make toner cartridges for Lexmark printers; Lexmark won an injunction in February that was still under appeal as of early 2004.

Civil libertarians (and yes, certainly some digital pirates) are also worried about further extensions of the DMCA by the states, laws that have been called "Super DMCA" laws. A number of states, including Illinois and Michigan, have passed laws that target the theft of pay-per-view TV signals or attempts to disguise or hide the origin of any electronic transmission (such as email). Many of these laws are patterned after model legislation crafted by the Motion Picture Association of America. These laws create a better dragnet for true pirates, but they also add opportunities to snare the innocent along with the guilty and to abrogate basic electronic privacy rights.

Fortunately for the U.S. citizenry, Verizon stuck to its guns in its litigation with the RIAA regarding turning over customer names. On December 19, 2003, the U.S. Court of Appeals overturned the Ninth District Court decision and ruled in Verizon's favor:

The district court rejected Verizon's statutory and constitutional challenges to § 512(h) and ordered the internet service provider (ISP) to disclose to the RIAA the names of the two subscribers. On appeal Verizon presents three alternative arguments for reversing the orders of the district court: (1) § 512(h) does not authorize the issuance of a subpoena to an ISP acting solely as a conduit for communications the content of which is determined by others; if the statute does authorize such a subpoena, then the statute is unconstitutional because (2) the district court lacked Article III jurisdiction to issue a subpoena with no underlying "case or controversy" pending before the court; and (3) § 512(h) violates the First Amendment because it lacks sufficient safeguards to protect an internet user's ability to speak and to associate anonymously. Because we agree with Verizon's interpretation of the statute, we reverse the orders of the district court enforcing the subpoenas and do not reach either of Verizon's constitutional arguments.

Note, however, how the Court has once again avoided dealing with constitutional or First Amendment issues by ruling in favor of Verizon only on the first count, but not speaking to the second and third. This will be litigated in future years, without a doubt.

## DESPERATELY SEEKING LIBRA

The Hopi have a word for it: *koyaanisqatsi*. It means "life out of balance." To our eyes, the DMCA, as it was written and as it is developing through case law, is out of balance. It weighs too heavily in favor of the well-heeled corporate copyright holder, and not the artist who created the work or the consumer. This is one of the reasons there have been a number of laws introduced in Congress to put limits on it. Congresswoman Zoe Lofgren (D: California), for instance, introduced a bill called the "Balance Act," intended to restore Libra's scale to equanimity. The bill would restore the legal right to make backup copies of digital media for play on different machines. The bill was introduced in 2002, died in committee, was reintroduced in 2003, and stalled again. In short, the legislative reflection and backlash to the DMCA has been fairly weak as other issues, such as war, terrorism, deficits, and re-election campaigns, occupy Congress's time.

Yes, of course, there are two sides to the DMCA argument. If you believe the purpose of copyright law is to afford the creator a fair and equitable return for his intellectual work but for a limited period of time and tightly circumscribed circumstances, then the DMCA is a bad law.

If, on the other hand, you believe the purpose of copyright law is to maximize the financial return for copyright holders and to protect their investments in obtaining the copyrights and making them valuable, then the DMCA is a good law.

In either case, the DMCA and the intent of the founding fathers seem as distant as the near quarter-millennium that has passed between the Copyright Act of 1790 and now, as we watch control of copyright increasingly pass from the hands of the many into the hands of the few.

# 6

# GLOBAL FALLOUT

You must understand, copying is a sign of respect in China. I am trying to create a new understanding. I am always giving lectures to the entire college, trying to convince students that it is better to buy software even if it costs more. You see, we charge so much for software that we are punishing our children for getting an education.[1]

**Sheen–Yan Torn, Vice Director, Intellectual Property Office, Taiwan**

From Red Square you take the Zamoskvoretskaya (green) line of the Moscow subway from Teatrainaya and go north three stops to Savyolovskaya, just one stop outside the main metro ring around Moscow. Exiting here, you hop-step along with the fast-moving crowd toward the stairs. You see all manner of goods for sale: people selling from card tables, in little stalls, and in little cubby-hole shops. Food, snacks, clothing, souvenirs, papers, books, music, gum, and computer software—all are for sale in the dark caverns of the subterranean walkway. Of course, if you've been out and about in Moscow for a day or two, you will have seen many such temporary, hole-in-the-wall retail establishments.

Capitalism in a suitcase.

But here, at Savyolovskaya, the closer you get to the exit, the more items you see in those clear 5" jewel boxes—music, movies, and software. But the

---

1. Interview with Sheen–Yan Torn, Vice Director, Intellectual Property Office, Ministry of Economic Affairs, Chinese Taipei, December 30, 2002. Mr. Torn is also a Professor of Computer Science at the National Taipei University of Technology.

trade seems desultory. The rush hour crowd moves along as we might in the underground tunnels at Grand Central Station in New York, past vendors selling pretty much the same things.

As you exit above ground, the concentration of electronic media sellers up and down the stairway thickens, and once you surface, you see you have entered a bazaar of one-story shops, each one only a few square feet and able to accommodate only a handful of customers at a time. There is a main concourse perhaps 300 meters long, shops jam-packed on both sides, and more around the corner.

It *is* a testament to capitalism. Colorful, thronged, and outfitted with absolutely the hottest goods and the latest point-of-sale technology. A little further on is a permanent structure selling electronics hardware: HP Pavilion notebooks, Dell Inspiron laptops, Nokia and Samsung cell phones, and Sony DVD players.

But in the gypsy camp lining the path to the hardware complex it's all software, music, and movies. And nothing but the latest: Microsoft XP, Autodesk 2004, Microsoft Project 2004, Microsoft SQL Server, Electronic Arts videogames, Disney's *Finding Nemo*, Eminem's *Sing for the Moment* CD.

Everything costs 80 rubles, or about $3, unless it comes packed three in a set. Then it's 200 rubles. Movies that would cost $25 to buy on DVD in the U.S., CDs that would cost $17, and software at $500, $1,000, or even more, all for the same price. In fact, since it's harder to copy books than CDs, if you want a computer manual or a book on programming, you might have to shell out more than the cost of the software itself.

What a deal! For Muscovites, who make, on average, 20,000 rubles a month, how could this not be good? Even if the source of all this content is suspect.

In fact, the economics are good enough that there is an entire underground economy in Russia supporting the illegal copying of software and other digital media—repackaging it and selling it at places like Savyolovskaya or less organized outlets, like the guy with a card table on Kalanchovskaya Street near the IDC Russia offices. The factories that pump out pirated software look little different from legitimate duplication and packaging plants. In fact some do both, distributing and manufacturing both legal copies of software and illegal ones. There is even some pride of creation— Russians point out that *their* pirated software is of higher quality than the pirated software that comes to the bazaars from China, Poland, Bulgaria, and the Ukraine.

But look closer. There is also Russian software for sale, although not nearly as much as from the multinational software firms. It *too* retails for 80 rubles.

For multinational software companies, like Microsoft, Autodesk, IBM, and BEA, Russia is just one bad spot in a mosaic of international markets. For local Russian packaged software vendors, however, Russia *is* the market, and 80 rubles a copy is the number they have to work with to make a living.

Here's a country with almost as many scientists as the U.S., more college graduates than all of Western Europe, and world-renowned skills at *writing* software, yet its packaged software market is only 12 percent of all the money spent on information technology in Russia. In neighboring Finland, it's 20 percent, in the nearby Netherlands, 24 percent. The share of that spending to homegrown software companies is negligible. Russia's PC software piracy rate[2] of 87 percent—87 out of 100 software packages running on PCs are pirated—means that any nascent Russian packaged software industry is permanently stillborn.

Instead of employing skilled, higher-paid (and higher tax-paying) software developers to drive its software industry, Russia is employing the equivalent of McDonald's counter people to distribute other people's purloined software.

The same is pretty much true for music and movies. Although the movie distribution business is booming in Moscow, over 90 percent of what's shown is from the U.S. In 2001, the Russian film industry produced only 30 features films. The music industry is just as beleaguered.

2.  This is the 2003 piracy rate for PC software calculated by IDC for the BSA. The rate excludes other types of software, such as that running on servers or mainframes. The piracy rate is the percent of total software installed during the year that has been pirated.

# HOW BAD IS PIRACY?

There is no general measure for all digital media piracy, although every year the U.S. government tallies best estimates from the music, movie, software, and game software industries and puts certain countries on various watch lists.[3] But the estimates are only for the countries on the watch lists and don't cover the impact of piracy in much bigger—but lower-piracy—markets.

The music industry, for instance, tracks the retail value of pirated CDs sold around the world—over $4 billion a year. But this doesn't get at the retail value of the music sold or the size of the Internet downloading losses. The movie industry looks at losses in the U.S. ($3 billion a year) but has no measure of what's lost outside the U.S. or by country-level filmmakers.

However, for a decade, the Business Software Alliance has estimated the amount of software piracy in the world.[4] The BSA, as you saw in Chapter 3, *Us Against Them,* is a trade group of leading multinational software companies with a mission to promote "a safe and legal digital world"—i.e., combat piracy. The study, because it has been published for almost a decade, has itself been studied, making software piracy the most consistently tracked and examined form of digital piracy. In 2004, IDC[5] conducted the study for the BSA.

The methodology for estimating piracy is a little arcane—it involves determining how many software packages are running on the PCs in a country and comparing that number to the total shipped by software companies—but it has stood the test of time.

In some countries, the amount of PC software piracy is astounding. The 10 worst offending countries as of 2003 are shown in Figure 6–1. Compare them to a country like the U.S., where the PC

---

3.   The industry submission is available at http://www.iipa.com/.

4.   Available at www.bsa.org.

5.   IDC is a major U.S.–based computer and communications industry market intelligence firm. Author Gantz is the company's Chief Research Officer and led the team that conducted the study mentioned.

| Vietnam | 92% |
| China | 92% |
| Ukraine | 91% |
| Indonesia | 88% |
| Zimbabwe | 87% |
| Russia | 87% |
| Algeria | 84% |
| Nigeria | 84% |
| Pakistan | 83% |
| Paraguay | 83% |

**Figure 6–1**  Top 10 PC software pirating countries. Source: IDC, 2004.

software piracy rate is 22 percent, or Japan, where it is 29 percent.

There are plenty of other offenders. In 34 countries, two-thirds of all PC software was pirated. In the study, the only good news is that PC software piracy has dropped from an average of 42 percent in 1994 to 36 percent in 2003. The low point was in 1999, when the rate was 31 percent. In the IDC study, the retail value of pirated PC software for 2003 was $28.8 billion.

*But that's not all.* If you consider *all* of the software pirated in the world, including software that runs on servers and mainframes, that retail value surpasses $42 billion. Even in the United States, which has the lowest piracy rate, the value of pirated software is over $10 billion. The piracy rate may be lower for the software that runs on enterprise computers—after all, it's a little hard to pirate quarter-million dollar database systems running on IBM 390s—but the losses add up. This is because PCs running Microsoft Word or Adobe Photoshop really only make up a small portion of the software used in a country. Over 70 percent of a medium or large company's software budget is spent on enterprise-class software: database management systems from companies like Oracle, complex suites of business management software such as SAP, and powerful customer relationship management applications from companies like Siebel Systems.

Figure 6–2 shows the retail value of all pirated software in 2003 in the 87 countries studied by IDC.

Okay. If software piracy suddenly dropped to zero, would the vendors be $43 billion richer? No, of course not. Many individuals and companies would probably just do without, write their own, or find cheaper alternatives. But *some* of that money would be recouped, resulting in an improved GNP, more jobs, more dollars spent on R&D, and a healthier economy worldwide. As you will see later, lower piracy would stimulate more activity in the software market, which would lead to purchases of *new* kinds of software.

It could be worse: We could be talking about the cigarette industry. According to the U.S. Customs Service, cigarettes are the number one counterfeit commodity seized at the border—38 percent of 2002's seizures.

At 29 percent, digital media, including software, was *only* number two.

## THE HIDDEN COSTS OF SOFTWARE PIRACY

While there are economic benefits to a "free" commodity—as pirated software is regarded in many countries—there are also economic costs. In a 2003 study for the BSA on the economic impact of software piracy, IDC quantified those costs. The study looked first at the economic impact of the current information technology industry in each of the countries and then computed how much more impact the industry would have if the piracy rate were lowered.

IDC found the tradeoffs for "free" software were lost jobs, lost GDP growth, and lost tax revenues. Local economies also lost productivity as the workforce dealt with out-of-date and unsupported software and suffered from a lack of the economic flexibility that comes from having a vigorous local software industry.

| COUNTRY | MILLIONS |
|---|---|
| **North America** | |
| US | $6,496 |
| Canada | $736 |
| **Western Europe** | |
| Austria | $109 |
| Belgium | $240 |
| Denmark | $165 |
| Finland | $148 |
| France | $2,311 |
| Germany | $1,899 |
| Greece | $87 |
| Ireland | $71 |
| Italy | $1,127 |
| Netherlands | $577 |
| Norway | $155 |
| Portugal | $66 |
| Spain | $512 |
| Sweden | $241 |
| Switzerland | $293 |
| United Kingdom | $1,601 |
| **Eastern Europe** | |
| Bulgaria | $26 |
| Croatia | $44 |
| Czech Republic | $106 |
| Estonia | $14 |
| Hungary | $96 |
| Latvia | $16 |
| Lithuania | $17 |
| Poland | $301 |
| Romania | $49 |
| Russia | $1,104 |
| Slovakia | $40 |
| Slovenia | $32 |
| Turkey | $127 |
| Ukraine | $92 |
| **Asia Pacific** | |
| Australia | $341 |
| China | $3,823 |
| Hong Kong | $102 |
| India | $367 |
| Indonesia | $157 |
| Japan | $1,633 |
| Korea | $462 |
| Malaysia | $129 |
| New Zealand | $21 |
| Pakistan | $16 |
| Philippines | $55 |

| COUNTRY | MILLIONS |
|---|---|
| **Asia Pacific** | |
| Singapore | $90 |
| Taiwan | $139 |
| Thailand | $141 |
| Vietnam | $41 |
| **Latin America** | |
| Argentina | $69 |
| Bolivia | $11 |
| Brazil | $519 |
| Chile | $68 |
| Colombia | $61 |
| Costa Rica | $17 |
| Dominican R | $5 |
| Ecuador | $11 |
| EL Salvador | $4 |
| Guatemala | $9 |
| Honduras | $3 |
| Mexico | $369 |
| Nicaragua | $1 |
| Panama | $4 |
| Paraguay | $9 |
| Peru | $31 |
| Puerto Rico | $11 |
| Uruguay | $10 |
| Venezuela | $55 |
| **Mideast/Africa** | |
| Algeria | $59 |
| Bahrain | $18 |
| Cyprus | $8 |
| Egypt | $56 |
| Israel | $69 |
| Jordan | $15 |
| Kenya | $12 |
| Kuwait | $40 |
| Lebanon | $22 |
| Malta | $2 |
| Mauritius | $4 |
| Morocco | $57 |
| Nigeria | $47 |
| Oman | $11 |
| Qatar | $13 |
| Reunion | $1 |
| Saudi Arabia | $120 |
| South Africa | $147 |
| Tunisia | $29 |
| UAE | $29 |
| Zimbabwe | $6 |

**Figure 6–2**
Retail value of pirated software in 2003.

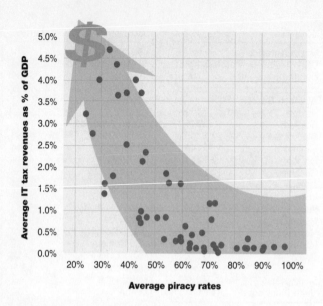

**Figure 6–3**    The trade-off between piracy and tax revenue. Each dot on this chart represents a country. In general, the more software piracy in a country, the less tax revenues available from legitimate sales. This is one of the prices paid for "free" software.

For the 57 countries studied, which account for all but 2 percent of worldwide spending on information technology, IDC found that lowering piracy by just 10 percent over four years would:

- Create 1.5 million jobs.
- Create $400 billion in economic growth.
- Add $60 billion to government tax receipts.

Lowering piracy by 10 percent in four years, by the way, has been done by over 75 percent of the countries in the study at one time or another.

Figure 6–3, from the IDC study, shows the correlation between tax revenues and piracy rate. Countries with high piracy rates clearly miss out on the economic benefits of a strong software industry.

The software industry ripples through almost every facet of a community and society. It provides jobs, revenue, and taxes, of course, but it also supports education and community development. It raises the standard of living in the community (programmers love sports cars, high-tech toys, and big-screen TVs) and it raises intellectual and cultural values as well. Software development is a clean industry that requires few resources except electricity. Consider Provo, Utah, a small post-industrial town until the startup of Novell, a networking software company, in 1983. As the business grew, the town became more prosperous, the nearby universities began cranking out more computer science majors, and more software enterprises started up. There are countless tales of how a software company transformed a community that previously was going nowhere.

The jobs and tax revenues, by the way, don't come just from software developers. A significant amount of the work done by IT services companies—who are mostly indigenous players—is the installation, deployment, and support of software. In countries with low piracy rates, software is also a high-margin category for distributors and resellers. Yes, they may obtain some business working with or selling pirated software, but really, how many wedges can you slice out of an 80-ruble pie to pay for service or distribution profit?

These ancillary businesses, like CompUSA, create economic and intellectual synergy in communities. For example, you buy a software package based on the recommendation of a knowledgeable and trained salesperson. You go back seeking advice on further enhancements, and then purchase service and support. Your documented problems and suggestions for improvement get fed back to the software developers. An enhanced chain of value is formed in these relationships for everyone concerned, and most often the customer benefits most—in ways that far outweigh the low cost of a pirated copy.

Back to Russia. Here, IDC found that lowering piracy by 10 percent over four years could grow IT-related tax revenues by 20 percent and software industry employment by 50 percent.

## ARE THESE NUMBERS REAL?

Would all that pirated software be turned into revenue if piracy disappeared overnight?

Yes and no. The 2003 IDC study on the economic impact of software piracy examined the legitimacy of using a linear ratio between falling piracy rates and rising industry revenues. In any one case, the chance that a software pirate would suddenly fork over list price for software if the hand of God somehow reached down and drove piracy to zero is slim. In the aggregate, however, the ratio is more linear than price-elasticity theory would lead you to believe. Lowering piracy stimulates more software production, which stimulates marketing, which stimulates demand. While an individual pirate might not buy a copy of his or her previously pirated software, somewhere else in the economy a different person would likely buy another type of software.

The cross-check on this assumption was estimating what a country's software spending would be if piracy were lowered a set percentage, followed by a comparison of the size (as a percent of all spending on IT) of the software industry to that of countries that already had the lower piracy rate. In most cases, the predicted new software industry would *still* be smaller than that of its new cohort.

In short, good things seem to happen when you lower software piracy. Would the same happen if you lowered music or movie piracy? Surely the filmmakers and songwriters of Russia, China, India, and other high piracy nations would say so. As we'll see in Chapter 9, *Angel on My Shoulder: What's in It for Me?*, some of the most vocal proponents for antipiracy campaigns are the local music and entertainment industries.

## WHAT DRIVES PIRACY?

You think it's price, right? Why *wouldn't* someone pirate software if it were easy, the risk of getting caught small, and the penalties light?

Yes, money is one reason. In a study conducted in 2000, Donald B. Marron of Charles River Associates and David G. Steel of McKinsey, UK, pointed out the strong correlation between income in a country and the piracy rate. In general, the poorer the people, the greater the propensity to pirate software.[6]

But that's not the whole story. When Marron and Steel plotted income versus piracy, they found some anomalies. Qatar and Kuwait, for instance, both nations in which the citizenry is well-heeled, sat well outside the normal piracy-income curve. In those countries there should be less piracy. South Africa was well below the curve; one would expect *more* piracy. India, too, if you took only the income of the people in the country who have at least a remote possibility of access to a computer, seemed to have abnormally high piracy.

That gets to another reason for piracy: culture.

Here's "Shashi," an Internet user in India weighing in on a discussion forum on *www.indianink.net* on the topic of rampant software piracy in India:

> I used to hear that one could sell only one copy of software in Asia because before you could make another copy, everyone would have a pirated copy of it. All this while I didn't think much about it. Now that I am here, I see that people who copy and distribute for profit are well-educated and quite wealthy. So, why are they copying?

> The buyers of software are from the upper classes, and have more than one car at home, large flat-screen TVs, and air-conditioned homes. High prices have not prevented them from purchasing these luxury items, so why do they need a lower price structure for software?

---

6.  Donald B. Marron and David G Steel, "Which Countries Protect Intellectual Property?" *Economic Inquiry*, Vol. 38, No. 2, April 2000, published for Western Economic Association International by Oxford University Press and available at http://ei.oupjournals.org/cgi/content/abstract/38/2/159.

The idea that culture might drive software piracy was tested by Marron and Steel.[7] They plotted software piracy rates by country against the collectivism in a country's culture using a measure designed back in the 1970s by Geert Hofstede, a researcher from IBM. In an individualistic culture like that of the U.S., institutions grew up to protect individual rights, chief among them the right to own property. In a collectivist country such as China, Indonesia, or Ecuador, institutions give their support to groups—families, friends, farms, collectives, and close associates—that value resource-sharing over individual rights.

If you plot countries by the Hofstede measure of individualism versus software piracy, lo and behold, you find culture does indeed have an impact. In fact, based on statistical measures, inbred cultural habits seem to be an even stronger impetus for piracy than economic gain.[8]

When you consider it, the idea that culture figures in the propensity for a community to pirate software makes some sense. People can shell out $1,000 for a new computer, but not $300 for their software? (Right, Shashi?) Then again, if Muscovites are used to buying counterfeit Gucci luggage, Bruno Magli shoes, Oakley sunglasses, and even Stolichnaya vodka, why would they flinch at buying somebody else's Adobe Photoshop? But digital media are a lot easier to copy than shoes, gloves, vodka, or other tangible products, and the results are not inferior knockoffs, but rather perfect copies.

---

7.  Ibid.

8.  An interesting perspective on this is propounded by Amy Chua in her book, *World on Fire: How Exporting Free Market Democracy Breeds Ethnic Hatred and Global Instability* (New York: Random House, 2003). While the title rather sums up her argument, she also makes this finer point: "Americans don't hate Bill Gates, even though he has owned as much as 40 percent of the American population put together. They don't feel cheated or exploited by him, or that he has humiliated Americans by making billions on their soil. Not so in societies with a market-dominant minority...[where] the plutocrats are ethnic outsiders. And while Bill Gates does not generate mass ethnic resentment in the United States, Indian tycoons in Uganda, Eritrean businessmen in Ethiopia, and Jewish oligarchs in Russia do" (pp.19–20).

Besides, even in America's individualist culture, getting stuff for "free" is a powerful marketing ploy. Buy a perfume or cologne, and get a handbag *free*. Buy one bag of potato chips, get one *free*. Buy a fast-food hamburger, and get the fries for *free*. Buy a computer, and get a lot of preinstalled software for *free*. You can even download plenty of legitimate software from the Internet for free. As Joni Mitchell sang in "Real Good for Free":

> Now me I play for fortune
> And those velvet curtain calls
> I've got a black limousine
> And two gentlemen
> Escorting me to the halls
> And I play if you have the money
> Or if you're a friend to me
> But the one man band
> By the quick lunch stand
> He was playing real good, for free.[9]

## WHO GETS HURT?

All right, so there's software piracy. What does it matter? Isn't most of the stuff just Microsoft software? It's not like Microsoft doesn't make a huge profit. It has billions in cash reserves—$50 billion in 2003 alone—which would be enough to pay operating expenses for three years even if the company didn't sell another nickel's worth of software. What's a little pilferage to them?

Actually, it's the local software sellers who get hurt the worst. The IDC study on the economic impact of software piracy found that 80 percent of lost revenue was from local players—software firms, service companies, and distribution points. It's your friends, your family, your associates, and your community. The missing revenues mean small computer repair shops never open their doors, Web designers never get employed, college enrollment languishes, and new high–tech enterprises never get off the ground.

---

9.   http://www.elyrics.net/go/j/joni-mitchell-lyrics/real-good-for-free)-lyrics/

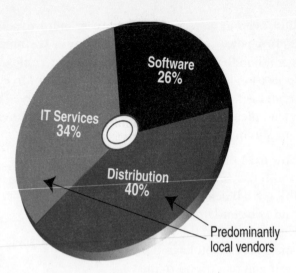

**Figure 6–4**    Who gains from lower software piracy?

If software piracy could be reduced, Figure 6–4 shows where the increased revenues would come from, by functional area. As you can see, the *non*-software industries have more to gain than the software industry.

This isn't just IDC talking. In September of 2000, the Chinese Ministry of Information Industry issued results of a year-long study of its own software industry. A quarter of the domestic companies felt that software piracy was the number one inhibitor of their economic success. One software company, Suntendy, which created the first Chinese language word processing software, claimed there were 10 pirated copies of its software in the market for every one sold. Remember, this is a study from China—the number two nation when it comes to software piracy.

Would the same hold true in the music and movie industry? Would the benefits accrue to more than just the content creators if piracy of their medium was lowered? Surely they would, with all sorts of enterprises benefiting, from film schools and movie theaters to sound technicians and mixing studios.

Without specific research, it's hard to quantify the benefts of lowering piracy for anything but the software industry.

But you'll see one indication in Chapter 9, *Angel on My Shoulder, What's in It for Me?*, where we discuss how Ghana revived its indigenous music industry when it cut down on music piracy. Cutting piracy helped the big multinational labels a little bit in a tiny market, but it had startling benefits inside Ghana.

## AN ECONOMIC ARGUMENT FOR PIRACY

There are those who think piracy isn't *all* bad for software and media companies. Carlos Osorio, a research associate at Harvard University, makes the case in a working paper published in June 2002 that piracy can help spread a vendor's installed base in a manner that can lead to future revenues.[10] His argument pits the negative impact of piracy on incentives for innovation against the beneficial network effects of having more copies in people's hands. Vendors can lock users in today and convert them to paying customers later.

It's an interesting argument, this one for "sponsoring" a market, and it isn't news to either the software industry or the music business. Many software companies offer free downloads of their program on a try-and-buy basis: Use it for 30 days, and then the license expires unless you make a purchase. Many of those who download songs from the Internet say they only do so to sample the music. If they like what they hear, they go out and buy the CD

Osorio's math actually computes the magic level of software piracy below which the benefits of the network effect aren't enough to compensate for lost innovation (and revenue). Above that, the network effects outweigh the deleterious effect of reduced innovation. It's almost an "if–you–can't beat–'em–join–'em" message, or at least sage advice to software vendors to

---

10.  Carlos A. Osorio, "A Contribution to the Understanding of Illegal Copying of Software," Working Paper, June 2002, available at http://itc.mit.edu/itel/docs/2002/osorio_ICS_workingpaper.pdf.

think about varying their approaches to dealing with piracy by
country. The good news in Osorio's work is that there *is* a
magic number. The bad news is that it's pretty high—81 percent—meaning that only in countries where 81 percent or
more of the software is pirated is there a decent network effect
from piracy. The reason: There are so many people using the
product that some may convert to paying users later.

In another study the same year, Dr. Philip McCalman of the
Department of Economics at the University of California at
Santa Cruz studied the nature of motion picture "diffusion"—
or releases—around the globe and discovered that the intellectual property porridge had to be just the right temperature.[11]
If intellectual property protection was too lax in a county, distributors would be slow to roll out new movies. If it was too
strict, companies would have enough market power that they
could restrict new movie releases to maximize revenues from
the movies already playing in theaters.

McCalman, too, came up with a magic number: 3.09. On a scale
of 1 to 5 measuring the strength of intellectual property protection in a country, 3.09 is the breakpoint above which stronger
protection creates market stagnation and below which it boosts
the market. The measure itself was developed by Juan Carlos
Ginarte from the World Bank and Walter Park from American
University a decade ago. The strength of protection was tied into
the duration of patent lengths, the amount of property covered,
the number of treaties in force, provisions against loss, and
enforcement. On the 0-to-5 scale, a rating of 3.00 is "low" protection, a rating between 3.00 and 3.75 is moderate, and a rating
over 3.75 is high. So, according to McCalman, if a country has a
rating below 3.09, stronger intellectual property protection will
increase movie distribution. But in a country with a rating of
3.75, increasing to over 4.0 might actually inhibit distribution.

And these magic numbers mean—what?

11. Phillip McCalman, "International Diffusion and Property Rights: An Empirical
Analysis," March 2002, available from the Society for Economic Research on
Copyright Issues at http://www.serci.org/2002/mcCalman.pdf.

They mean that there is a law of diminishing returns at work here. You can increase intellectual property protection to a point—but not beyond. Governments and vendors need to think about how hard they want to push it. Not enough protection and local industries suffer; too much, and innovation lags.

## WHY DON'T GOVERNMENTS DO SOMETHING?

Most governments at least pay lip service to intellectual property protection. They must, in order to trade with the developed nations under the GATT (General Agreement on Tariff and Trade) and TRIPS (Trade Related Aspects of Intellectual Property Rights) agreements that were an annex to the formation of the World Trade Organization in 1995. Officials we spoke with at the Taiwanese Intellectual Property Office in Taiwan told us that the United States government would like them to adopt its intellectual property and copyright laws *in toto*. While Taiwan and other countries are not entirely reluctant to meet U.S. requirements, sometimes the U.S. requirements are much stricter. That can be unfair, taking a great deal of time and money to implement.[12] Developing countries are also encouraged by their First World trading partners to sign the WIPO Copyright Treaty.

For instance, to join the World Trade Organization (WTO) in 2002, China had to improve its own practically nonexistent intellectual property laws up to the TRIPS level and agree to step up enforcement to international norms.[13] Thailand has ratified some terms of the WIPO treaty and established a Central Intellectual

---

12. In Taiwan's case, there are political overtones as well. In addition to working to control media piracy, Taiwan is number three in filing for U.S. patents, right behind Japan and Germany, meaning it's a powerful trading partner, not just in electronics but in other products, from bicycles to drill presses. TSMC, the largest semiconductor maker in Taiwan, is number 40 in U.S. patents. The U.S. refusal to support Taiwan's bid for membership in the United Nations, in deference to the People's Republic of China, rankles those working to support protection of U.S. intellectual property.

13. As reported by the U.S. Department of State Office of International Information Programs, http://usinfo.state.gov/regional/ea/iprcn/facthurt2.htm.

Property and Trade Court, as well as a Department of Intellectual Property, all as part of its ICT2010 Initiative. The Philippines signed the WIPO treaty in 2002 and launched a Go ICT Stop Software Piracy campaign. And so on.

There are political trade-offs (surprise) involved with digital piracy. Taiwan, for one, has taken steps to please its major trading partner, the U.S., by foregoing the immediate gratification of "free" software, music, games, and movies for the long-term gratification of a healthier, richer, and more diverse economy. While China has agreed to step up enforcement and the government in Beijing has taken some action, little had changed at the street level by the two-year anniversary of China's entrance into the WTO. Then Microsoft's relationship-building fell into ruin in late 2003 when Beijing decreed that its ministries would purchase a domestic version of Linux instead of Microsoft Windows. This was viewed as a political response to Microsoft's demand that the Shanghai Education Commission pay full price for licensing Windows and Office. China will also replace Office with a homegrown application suite, Kingsoft WPS.[14] In this and many other areas of its commerce, China appears anxious to learn from its foreign trading partners, only to bring what it's acquired back as a home-court advantage.

In Moscow, Yury Luzhkov, the pro-business mayor at the time of this writing, is vocally antipiracy. He led Moscow City in implementing the first law in the country against the sale of pirated CDs, prompting a number of very public CD destructions. Of course, down in the streets the city police turn a deliberately blind eye to the sale of pirated software, "commissions" from which bring them extra income.

One of the most anti-American examples was Iraq. During Saddam Hussein's regime, partly because of the boycott by multinational software firms, the government actively encouraged software piracy as a way to strike back at the West and as a way

---

14. Jen Lin-Liu, "Microsoft Suffers Chinese Triple Whammy," *IEEE Spectrum*, October 2003, p. 18.

to keep costs down. In the words of Hussain Kubba for the *Baghdad Bulletin* (July 7, 2003):

> This piracy was nurtured under the eye of the previous regime without any regard to its ethical, legal, and economic implications. It has matured into a culture that considers all software a free public good available to all.

Of course, for reasons too obvious to elaborate, that will change.

## THE RULE OF LAW

In their analysis of the causes of software piracy, Marron and Steel[15] charted a third major force besides economics and culture: the quality of the economic institutions protecting intellectual property. The variables they looked at included the country's tradition of law and order, the government's propensity to repudiate contracts, the quality of the bureaucracy, the extent of corruption, and the risk of expropriation.

No surprise here: "Countries with weak economic institutions have significantly higher piracy rates than do countries with strong institutions." If countries can't protect *tangible* property, how can they be expected to protect *intellectual* property?

To see the connection more directly, we decided to compare piracy rates to a measure of how easy it might be to get around the institutions of a country, namely the "Corruption Perception Index"[16] computed by Transparency International, an organization that tracks corruption around the world. The index ranks

15. Op. Cit., ff. 7.
16. The Corruption Perception Index is based on multiple sources that draw from surveys of thousands of business executives, academics, and government experts in over 100 countries. Scores range from 1 to 10, with 1 being high in corruption and 10 being low. The data plotted in Figure 6–3 are from the 2003 study. The country with the lowest score in 2003 was Bangladesh (1.3); the country with the highest was Finland (9.7). Transparency International, based in Berlin, Germany, but with over 85 national chapters, is an organization that tracks and fights corruption around the world. See www.transparency.org.

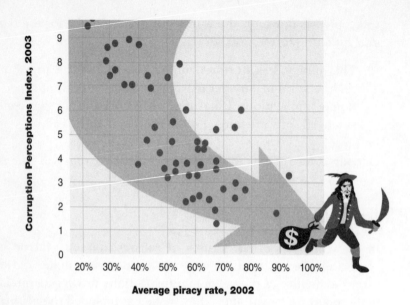

**Figure 6–5** Software piracy and corruption—each mark represents a country. A high score on the index means a low level of corruption. In general, corruption and software piracy go hand in hand, but there are some countries outside the band. Hong Kong and Kuwait, for example, have higher piracy than their corruption perception index would warrant. The Czech Republic and the United Arab Emirates have less piracy than their corruption perception scores would indicate.

countries in terms of the degree to which corruption is perceived to exist among public officials and politicians. Figure 6–5 shows how 82 countries stack up—clearly the more corrupt a country is perceived to be, the higher software piracy is likely to be.

Consider China again. The country didn't even have its own copyright laws until 14 years ago. It only tightened them recently in order to become a member of the WTO and, since then, hasn't been particularly diligent about enforcement. In an article in *Forbes* in February 2003 about Microsoft's attempts to deal with software piracy in China, the author, Robyn Meredith, writes: "The uniformed policeman strolling Beijing's Silk Market ignore counterfeiters, instead watching out for pickpockets." Couple China's "weak economic institutions" with a culture that apparently doesn't respect the idea of intellectual output as property (and doesn't want to be economically dependent on the West—or anyone else, for that matter), and you have a tough nut for digital media makers to crack.

It doesn't always have to be culture or corruption, though. It can simply be the institutional view. In Milan, Italy, in 2000, a judge threw out a criminal case against a businessman from Turin who copied all sorts of office software for use on other computers in a company, ruling it was okay as long as it wasn't copied to sell for a profit.

## THE GLOBAL PUSH TO LOWER PIRACY

In the 10 years the BSA has been tracking PC software piracy, the worldwide rate has dropped 13 percent, although it's still up a few points from its low in 1998. Twenty–two of the countries have dropped their piracy rate more than 25 points since 1994; 12 have dropped it more than 30. Figure 6–6 shows both the 10 countries that have dropped piracy the most and the 10 that have dropped it the least.

The reason to beef up intellectual property protection is a combination of enlightened self-interest and arm-twisting on the part of

**Top 10 High Performers**

| Country | 1994 | 2003 | Difference |
|---|---|---|---|
| UAE | 86% | 34% | 52% |
| Slovenia | 96% | 52% | 44% |
| Israel | 78% | 35% | 43% |
| Japan | 66% | 29% | 37% |
| Hungary | 76% | 42% | 34% |
| Ireland | 74% | 41% | 33% |
| Spain | 77% | 44% | 32% |
| Oman | 96% | 65% | 32% |
| Netherlands | 64% | 33% | 31% |
| Malta | 77% | 46% | 31% |

**Top 10 Holdouts**

| Country | 1994 | 2003 | Difference |
|---|---|---|---|
| Chile | 70% | 63% | 8% |
| Vietnam | 100% | 92% | 7% |
| Thailand | 87% | 80% | 7% |
| Australia | 37% | 31% | 6% |
| India | 79% | 73% | 6% |
| China | 97% | 92% | 5% |
| Kenya | 82% | 80% | 1% |
| Venezuela | 72% | 72% | 0% |
| Nigeria | 82% | 84% | -2% |
| Zimbabwe | 63% | 87% | -24% |

**Figure 6–6**  PC software piracy rate change: high performers and holdouts.

trading partners. Israel is now a net software package exporter with a strong local software industry. South Africa, after sanctions were lifted in 1995, wasted no time entering the First World when it comes to intellectual property protection.

Ireland's dramatic drop accompanied its rise as a software distribution point—the country now ships about 60 percent of the software that goes into Europe, so quelling piracy is a real issue for the Irish economy. The country can't very well lobby other governments to crack down on piracy without having its own house in order.

Some of the other countries with steep drops in piracy have seen concerted government efforts to lower piracy. Taiwan, for instance, named 2002 the "Action Year for Intellectual Property Rights (IPR) Protection," which entailed tightening its copyright laws, clearing court dockets, and putting pressure on local police forces and prosecutors to track down counterfeiters and pirates. A task force was put in place that raided the night markets selling pirated optical disks. A separate IPR police force in 2003, manned by 220 officers, was established to stay on top of piracy.

The "Action Year for IPR Protection" paid off. Taiwan's software piracy rate dropped 10 points in 2002 to 43 percent, the same as France.

The United Arab Emirates (UAE), which dropped an amazing 52 points in 10 years, now has a piracy rate lower than Canada or Italy. In 1990, there was a generational succession in government that brought in several younger rulers, who launched another level of modernization. By 1992, the country had enacted new intellectual property protection laws (which hasn't hurt foreign direct investment) and followed up by signing onto the international intellectual property rights treaties. As a result, in one year, 1996, software piracy dropped 37 percent to 47 percent. The country is still tightening up its laws and increasing enforcement.[17]

17. There is an irony here. According to Hassain Kubba of the *Baghdad Bulletin*, most of that pirated software used in Iraq is smuggled in from the UAE. It must be okay to export pirated software, just not use it within the country.

Of course, in some ways the holdouts are more interesting than the success stories. What is it about China that makes it so intractable?

It's not that there hasn't been movement from Beijing. China's copyright law was penned in 1990 and amended in 2001 in preparation for joining the WTO. The country has a National Copyright Center, a State Intellectual Property Office set up in 1998, and special intellectual property panels in its court system. There is even a Web site sponsored by the IPR Tribunal of the Supreme People's Court and full of content written by working IPR judges. And according to the State Intellectual Property Office, while China pursued only 2,143 intellectual property violations in the five years from 1996 through 2000, it handled over 45,000 in 2001 and destroyed over 90 million illegal video and audio disks.

Still, there's that 92 percent software piracy rate, only five points better than it was in 1994. By U.S. Department of Commerce estimates, 90 percent of other media are pirated, too. In fact, something like 20 percent of *all* consumer goods sold in China are counterfeit. Piracy and counterfeiting don't seem to be abating.

Perhaps it's a perfect storm of the three factors listed by Marron and Steel that lead to China's piracy:

■ Low salaries even for skilled (and PC–wielding) workers.

■ A culture that puts China on the top of the U.S. Customs list of nations with seizures of counterfeit goods at the U.S. borders (49 percent of all seizures).

■ Economic institutions that are still weak in administering property laws, much less *intellectual* property laws.

Globalizing the world to the Western intellectual property point of view ain't easy.

## WHAT'S THE GLOBAL FALLOUT?

The software industry may have the best measures of the impact of piracy—after all it's about six times the size of the recorded music industry and nine times the size of the motion picture industry—but piracy affects the whole meghilla. If the Motion Picture Association of America thinks it loses $3.5 billion a year to piracy just in the U.S.—*but isn't counting Internet download-ing*—couldn't the losses really be much bigger? And the Record-ing Industry Association of America's $4+ billion—couldn't that be bigger on a global basis?

Whether you buy all the industry association arguments or even the IDC global study, you have to believe that there is *some* nega-tive impact from piracy.

Consider the Chinese film industry. In 2001, director Feng Xiaogang discovered bootleg copies of his breakthrough movie, *A Sigh*, in the market days before its Chinese premier. As he told the *Financial Times*, "Piracy has eaten up half my box office." A year later, at the debut of the martial arts movie *Hero*, starring Jet Li, movie officials videotaped its premier audience and required them to check all cell phones, watches, lighters, car keys, neck-laces, and pens at the door. At the beginning of each perfor-mance, a recorded announcement was played warning the audience that any videotaping was against the law and offenders would be summarily arrested as they sat recording in their seats. Industry staff watched the audience during the movie with night vision goggles.[18]

There is probably something to all the academic research that says piracy isn't just about getting expensive stuff for free. People use a complex set of factors when making decisions about pur-chases, some conscious and some not, some rational and eco-nomic, and some cultural or formed through personal values. In other words, it isn't simply a pricing decision. Certainly it couldn't hurt for people to be made more aware of the facts of copyright laws and global economic consequences, but ratcheting up too much intellectual property protectionism might boomer-ang and exacerbate the situation.

---

18. As reported by the U.S. Department of State Office of International Information Programs. See http://usinfo.state.gov/regional/ea/iprcn/nyt14nov.htm.

Nor can we do nothing. The "invisible hand" of economics isn't going to fix the problem. Raising awareness of the economic consequences of individual pirating actions is one of our missions in this book—raising the social consciousness, if you will.

A perhaps apocryphal story is told that during the 1940s, people living in Kansas and Nebraska were unaware that a world war was going on. It's unlikely such isolation could happen today, at least in the economic realm where computers and networks are making us into one large global community. The piracy in one place or one medium affects the market, R&D investment, and user behavior in another. Jackie Chan learns English so his movies will sell better in the U.S., where piracy is lower. Russian software developers move to Western Europe to find an outlet for their talents. The shutting down of one U.S. file-sharing service, Napster, leads to the creation of another, KaZaA, based in a locale that makes it hard to go after legally. Adobe considers no longer offering local language versions of and support for its products in some Asian markets because the localized versions are so popular with pirates.

So, yes, the fallout is global. Piracy "benefits" some countries and economies but only for a limited time. Others suffer because the disparity between haves and have-nots is too great, and the country is not far enough along in its economic development to compete with pirated goods. Which side of the scale weighs more heavily may vary by situation, market, country, or culture.

But just as there is no such thing as a free lunch, there is no such thing as "free" pirated software, music, games, or movies. It may just be a question of who's picking up the tab and whether it's in lost coin, lost jobs, lost economic growth, or lost innovation.

# DUDE, WHERE'S MY MP3?

If this was just a revolution of machines it would be a revolution that mattered to about 15 propeller heads in Silicon Valley and the rest of us could get on with our lives. Quite simply digital technology is the solvent leaching the glue out of old much cherished social, political and business structures. We're in a period where everything is changing, everything is up for grabs and nothing makes any sense and probably won't make any sense for two or three more decades. Now the good news is that all of that uncertainty also spells opportunity. It's created new opportunities for businesses, new kinds of jobs. This is a full employment act for everybody touched by information technologies. At a social level though it could be very good, but it could also be very bad. We really are performing a great unwitting experiment on ourselves and it's anyone's guess how it's going to come out.[1]

**Paul Saffo, Director of the Institute for the Future**

Sociologically speaking, it would be interesting to note exactly when $MP3$[2] became the generic term to refer to a song. A song used to be a work that you listened to on a record or the radio. It had distinctive characteristics: the composer, the artist, whether it was live or studio, and perhaps even an association with a particular event or time in your life.

An MP3, in and of itself, has none of these characteristics. It is a computer file that comes from somewhere in the ether. It lacks associations in time

1. Paul Saffo, director of the Institute for the Future, in an interview for the *Frontline* television show, "High Stakes in Cyberspace" (WGBH/PBS, http://www.pbs.org/wgbh/pages/frontline/cyberspace/) broadcast October 31, 1995.
2. MP3 is short for MPEG3, the standard developed by the Motion Pictures Expert Group in 1987 for data compression. Originally created for images, it was also adopted for use with audio files. MPEG4 is a standard used to compress video.

and space. It is a commodity, something to acquire and store on your hard disk. You don't gaze at it and remember your first love or when you attended the concert where you heard it played. You don't sit in front of your stereo and lean nostalgically into the speaker; instead, you probably stare at your computer, listening while you're multitasking away or perhaps downloading more MP3s.

Songs have mood, texture, memories, cachet, and sonic nuances. We remember our favorite is the fourth track on the album with anticipation and an assortment of emotions. MP3s, as "cuts" taken out of context, have no physical attributes, and they are often of inferior sonic quality. We use them, but they don't convey the same aura as a song on an album—for instance, listening to the Who's *Tommy*, we lose the segue between "Overture" and "It's a Boy."

Yet MP3s are a clear harbinger of our digital future. They portend a radical shift in how we entertain ourselves and what devices we use to play our media. MP3 quality will improve; indeed, it will eventually become the finest quality media we have ever heard or seen. It will have nuances, cachet, and texture, and will transport us in heart and mind and senses with its multimedia capabilities.

All this will come to pass in the digital millennium, because today's youth will demand it as they simultaneously make it happen. Let us, then, explore this new world where young people have learned, ever so quickly, how to satisfy their cravings for various forms of entertainment media and software, learning how they acquire MP3s while considering what our research says about how these matters are profoundly changing life as we know it in this new millennium.

---

# THE DAWN OF MP3 DOWNLOADING

Shawn Fanning, a 19-year-old freshman at Boston's Northeastern University in 1999, knew there was a problem. No, it wasn't that the world needed a new paradigm for the music industry or that music lovers needed 70 million new friends with whom to share tunes, but simply that he and his dorm mates were having trouble finding good music—music they liked—on the Internet. From Internet chat rooms and word-of-mouth, Shawn and his buddies knew there was a bunch of good music on the Net, stored in a file format called MP3, but finding actual songs was difficult. Nobody knew who had what songs where. For Fanning, who was bored with school and interested in programming, the problem became a project, which became a program—and ultimately a paradigm! After an intense period of programming, during which he quit college, he developed a software application that married file-sharing and Internet searches with instant messaging, and thus solved the problem of finding MP3s on the Internet. He named his program Napster (his college nickname) and, in a trice, revolutionized the music business and set 100 million music pirates loose.[3]

Prior to Napster, music sharing on the Internet was small potatoes—probably fewer songs were swapped than CDs lost to mice in warehouses. Nobody in the media really worried about copyright violation. Napster caught on like wildfire, however, swelling to millions of users in months and spawning copycat services. Napster became a company, got venture financing during the peak of the Internet stock boom, and within a few years, file-sharing and the appellation "MP3" replacing "song" was here to stay.

Caught up in the frenzy, few of Napster's growing hordes thought much about copyright violation. Stuff on the Internet is free, right?

Across all our focus groups, interviews, casual discussions, and surveys, the prevalent attitude seems always to have been that the technology and resources are in place for downloading, so why not do it? Yet isn't this like walking through an open air

---

3.  The number of Internet users under the age of 35 in 1999. At its peak in February of 2001, Napster had 70 million users who downloaded over 295 *billion* songs.

market and deciding that because the merchant isn't standing next to the produce, it's okay to take whatever you want? Of course, if you take the merchant's apples, there aren't as many there when you leave—which is not the case with downloading copies of files from other people's computers. The kids we talked to were smart enough to see—or at least rationalize—the difference between shoplifting and downloading.

## DIGITAL COPYING: THE LEGAL AND THE ILLEGAL

MP3s are not illegal, immoral, or even improper. In fact, it's quite legitimate to buy MP3s from music services and Web sites such as Apple's iTunes online music store, Musicmatch, and others. In the coming years, as more entertainment companies get their business plans together, you will be able to buy movies and television shows as downloadable files, in much the same way you buy them on DVD or as satellite/cable pay-per-view today.

All creative media—literature, music, dramatic works, pantomimes and choreographic works, dance works, photos, graphics, sculpture, paintings, motion pictures, sound recordings, and all types of audio-visual and multimedia works—are automatically covered by Federal copyright law. You don't even have to register your claim to copyright, as you once had to do; it is inherent in the act of creation. The danger in this is that you may not actually know what's copyrighted; therefore, always assume that everything is.

The MP3 is, after all, just a file format designed to compress and save media that, by their nature, are too large to conveniently send over the Internet or store. Media files aren't always MP3s; the binary file format is also used—for example, for software or games. So if the file format is benign, what can you do legally with media that has been copyrighted by someone other than yourself?

■ Making a complete copy of any form of copyrighted work for other than your own personal use is against the law. This applies whether you give the copy away or sell it. That means all forms of Internet file-sharing and burning copies of CDs for other people is illegal.

■ You may not make a copy of a copy-protected CD or DVD, but you may make a copy of a non-copy-protected disc for personal use or for a safe (archival) backup copy.

■ You may copy CDs you bought to your personal computer or to another medium, such as a cassette, so long as you do not distribute (freely or for sale) to others.

■ You may not, under any circumstances, upload to or distribute copyrighted media on the Internet, unless you have a licensing agreement with the copyright holder to do so.

## HOW MP3s ARE SHARED

Today, over 60 million people share files around the world. At any given time, there are at least 3 million people on KaZaA, sharing half a billion files or more. KaZaA, while the most popular, is only one of several dozen file-sharing programs. Moreover, there are two additional venues for file-sharing: Internet Relay Chat (IRC) sites (many of which are utterly off the Web-viewing radar screen) and newsgroups. Both are like private clubs whose use requires a more sophisticated level of computer expertise. In the aggregate, there is far more file-sharing on IRCs and newsgroups, of far more precious kinds of intellectual property than just MP3 songs, than you can imagine. This is a tsunami that will not recede.

One focus group student said he would download if only he knew how. Several others quickly replied they could teach him in just a few minutes. Indeed, it is quite simple. Here's how it works.

Computers store information in files. A *file* is a bucketful of information, whether words, numbers, music, video, or whatever. Files are created with software programs, and the program that created a given file is also required to use, view, or play back the file's information. You write a story using a word processor and save it as a file. You give the file to someone else, who must also use a word processor to read your story—or to print it out for later reading. Similarly, you insert your music CD in your computer's drive and use a program such as Microsoft Windows Media Player or MusicMatch Jukebox to copy it to your hard disk. Each song is stored as a separate file, commonly in .wav or .wma file formats (with Windows PCs; Macs use different media file formats). Next, you open a utility program, such as ImTOO CD Ripper or MP3 Wave Converter, which converts the media file to an MP3 file or vice-versa.[4]

This is where the Internet comes in: It can be used to convey the file from one computer to another. People often use email to send a file as an *attachment* to the email message. However, it is also possible to transfer a file between two computers more or less by simply clicking and downloading. The techie term for this Internet computer configuration is *client-server*. Servers are computers that have lots of files on them from which clients select those they want to copy. There are many, many Web sites that offer downloading services for all kinds of legitimate purposes. Similarly, it's possible for you to transfer, or upload, a file from your computer to someone else's computer, making your computer the server. Transferring files between two computers is called *peer-to-peer* computing, where all the computers act as both clients and servers, downloading and uploading from each other.

What Shawn Fanning did was to create a peer-to-peer computer network where people accessed his Napster server computers,

---

4. You can find programs like these by the score at www.download.com. Some are free; others are shareware and inexpensive to purchase.

where a database of available files for download was stored. From there, you connected directly to the peer computer where the files were stored to download the tunes you wanted to your own peer computer.[5]

Once the music industry got wind of all these people making songs available to others for free, it moved quickly to put Napster out of business. The courts held that Napster was indeed violating the copyrights of record companies because it was, for a time, in possession of and responsible for distributing media owned by someone else. Napster shut down its servers in 2002 (although it revamped and came back as a for-pay music service in late 2003).[6]

But in a trice, clever people came up with an alternative: the music, movies, games, and software would not be stored on a central server; rather, they would be stored on each individual's client computer, and clients would share files directly with each other, with no central server involved.

## AN ANATOMY OF DOWNLOADING

Today, when we think of peer-to-peer, we often think first of KaZaA.[7] Risen from the ashes of Napster, it's where the kids flock

---

5. You may also hear the term *warez* in conjunction with Internet file-sharing. The term predates Napster and is thought to be a snide send-up of the term wares, or products for sale. Warez groups are generally quite sophisticated, "cracking" new software programs and distributing them around the world; they are often the target of law enforcement antipiracy efforts. Most people would consider them a more serious breed of cat than Napster or KaZaA downloaders.

6. Meanwhile, Shawn Fanning has a new startup business, Snocap, which has developed a technology that identifies music files on file-sharing services and then charges a fee for their use.

7. KaZaA software has gone through several versions; the original was replaced by KaZaA Lite, which was purportedly less prone to viruses and other computer diseases; then came KaZaA Lite K++, which offered other enhanced features, such as ad blocking and a way to block servers thought to be operated by the RIAA in order to apprehend downloaders. As of 2004, KaZaA went semilegitimate, offering version 2.6 (aka Media Desktop) for free, as well as in a for-sale version for $29.95 with no ads, more download "channels," and select content for purchase.

if they have Windows PCs. If they're on Macs, they might use LimeWire instead. There are others, numerous others, but from a digital dining perspective, you might say KaZaA is the McDonald's of MP3s.

You begin at *www.kazaa.com* and download a copy of KaZaA, the software program you must have to share files. Another click or two and it is installed on your computer. Now you have a window on the world of online free media.

Once you've started the KaZaA program and are online, you simply type in the name of the group, song, movie, software, book, game, or whatever you're looking for into the Search box. Within a few seconds, you'll see a directory of all the computers that have what you're looking for. A click or two and the downloading begins; soon it's yours, the file stored in a KaZaA folder on your computer's hard drive. This folder is called Shared Files; once you have some files stored in it, you become a peer-to-peer resource on KaZaA as well. In other words, the files in that folder become available to everyone else who's using KaZaA—unless you disable that functionality, which can be done by going to the Options menu (see Figure 7–1).

KaZaA is finicky and in some ways downright dangerous. A common occurrence when requesting a file is the "More sources needed" message, which means that the file is unavailable for download. The free version of KaZaA also spawns innumerable popup and banner advertisements, some of which are just a nuisance but others of which implant cookies on your computer that can broadcast your computer's IP address and other information back to the Web site from whence they came. Another undesirable side benefit is spyware, such as Altnet, which burrows into your computer and can harness your computer's excess microprocessor power to help speed up file transmissions over the network, similar to the way bicyclists draft each other in a race.

Another danger is that hackers lurking on KaZaA can sneak into your computer through file-sharing, peek at your private files, embed a virus, and snitch passwords and credit card numbers—and just about anything else they feel like doing. When your

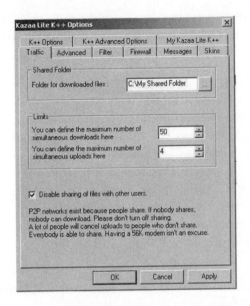

**Figure 7–1** How to disable file-sharing in KaZaA.

Shared Folder is available to others, the potential for intrusion is very strong. Even though KaZaA Lite K++ and 2.6 purport to address many of these problems, the possibility of downloading viruses and other risks is extremely high, around 45 percent according to a research study by TruSecure.[8]

Welcome to the world of file-sharing, where your privacy is invaded, your computer becomes an accomplice after the crime, and you're at risk of catching computer diseases. To make matters worse, many of these intruders are pornographic Web sites, which is not only embarrassing but potentially damaging—they invade your computer like cockroaches in a New York apartment, planting Web addresses in your History folder and changing your browser's home page to one of their own without your permission.

8.  See www.wired.com/news/business/0,1367,61852,00.html?tw=wn_tophead_1.
    TruSecure, a security services provider, is at www.truesecure.com.

So there truly is no free lunch, nothing is ever really free, and you can still end up becoming someone's unwitting dupe.

# THE DARKER SIDE OF DOWNLOADING

Such are the risks when attempting to get something for nothing. That's why Internet Relay Chat emerged as another venue for digital dining—let's say it's the TGI Friday's of MP3s. IRC is a very old Internet service that has grown from simple interest groups where people gathered to talk—er, type—about some favorite topic or other. But IRC is a network unto itself, where the threshold for admission and the benefits of privacy and anonymity are much better developed than on mass-market download services such as KaZaA.

Finding IRC sites is no mean feat. You can Google a query and find some, but you may not know what to look for once you're at the site page. What's more, you won't be able to enter. IRC sites are probably more appropriately deemed portals: The site page may look something like Figure 7–2, but it's only the mouth of the cavern. The real entrance lies somewhere within.

In order to partake of the file-sharing benefits of IRC sites, you must first download and install an IRC client program such as mIRC.[9] The IRC client is your guide and secret password, so to speak, into these private file-sharing realms. Using this client program to find and to navigate IRC file-sharing server sites requires both practice and advanced computing skills, which means IRC is not for everybody.

Once you get to a file-sharing site, you still need to perform some *parlez-vous* to get what you want. You'll encounter chat groups—often hundreds of them—which you must join in order to gain the next level of admittance. (See Figure 7–3.) That's why IRC media are cleaner, safer to acquire, and usually better quality. Whereas KaZaA content is Top 40 radio or cable-channel movies, IRCs have a lot of first-run stuff: movies that haven't even been

---

9.    Available at www.mirc.com. There are other IRC clients as well.

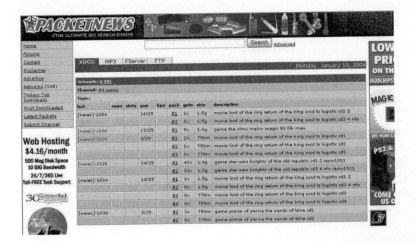

**Figure 7–2** This Web page displays warez for the taking, but you'll need an IRC client to partake.

released, esoterica, computer software, and games. You want the just-released version of Microsoft Office or Adobe Photoshop? It's here.

Even more and better content is available on yet another older Internet service, Usenet news. Usenet is a collection of special-interest newsgroups (most begin with the prefix alt—for example, alt.binaries.sounds.mp3) where, among other things, you can find—you guessed it—downloadable media such as music, movies, games, and software. Newsgroups are premium file-sharing services—let's call them the Morton's Restaurants of MP3s—and many require a paid subscription. You might need to purchase an agent in order to download, and your subscription might be based on the quantity (e.g. 10, 20, 30 GB) of the media you download per month. That lets you in and keeps the RIAA and Feds out. Newsgroups often specialize in software programs, hence the reference to binaries (as in binary files). Newsgroup content is more readily available, and while it may mirror IRC content, it's usually newer stuff and always easier and faster to download.

**Figure 7–3** An Internet Relay Chat screen; each line represents a chatter who has the named media available for downloading. This screen is constantly scrolling, meaning files are constantly being shared. Note that in this time frame, only a few seconds, 623.9 *giga*bytes had been transferred. On the date this screenshot was captured, several of these films were either not yet released or in their first week or two of theatrical release.

## THE POWER OF YOUTH

Young people are not the only ones who will listen to tomorrow's MP3, nor will they be the only ones to download digital files from the Internet. But they are the vanguard of the trend, and that makes them worth studying. Consider these somewhat staggering statistics:

- By the end of 2002, according to a survey by Ipsos Reid,[10] one out five U.S. respondents 12 or over had downloaded music

---

10. Quarterly *Tempo* music study conducted in December 2002 of a nationally representative sample of 1,112 U.S. respondents 12 years or older by Ipsos-Reid. Released on February 20, 2003, and available at www.ipsos-reid.com.

from a file-sharing service like KaZaA. Over *half* of kids 12–17 had done so. Forty-four percent of people 18–24 had done so.

■ According to a study by the Pew Internet & American Life Project in mid 2003,[11] 35 million Americans were already music downloaders, with 52 percent of Internet users between the ages of 18 and 29 having downloaded music.

# THE TECHNO-ELITE

The Pew Internet and Modern Life Project released another report in November 2003, entitled "Consumption of Information Goods and Services in the United States."[12] The report describes the emergence of a "technological elite," whose technology skills go beyond merely using a particular technology—cell phone, DVD player, personal computer—to being able to personalize and manipulate the technology. For example, the techno-elite personalize their Web home page in their browser program rather than accept what the ISP installed as the default.

Two categories the Pew study detailed were:

■ *Youthful tech elites*: Average age 22, mostly male, comprising about 6 percent of the U.S. population. As the heaviest technology users, over 80 percent have cell phones, while all use the Internet, most of them interactively—downloading media, creating Web pages, and participating in interactive games, group activities, or blogging. Pew reports that youthful tech elites spend on average $161 per month on information resources and goods.

■ *Wired GenXers*: Average age 36, equally male and female, comprising 18 percent of the U.S. population. All are Internet-savvy, and 82 percent use cell phones. They engage in the same kinds of online activities as young tech elites, including

11. From a survey conducted by the Pew Internet & American Life Project, funded by the Pew Charitable Trusts, of 1,555 U.S. Internet users. Released July 2003 and available at www.pewinternet.org.
12. See www.pewinternet.org/reports/pdfs/PIP_Info_Consumption.pdf.

those interactive, and spend an average of $169 monthly on information goods and services.

Both of these groups say the computer and the Internet are their media of choice. Many are moving away from wired telephones toward exclusive use of cell phones, and likewise many prefer wireless Internet access, *a la* sitting at Starbucks sipping a mocha latte while checking email or Web surfing. Although this may come as no surprise, Pew notes that fully 69 percent of the population—mostly baby-boomers and young marrieds—are not part of this "technological elite." Clearly, a new generation of technology "haves" is emerging and, even though its number may now be smaller than the technology "have-nots," it is the dominant force, if only by virtue of two facts: one, low-tech and no-tech people are in the aging population, and two, those who possess the best information resources are the most powerful.[13]

## VIEW FROM THE STREET

In our own less scientific survey of colleagues, friends, and their colleagues and friends, we found that the younger the respondent, the more likely he or she was to be a music downloader, as shown in Figure 7–4.[14] Our data confirm that the front-line position has been taken by youth in the war of intellectual property. Even so, the real surprise here may be that so many middle-aged and even older people also download.

In the movie, *Dude, Where's My Car?*, Jesse and Chester are two young guys whose partying the night before was so intense that they can't remember where they parked their car. Their quest in the movie is to find it, fill in the memory gaps from the night before, and make up with their angry girlfriends—the behavior of

---

13. To paraphrase, with apologies, Sir Francis Bacon.
14. See Chapter 3, *Us Against Them?*, for more information on the survey. These results mean that 95 percent of the respondents to the survey who were under 18 years of age had downloaded music, not that 95 percent of all kids that age had done so or that 95 percent of music downloaders are under 18.

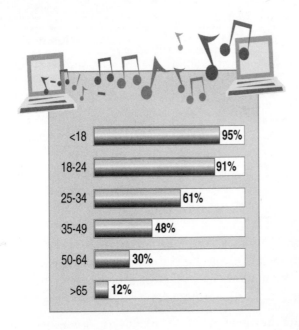

**Figure 7–4** MP3 downloaders by age.

simple organisms. Along the way, of course, they save the world from an alien invasion.

Just as Jesse and Chester didn't realize where their search would lead them, today's youth didn't intend to change the music world, set intellectual property law on its ear, or pit hardware companies against software and content companies. Youth may also be the vanguard of the downloading trend because they are generally more technically adept, but in truth they simply wanted easier access to more music (and movies, games, and software). Yet in so doing they have characterized a whole new generation of computer users.

## IT'S NOT JUST MP3s

While Napster was strictly designed for sharing MP3s, later file-sharing programs like KaZaA and dozens of others were designed

| Type of File | Number |
|---|---|
| Movies | 8,257 |
| Adult XXX Movies | 6,534 |
| Games | 4,935 |
| Programs | 4,753 |
| Ebooks | 735 |
| MP3s | 84,562 |

**Figure 7–5**    Downloads available at a German site.

to share *any* files. And file-sharing tools abound, from Bearshare, which makes using the Gnutella network easier to use, to eDonkey, which allows users to access files before they are done downloading, to Earthstation, which offers user anonymity.

To date, however, most downloads are still music. At one German file-sharing site we sampled in 2003, we found the types of files shown in Figure 7–5.

One of the reasons MP3s are so popular, of course, is that they take less time to download. A typical MP3 song is 3–4 MB of data, about the equivalent of a 300-page term paper, and takes just minutes to download over a campus network. Movies often take hours.

This will not be true forever. In 2003, a new file-sharing technique caught on which relies on a file transfer protocol, created by former hacker Bram Cohen, that splits files into smaller parts and distributes them across multiple computers. Called BitTorrent, it's referred to as a "swarming, gathering, and scattering" file transfer protocol where the unused bandwidth of network users is tapped to speed downloads across the net. BitTorrent has legitimate uses—such as software distribution— but now is more often used to distribute pirated TV shows and movies. The odd thing is that the more users there are online, the faster the downloads.

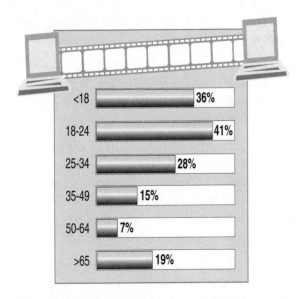

**Figure 7–6**  Movie downloaders by age.

The impact on the movie and TV business could be immense. *Wired* called BitTorrent "Napster for the Movies," and already European broadcasters who pay to distribute U.S. TV shows six months to a year after they first appear in the States have found their shows on the Internet months before they are ready for European distribution.

Once again, youth leads the way. Drawing on our survey of the fall of 2003, as shown in Figure 7–6, we find that college (and grad-school) aged young people are the most likely to download movies.

Our data were not too different from some collected in a more rigorous study by the BSA. Conducted for the BSA by Ipsos-Insight and published on September 16, 2003,[15] the study found that while 64 percent of students downloaded music without paying for it, 25 percent downloaded movies without paying for

15.  Available at www.bsa.org.

them. The study, "Internet Piracy on Campus," polled 1,000 college students and 300 faculty and administrators.

Sixteen percent of students surveyed also downloaded software programs without paying for them. The report also points out that "students who download pirated music are much more likely to download pirated software without any qualms about doing so."

The study also found that two-thirds of the students didn't know if their school had an official policy against using unauthorized software, although 88 percent of administrators said there *was* such a policy. Only one in eight students felt the school's policy was effective, compared to two–thirds of the administrators. Does it seem like we have a communication problem here?[16]

Did we say that young people are the vanguard of the trend? Given their computer skills, the hubris of youth, the Internet, and billions of files at their fingertips, they'll start a revolution. Correct that: They *started* a revolution, and got that new moniker from Pew Research, "techno-elite," in the bargain.

## STUDENT ECONOMICS

The youth we met with and talked to are not all technology wizards, but by and large they are quite savvy and street-smart about what's happening to them on an economic level. Many felt that the business world, especially the media, arts, and entertainment businesses, no longer seek a reasonable profit, but rather profits without limit. As one student succinctly put it, "Monetary interests precede art."

For the average college kid, most digital media, including textbooks, are beyond his or her budget. Consider one who goes to a good private college. Mom and Dad may shell out up to $40,000 a year in tuition, room, board, travel, fees, and health care. Yet the students themselves often have very little spending money, and if they have any appreciation for the largesse of their parents, loan

---

16. Policies vary—widely. We asked a student who attends Cornell what the school policy was on file-sharing. "Don't get caught," he replied.

sponsors, or the scholarship fund, feel guilty about spending it. For the most part, from what we learned in the focus groups we conducted in the fall of 2003, all students—rich and poor alike—feel poor. And what money they actually have spending control over goes fast:

- A computer is no longer an option, but a must. The old family PC running Windows 98 won't cut it: Students' computers must be a close match with the school's technology resources, and students usually must buy their own software. For instance, Adobe Photoshop 8 is $275, Microsoft Office 2003 is $199, Symantec Norton AntiVirus is $50, and FinalCutPro 4.0 is $700—educational pricing![17]

- Textbooks for four or five courses each semester average $500–$700.

- It costs eight or nine dollars to see a movie (and the amount doubles if you add popcorn and a Coke).

- CDs average $15 and DVDs $20, limiting how many one can afford.

For the average college student who doesn't have much discretionary income, the cost of going to college while enjoying a modicum of entertainment diversions is quite high. In fact, you could go so far as to say that media companies are pretty rapacious when it comes to the youth market. Some software publishers, like Microsoft, offer reasonable discounts for college students, but many do not. Textbook publishers penalize students for selling their used books by raising the prices of new texts ever higher. Of all the media businesses, movies on DVD seem to be the most reasonable. And whatever happened to the long-promised reduction in the price of CDs?

Factor into the answer to this somewhat rhetorical question the fact that most of the students in the six focus groups we conducted in the fall of 2003 don't buy more than one or two CDs a year anymore, and often don't even own stereos or boom boxes.

---

17. January 2004 street (not suggested retail) prices.

Instead, they listen to music on their PCs, and for portable listening, they like MP3 players, which hold hundreds of songs.

Although it's only partially *because* of economics that students and teens download so much, the economics are certainly good. Of the students we met, those who downloaded (and some did not!) had hundreds of songs on their computers, generally between 400 and 1,000. If you had to buy all the albums it would take to compile a playlist of all these songs, you could be talking a retail value of $3,000–$5,000. Double that for the kid who told us he had 2,500 songs, some going all the way back to the original Napster days.

What's so disheartening to the music industry, of course, is that the defectors are mostly young people, the heart of the music market. In 1992, the largest purchasing segment in the $10 billion music industry was comprised of kids from 15–19 (17 percent); the second was 20–24 year olds (15 percent). Together they accounted for 32 percent of music sales. By 2002, however, that aggregate percentage had dropped to 25 percent, with the youngest teens down to 13 percent of the market.[18]

## INTERNET-BASED INFORMATION IS *REAL* POWER

The Internet's information resources have been, by and large, free for the taking. Sure, there's been some plagiarism and copying from Web sites sneaking into term papers, but these acts didn't originate with the Internet. More to the point, there has always been a ton of free resources on the Internet. Bands put a song or two or three from their latest album on their Web site. Booksellers post a chapter from a book. Software companies offer demonstration versions, free for downloading. Yet from the copyright owner's perspective, this small portion of the intellectual property is provided in the spirit of fair use, to interest you in buying the product.

---

18.   Benny Evangelista, "Music Industry Changing Its Tune," *San Francisco Chronicle*, June 16, 2003, available on www.sfgate.com.

Next thing you know, the media is all over the place because the Internet is the world's fastest and most reliable source of information dissemination. The Chicago band Low Skies found this out when its first album, *The Bed*, debuted on the Web at both Amazon and eBay. The former was selling new copies of their Flameshovel Records CD for $12.99, while the record stores, college radio deejays, and magazine reviewers who had received promotional copies were selling them for around four bucks apiece.

Of course, even more devastating is seeing your music distributed for free after all the hard work and effort that went into making the album. Losing a thousand or so sales due to the free promo copies being sold can devastate a small label like Flameshovel. As one of the band members pointed out, they pay more than $4 to buy copies for themselves. The Web, and in particular, sites such as eBay, Craig's List, or Half.Com, turn out to be a global flea market for whatever it is you want to get rid of.

That's economics. The law of supply and demand. The invisible hand, moving through whichever medium has the most efficiency, like electricity, connecting buyer and seller in their transaction. A hand that knows no right or wrong, ethics or morality.

If that's the case, should Low Skies buy up all those promo copies and be done with it?

Well, the model for the relationship and behavioral pattern on the Internet is that transactions ought to be essentially free. Indeed, that's how it was conceived by the likes of Vincent Cerf, Tim Berners-Lee, and others. The people who advocated a free Internet were there first: students, academics, researchers, and people who possessed information and knowledge they simply wanted to share with the rest of the world. Free. Businesses using the Internet to sell goods and services came later and at first weren't entirely welcome.

Today, business runs the Internet. Commerce is driving Internet growth by using it as a computing platform for business-to-business transactions and to foster ever more business-to-consumer sales. Those in the media and information business have had copyright laws rewritten to their advantage. Often they have deployed sophisticated software programs to protect their copy-rights or in other ways thwart the pirates of the digital millennium.

Yes, this is what Paul Saffo warned us about.

Media executives probably think they are very smart, having pro-tected their business interests thus, but we know that the kids are smarter—a *lot* smarter. As one said in a focus group, no matter what "they" come up with to protect their media assets, a hack for it will be available within 15 minutes. That's what a lot of these young people *do*. It is the new millennium equivalent of excelling at spelling, basketball, or skateboarding. Many of these kids are at the mind-meld level of intimacy with their computers, and as was the case when Steve Jobs and Steve Wozniak were creating the Apple II, nobody can tell them something's impossible.

But what if it's against the law? What if you're breaking the Digital Millennium Copyright Act by using a tool that allows you to download or make copies of media? "Does that mean hitting the Shift key is illegal?" one student asked.[19]

See what we mean?

## ETHICS FROM WITHOUT

Are what the students doing wrong? If so, it's an issue. Ethics cannot be taught. Ethics can only be learned through observing ethical behavior in others—in particular, those whom one respects or admires. In ancient Greece, the Stoics were the first to propound a theory of ethics, based on what they believed was innate human reason, that still works today. They believed that human behavior was governed by the laws of physics, or nature, and that the highest order of living was to act in conformance

19. In a widely publicized, embarrassing moment, in late 2003 the Bertelsmann Music Group (BMG) used a new CD copy protection scheme from SunnComm that prevented copying CDs to PCs—unless one loaded it in while holding down the shift key!

with nature. Indeed, they said, it is not possible to do otherwise! Humans are rational creatures, and to live rationally means to live in virtue; to live in virtue means to comport oneself morally and ethically. We cannot act against nature, for it would be acting against our own selves, and we always act out of a sense of personal necessity.

It's interesting to see how that argument, those "laws of physics," might be applied both for and against the ethics of downloading. Think of the guy in the dorm calling out, "Dude, where's my MP3?" Is he acting out of a sense of personal necessity, and thus ethically? Or he is acting out of a sense of willfulness that is selfish, irrational, without virtue, and in opposition to reason—e.g. physics and nature? If you've met enough teens and students, you know that he will think of his MP3s as a necessity. If you are the RIAA, you have a different view.

Perhaps one of the reasons that students lead the revolution is that they live in a different "nature" from the rest of us. They live in an environment in which being a geek is no longer a social stigma, where nerds are popular, where music plays 24 hours a day, where they live surrounded by their own kind, and where they have access to almost unlimited bandwidth and technological resources.

Colleges are Petri dishes for piracy.

Until recently, schools pretty much turned a blind eye, worried more about consumption of their computing and networking resources from file-sharing and plagiarism than copyright violations outside the classroom. There are experiments now, however, that may change that climate—that "nature" that drives ethics, according to the Stoics. (You and I might just see this as the imposition of some limits to change behavior.)

One of these systems, admittedly somewhat draconian, was installed at the University of Florida in the summer of 2003. Called Icarus (for Integrated Computer Application for Recognizing User Services), it scans network users' computers for viruses, worms, and file-sharing software such as KaZaA. When students register with the University network, they are required to certify that they won't share copyrighted files. If they do try to share files, the first time they get a popup on the computer screen warning them not to and a follow-up email message, and then are disconnected from the network for 30 minutes. If they do it again, they lose network privileges for five days. A third attempt and they are subject to school discipline and indefinite loss of network privileges.

The school's motivation for devising Icarus was practical. Before implementation, the university was fielding 40 copyright violation notices a month; during peak evening Internet usage, 90 percent of the student network traffic was file-sharing.

At implementation, Icarus spotted over 700 first-time offenders. Ninety tried to share files twice. Only four tried it a third time.[20]

Other solutions use more carrot than stick. Penn State, for instance, signed a deal in late 2003 with the reconstituted, fee-based Napster to offer its premium music service for free to students. The service offers kids unlimited streaming and tethered downloads along with 40 radio stations and an online magazine and message boards. For a buck, the students can buy the right to download a song permanently and copy it onto other media. Student reaction was generally positive, although many felt that since the "free" service was being paid for out of their $160 IT services fee, they were, in effect, still paying for the service. Many said they expected to continue using other file-sharing services to download.[21]

## ARE NEW MORAL GROUND RULES NEEDED?

It is human nature to look at something, figure out a way to turn it into a tool, and use it for our own purposes. Call it problem-solving or call it the challenge to create the next big thing in the world. To deny this characteristic, which we humans alone

---

20. Reported in *Wired News* on October 3, 2003, article "Florida Dorm Locks Out P2P Users."

21. The songs are only available on the computer and protected against copying. When the students leave Penn State, the songs disappear.

among all the animal species possess, is to deny our very humanity.

Had Shawn Fanning not devoted half a year of his life to writing the software code that spawned Napster, someone else would have. Surely, it would have been someone young, just as it would have been young people who would have been the first users. They are the soul of the music market, as well as the pulse of the hacking community.

But why do kids take copyright so lightly, and why are adults fast on their tails? In our quest to answer this question, we spoke with David Greenfield, Ph.D., a practicing psychologist in West Hartford, Connecticut, author of *Virtual Addiction,* and head of the Center for Internet Studies, where he works with abusive and addictive cyber-behaviors. He told us:

> There is virtually no authority or accountability on the Internet. It's an asocial, amoral technology. But conscience and morality are embedded in social interaction or context, which makes sense from a biogenetic perspective, because all sense of rights and wrongs are embedded in social culture. (The Internet's) convenience decreases the threshold of moral objectionability.
>
> As the ease of duplication increases, so does the moral relativity. Theft of intellectual property is a very impulsive act. The Internet, by its nature, has little direct connection with the physical activities you're engaged in. It encourages dissociation. The ease bends morality. The Internet has no soul. It's what we call in medicine an *iatrogenic* effect of the digital age. (Iatrogenic refers to what happens when a medical treatment actually causes an illness.) It creates distortion in the cognitive process. People don't think through things the same way they normally process information. It distorts what people think is intellectual property and what is not.
>
> Copyright isn't physical any more. The move from physical to virtual means that copyright doesn't mean the same

thing. For example, Staples won't photocopy a Stephen King novel for you (because it is such an overt copyright violation). But it's different when it's available in digital technology, which may have to do with ease of access and the ease of the process of doing it.[22]

Is it, then, the technology driving new ethical and moral perceptions about media ownership that will utterly change the world? Or is all this downloading just a fad, likely to go away in time as people get bored with free and easy access to media?

It will, as Paul Saffo suggested at the chapter opening, be interesting to see how all this shakes out 10 or 20 years from now.

---

22. Interview with author Rochester, November 2003.

# 8

# ELIOT NESS OR KEYSTONE KOPS?

Press Release
For Immediate Release
October 2, 2003

## Federal Investigation Leads to Prosecution of Internet Software Pirate

United States Attorney Kevin J. O'Connor and Special-Agent-in-Charge Robin Avers of U.S. Immigration and Customs Enforcement announced today that TRAVIS MYERS, age 29, of Yakima, Washington; TERRY KATZ, age 26, of Yorktown Heights, New York; WALTER KAPECHUK, age 55, of Schenectady, New York; and WARREN WILLSEY, age 53, of East Berne, New York, all waived indictment and pleaded guilty to charges of Conspiracy to Commit Criminal Copyright Infringement. These criminal prosecutions are the first cases to be brought as a result of the fifteen-month, software piracy investigation known as Operation Safehaven.

According to documents filed in federal court, MYERS, KATZ, and KAPECHUK were all participants in the "warez scene"—an underground online community that consists of individuals and organized groups who use the Internet to engage in the large-scale, illegal distribution of copyrighted software. In the warez scene, certain participants (known as "suppliers") are able to obtain access to copyrighted software, video games, DVD movies, and MP3 music files, often before those titles are even available to the general public. Other participants (known as "crackers") then use their technical skills to circumvent or "crack" the digital copyright protections; and yet others (known as "couriers") distribute the pirated software to various file servers on the Internet for others to access, reproduce, and further distribute.

... When sentenced by United States District Judge Ellen Bree Burns, MYERS, KATZ, and KAPECHUK each face a possible punishment of up to five years' imprisonment, three years' supervised release, and a fine of up to $250,000. WILLSEY faces a possible punishment of up to one year's imprisonment, one year's supervised release, and a fine of up to $100,000.[1]

## File-Sharing Companies Offer to Pay Girl's Settlement

Frank Ahrens
*Washington Post* Staff Writer
Thursday, September 11, 2003; Page E05

A coalition of companies that run Internet song-sharing services offered yesterday to pick up the cost of the $2,000 settlement a Manhattan mother reached with the music industry after it sued her 12-year-old daughter for copyright infringement.

Honor-roll student Brianna LaHara was one of 261 defendants targeted Monday by the major record labels and their industry trade group, the Recording Industry Association of America (RIAA), in a broad legal assault on people who swap songs for free over the Internet.

The precocious youngster, who downloaded Mariah Carey tracks, television theme songs and hundreds of other tunes on her computer, has become a symbol for critics of the music industry's aggressive legal tactics.

---

1.   From the cybercrime Web site maintained by the Computer Crime and Intellectual Property Section of the U.S. Department of Justice, http://www.cybercrime.gov/myersPlea.htm.

"These people give Joe Stalin a good name," said Wayne Rosso, president of Grokster Ltd., an Internet peer-to-peer file-sharing system that allows users to download and trade music for free. "It's cynical and hypocritical. I read the statement from (RIAA President) Cary Sherman: 'Nobody wants to play the heavy.' Then why the (expletive) are they playing the heavy?" [2]

Rosso's Grokster is a smaller player in the peer-to-peer world, averaging 50,000 to 60,000 music downloads per week, while KaZaA, the largest, averages 2.5 million per week. Grokster is a member of P2P United, the lobbying group formed in July representing six file-sharing services that offered to pay Brianna's $2,000 settlement.

Although it's nearly impossible to consider both of the above stories as describing the same type of crime in the same breath, they are nevertheless both prosecutable, with similar fines and sentences.

How can this be?

In the spring of 2003, according to most analysts and surveys, there were over 60 million active users of peer-to-peer services downloading[3]

---

2.  Wayne Rosso, at the time president of Grokster, a file-sharing service, about the RIAA to the *Washington Post Tech News*, "File Sharing Companies Offer to Pay Girl's Settlement," September 11, 2003; http://www.washingtonpost.com/wp-dyn/articles/A57424-2003Sep10.html. Joseph Stalin (1879–1953) was the brutal dictator of the Soviet Union who killed millions of Russians whom he deemed "enemies of the people." On October 15, 2003, Rosso left Grokster to become CEO of Optisoft, a peer-to-peer technologies company that offers Blubster and Piolet, products that compete with KaZaA. Optisoft is based in Madrid, Spain, and does not have a Web site. It would appear the market for peer-to-peer down-loading software is not abating.

3.  As mentioned earlier, downloading from these services might better be called file-sharing, or perhaps mass sharing. With KaZaA, as with its predecessor Nap-ster, songs are actually plucked off the PCs of other users on the network, not off some master cyber-jukebox. The software for making this happen also makes it possible for others to pluck songs off your computer. Uploads and downloads are going on simultaneously. It *is* possible to disable the upload function, but most people don't bother, don't realize they can, don't know how, or don't even know songs are being uploaded off their computers. We actually show you how to dis-able file-sharing in Figure 7–1.

copyrighted songs.[4] Over 300 million people have downloaded copies of the KaZaA software, making it one of the most popular software packages of all time. At its peak, Napster could have as many as 10 million users trading songs; today, KaZaA and other file-sharing services may have even more users online, simultaneously trading not just songs, but movies, class notes, research papers, photographs, and even software programs.

Are we talking about 60 million potentially prosecutable citizens? Are we heading toward a nation—indeed, a world—where Eliot Ness[5] and his boys turn into the gangbusters of the media industries, or where scofflaws turn law enforcement officers into Keystone Kops?[6] In this chapter, we take a look at the moves the media, software companies, and law enforcement agencies are making—and the countermoves of their opponents. It's a tale of cops and robbers, corporate intrigue, and rascals against the empire. While a deadly serious business, the antipiracy crusade is also oddly entertaining. You'll see.

---

# A MUSIC INDUSTRY OFFENSIVE

Let's start our story with the music industry. After a year or two of Napster, during which online music sharing grew from a trickle to a torrent, the music industry knew it was in trouble. CD sales were falling, the Internet wasn't going away, and industry-sponsored music downloading sites had few customers.

---

4. An observed KaZaA usage statistic on November 19, 2003, 12:30 PM: "3,886,894 users online, sharing 689,275,396 files (5,240,064GB)".

5. Eliot Ness was the lawman who pursued organized crime during prohibition and was responsible for putting Al Capone in jail. In 1957, he wrote about his experiences in a book, *The Untouchables*, named for his incorruptible crime fighting team. The book was later made into a TV series and a movie.

6. In the early days of silent film, Mack Sennett produced a series of slapstick films about a group of seriously inept policemen, the Keystone Kops. Pie-in-the-face scenes were commonplace. They debuted in 1912; their first big film, *The Bangville Police*, was released in 1913.

**Figure 8–1** 2003 was the year file-sharing became big news.

By 2003, apocryphal cover stories, like those depicted in Figure 8–1, from the February 2003 issue of *Wired*, published by Condé Nast, and the May 2003 issue of *Spectrum*, a publication of the Institute of Electrical and Electronics Engineers (IEEE), foretold the fiery doom of the music industry.

The message got across. On September 8, 2003, after months of making warlike noises, the RIAA issued subpoenas to 261 people it claimed had illegally copied or shared songs for which RIAA members owned copyrights (see "The Strange Story of Ross Plank" in Chapter 5, *Inside the Sausage: The Making of the Digital Millennium Copyright Act*). "Swap Swat" was the headline in the *Boston Herald*. The RIAA also offered a so-called "amnesty" program to those who would voluntarily admit their guilt and promise never to do it again—but very few people took advantage of it because it required an admission of guilt that could be used in litigation by other music publishers besides those represented by the RIAA.

The publicity was immense: stories in every newspaper in the land, follow-up stories on those who had been subpoenaed, sidebars on the story of Brianna LaHara (see Chapter 3, *Us Against Them?*), pros and cons from the print pundits, special in-depth segments on the TechTV channel, interviews with students, RIAA spokespeople, Congressmen, eggheads, and special teach-ins at colleges and high schools across the U.S. The lawsuits, the ethics of downloading, the lives and fortunes of artists—it all became grist for the conversational mill. It was an intergenerational topic.

Despite all the sound bites, fury, and brouhaha, the chances of getting caught and subpoenaed by the RIAA were less than one in 200,000—about the same as being struck by lightning. No one is really sure what the chances of a warez thief getting caught might be.

The RIAA did a lot of detective work to find its victims—er, the perpetrators. First, it used the peer-to-peer networks themselves to find heavy downloaders, and then uploaded songs from them. Once heavy potential uploading violators were found, the RIAA used information from the file-sharing service to determine the screen name and Internet address of the user, from which they got the actual name and address from ISPs under provisions of the DMCA (see Chapter 5).[7]

To determine if the songs it had uploaded had violated copyright, the RIAA used software detection tools that looked at some of the digital information describing the compressed content of the MP3 songs (called the hashing algorithm). These tools could be used to trace the lineage of a single illegal song as it passed from user to user—in some cases all the way back to the original Napster download. This is technology similar to that used by the FBI to track computer hackers. Eliot Ness would have been proud.

But there was a lot of backlash over the RIAA move. There was sympathy for 12-year-old Brianna, there were a number of

7. How invisible are you on the Internet? Not very. Your computer constantly "broadcasts" its unique identifier, called an *IP address*. To learn what yours is, go to www.whatismyip.com.

embarrassing mistaken identities, one of the most public of which was that of Sarah Ward, a 66-year old retired school-teacher from Boston (see Chapter 3, *Us Against Them?*), and there were all manner of editorials questioning the RIAA's tactics. The concept of the record labels suing the kids who make up the sweet spot of their market seems comical, if not pitiful. Something suitable, it would seem, for the Keystone Kops.

As law enforcement, maybe the lawsuits weren't elegant. But as PR and public education, the September blitz was brilliant. Kids had just gotten back to college—downloading spikes during the school year—and most had been warned by their colleges about the risks of downloading. The RIAA had conducted highly publicized softening-up campaigns the spring before, starting by announcing that they would be going after individual file-sharers in a press release in June, and then going to court to get the ISPs to turn over names and addresses, and even attempting to get colleges like Boston College, Boston University, Columbia University, Loyola, the University of Southern California, and MIT to agree to turn over the names of students downloading over the college networks. In the latter action, the Massachusetts schools won a reprieve when they fought the subpoenas on the grounds that they were issued in Washington, DC, and not the Commonwealth; but they told their students that when the right papers were filed, they would comply.

Headlines around the time were plentiful, as shown in the clips in Figure 8–2.

In retrospect, the RIAA didn't really expect to lock anybody away for violating copyright—or even make back in settlement fees a fraction of what it spent on enforcement, but that was not the goal.

The goal, pure and simple, was to scare the dickens out of downloaders.

Less than two months after the subpoenas, RIAA president Cary Sherman was quoted in an interview with *Boston Globe*

**Figure 8–2**    Examples of the free publicity garnered by the RIAA during its fall 2003 antipiracy campaign waged against the citizens of the United States. Clockwise from top: *Boston Globe*, September 9, 2003; *Newsweek,* September 22, 2003; *Boston Herald*, September 9, 2003; *Boston Globe*, September 14, 2003; *Boston Herald*, September 9, 2003; *BBC News*, September 3, 2003.

writer, Hiawatha Bray:[8] "We think it's been a remarkably small public relations backlash. We actually thought it would be worse." He pointed out that the RIAA got some editorial support from major newspapers, as well as support from Congress. In other words, the message was loud and clear: *En garde!*

Before the month was out, the RIAA had pulled back from its confrontational lawsuits, sending letters out to potential sub-

---

8.    Hiawatha Bray, "Cary Sherman, RIAA President, on Battle vs. File Swappers," *Boston Globe,* October 26, 2003.

poena recipients and offering to settle before litigation and even testifying to Congress that it was moving away from its shoot-first-ask-questions-later tactics.

And why not? Mission accomplished.[9]

As much as you might like to think the RIAA was running amok like Chief of Police Teeheezel and his Keystone Kops, make no mistake: This was an operation more worthy of Eliot Ness and his Untouchables. There was nothing slapstick about this operation—not at all.

## WHERE ARE THE COPS WHEN YOU NEED THEM?

While the RIAA's highly publicized bust stole the antipiracy headlines in 2003—there are over 67,000 Google references to the RIAA dated September 2003 alone—in another space-time continuum, traditional law enforcement was hard at work but hardly working, as the old saw goes.

Here's what we mean. According to statistics kept by the U.S. Department of Justice (DOJ),[10] the federal government gets leads on about 200 criminal cases on intellectual property a year, files 100 cases or so, and gets a guilty plea or verdict about 75 percent of the time. But only a third or so of the perpetrators ever do jail time, and when they do, it's usually a year or less.

The DOJ intellectual property crime categories include:

■ Trafficking in counterfeit labels for records, CDs, and movies

■ Criminal infringement of copyright

---

9.  Within six months, in April 2004, the Pew Internet & American Life Project reported that one in seven U.S. Internet users who had once downloaded songs over the Internet had stopped. Of course, at the same time a number of new users had started, increasing the number of U.S. downloaders from 18 million in December 2003 to 23 million in April 2004. Information from comScore Media Metrix that was part of the same study showed that the number of Internet users running popular file-sharing applications, such as KaZaA, had dropped from a peak of 25 million in June 2003 to 20 million by March 2004.

10. See www.cybercrime.gov.

| Commodity | Domestic Value | % of Total |
|---|---|---|
| Cigarettes | $35,579,894 | 38% |
| Media | $28,396,287 | 29% |
| Wearing Apparel | $9,294,975 | 9% |
| Consumer Electronics | $5,307,407 | 5% |
| Watches/Parts | $3,919,331 | 4% |
| Handbags/Wallets/Backpacks | $2,927,194 | 3% |
| Toys/Electronic Games | $2,150,847 | 2% |
| Cigarette Rolling Papers | $1,142,523 | 1% |
| Sunglasses/Parts | $1,074,798 | 1% |
| Headware | $1,043,252 | 1% |
| Other | $6,153,833 | 6% |
| **TOTAL** | **$98,990,341** | **100%** |

**Figure 8–3**   U.S. Customs Service Counterfeit Seizures. Source:
www.iacc.org/teampublish/109_476_1742.cfm..

- Unauthorized music recording and redistribution
- Trafficking in counterfeit goods (CDs, DVDs, VHS tapes, etc.)

If you search in other areas, you might find some additional
cases, ranging from stealing satellite signals to pirating engineering drawings, but let's do some math. According to the DOJ
Cybercrime data, we're talking about 75–100 criminal convictions a year. Perhaps more take place at the state and local level,
but to our untrained eye, this still doesn't look like much. Nation-
wide crime statistics indicate we put away more than 15,000
murderers in the U.S. each year. There are a million or so cases of
shoplifting reported a year, and at least 100,000 arrests. It's hard
to believe only 75 people commit intellectual property crimes.
Does anyone in blue take this seriously?

Another way to see how small the drop of apprehensions is in
comparison to the bucket of intellectual property crimes can be
seen in U.S. customs seizures of counterfeit goods. In fiscal 2002,
the U.S. Customs Service made 5,793 such seizures, with the
value of counterfeited goods shown in Figure 8–3.

Such is the yield from over 450 million checks of travelers and cargo a year in the U.S. Yet the value of all counterfeit goods seized around the world, even if it is $500 million, is a pittance compared to current estimates that counterfeiting accounts for over 5 percent of worldwide trade, or something upwards of $500 billion! These are good odds for crooks.

In fact, intellectual property piracy has such good odds that it is one of the least risky and most lucrative criminal enterprises. Ronald K. Noble, General of Interpol, in testimony before the U.S. Congress,[11] pointed out the links between intellectual property crime and terrorism. Some of the examples cited by Noble and others:

■ The black market in Kosovo, which operates freely even though the province is administered by the U.N., puts money in the hands of criminal organizations that, in turn, help fund ethnic Albanian extremist groups.

■ In 2000, a joint operation by Russian law enforcement and private industry led to the takedown of a CD manufacturing plant that had been funding Chechen rebels. The plant was earning about $600,000 a month.

■ Investigations in Denmark in 2002 led to a connection between counterfeiting and al-Qaeda; in the same year, a major software and games pirate of Lebanese origin was arrested in Paraguay and found to have been funneling money to Hezbollah.

■ The Irish Republican Army is known to have financed some of its activities through sales of pirated versions of Disney's *The Lion King*.

One of the reasons that digital piracy works so well for criminals is that white collar crime in general, and intellectual property crime in particular, are just not highly visible on law enforcement radar screens. Says Interpol's Noble: "IPC crime is a low priority for law enforcement agencies and investigations are poorly

---

11. Testimony on July 16, 2003, before the U.S. House Committee on International relations, available at www.interpol.int/Public/ICPO/speeches/SG20030716.asp.

resourced when compared to illicit narcotics or counter-terror-
ism investigations. There is also a lack of generalized expertise
among law enforcement agencies in recognizing and investigating
counterfeit and pirated goods."

In his testimony, Noble pointed out the low-risk, high-reward
nature of piracy. In 2002 in Europe, a kilo (2.2 lbs.) of CDs was
worth €3,000, while a kilo of cannabis resin was worth €1,000. A
counterfeit computer game might cost €0.20 to make and sell for
€45, while a gram of cannabis could cost €1.52 to make and sell at
€12. You don't need a degree in finance or a euro-to-dollar conversion table to see which is the more lucrative.

Moreover, the risks are lower. In France, for instance, at the time
Noble testified, the maximum punishment for counterfeiting was
a fine of $150,000 and two years in prison, while the punishment
for drug trafficking was a $7.5 million fine and 10 years in prison.

If you needed money quickly and didn't care how you got it,
which business would you invest in?

Big-time counterfeiters have gotten big-time sophisticated. Some
are legitimate businesses by day, counterfeiters by night. Some
are hidden in the jungles and protected by armed guards in
enclaves worthy of a Colombian drug cartel. Many employ computer scientists to duplicate code, defeat its antipiracy provisions,
and remaster it. The counterfeiters copy packaging, labeling, and
authentication certificates, then use million-dollar replicators to
pump out the fake CDs. They smuggle CDs like drugs, selling
them to unsuspecting—or uncaring—consumers, businesses, and
governments.

## CHASING BUCCANEERS

The cops may not make many intellectual property busts, yet
when they do, they like to toot horns, blow whistles, and bang
drums. There are so few cases, it appears they issue a press
release and post the news to their Web sites whenever one
occurs.

For the U.S. Department of Justice, one of the most satisfying busts was that of John Sankus, Jr., in February 2002. Sankus was co-leader of a "warez" group known as DrinkOrDie, which distributed pirated copies of high-end software and utilities over the Internet. The operation was not small: Sankus supervised about 65 people in countries as far away as Australia and Sweden. Their job was to acquire software, often from company insiders, defeat any embedded software protections (an illegal activity called *cracking*), and distribute it from multiple Web sites. Communications over the Internet didn't go via the familiar Web, but over IRC channels in encrypted signals. Sankus, an icon in the warez world, used a screen name "eriFlleH," or "HellFire" spelled backwards.

For the software world, Sankus *was* hellfire. The software cracked and "released" by his operation could make it to over 10,000 illegal distribution sites in a day. The software came not only from giants like Adobe, Microsoft, and Autodesk, but also from tiny companies that could ill afford losses from piracy. In a single year, DrinkOrDie illicitly distributed over 270 titles.

Sankus' capture was the result of a 15-month operation code-named "Buccaneer" undertaken by the U.S. DOJ, the U.S. Customs Service, and the U.S. Attorney for the Eastern District of Virginia. They not only nabbed Sankus on December 11, 2001, but also 70 others in a coordinated raid in six countries. In similar operations over the next year, the U.S. also shut down several other major operations (Rogue Warriorz, Razor1911, Apocalypse Crew) and even developed one of the better warez sites on the Internet as part of its undercover operation.

From an intellectual property prosecution standpoint, the judge threw the book at Sankus: 46 months in prison, and a big press release announcing his conviction.

The Sankus conviction was topped in early 2004 by the Razor1911 bust, when Sean Michael Breen, 38 years old, of Richmond, California, was sentenced to 50 months in prison for two counts of copyright infringement and three counts of mail fraud. Breen and his accomplices specialized in computer games, releasing versions of Quake, Red Alert, Terminal Velocity, Warcraft II, and Warcraft III on IRC sites before they were published. Yet it was more than likely Breen's buying networking hardware under false pretenses from Cisco Systems and having it shipped to a phony storefront that got him caught, not his IRC activities.

Sadly, the tide is not in favor of Eliot Ness. The Sankus and Breen takedowns barely made a dent in the underground trafficking of warez.[12] By virtue of their underground nature, it's difficult to even ascertain how many warez IRC sites exist. They're like a resistance movement, appearing and disappearing, shutting down and reopening elsewhere, new ones appearing all the time. No matter how tightly the gangbusters squeeze, there will always be customers looking for a free copy of something digital. And it's likely there will always be a Web site where they can find it.

## CHASING BUCCANEERS ABROAD

Outside the U.S., where digital piracy is even worse, law enforcement operates pretty much under the same publish-or-perish conditions. If you make a bust, tell the world about it. Some examples from 2003:

- A 23 year-old student, Bilal Khan, was sentenced to 15 months in prison in England for producing and counterfeiting business software that he sold on mail-order Web sites he created and over eBay. Khan had been traced by the police when a consumer who inadvertently bought some counterfeit software turned his name over to the police; he jumped bail, left London, and went to Pakistan where he continued his business. He returned to London and was captured when he was stopped on a routine traffic violation.

---

12. Another big raid, even bigger than the one that netted Sankus and Breen, Operation Fastlink, took place in April 2004. The Feds and their international counterparts conducted searches in 27 states and 10 countries, netting over 100 people involved in piracy of over $50 million in movies, games, music, and software. One server had over 65,000 titles on it. The warez groups targeted were known by names like Fairlight, Kalisto, and Project X.

▪ A court in Germany sentenced a 42-year-old man, known to the U.S. press only as Mr. M., to three years in prison for selling 20,000–30,000 illegal CD software, game, music, and video compilations. Downloading software illegally from servers in Taiwan, Hungary, the UK, and the Netherlands, he burned CDs and distributed them through resellers in Germany, Greece, Italy, and Switzerland.

▪ Police in Thailand arrested Maksym Kovalchuk, *aka* Maksym Vysochansky, perhaps *aka* many other names, a 25-year-old Ukrainian and the alleged mastermind of a vast software pirating network, as he was visiting an ice cream parlor in Bangkok. Agents had tracked him from the Ukraine to Thailand. To communicate with buyers, he used online aliases and multiple email accounts. He was also wanted for money laundering, possession of unauthorized credit card information, and computer hacking. By late fall, there were rumors of other criminal connections in the foreign press[13] and suggestions that there was something mysterious about his extradition.

## CHASING A MIRAGE

"There's something happening here," sang Buffalo Springfield, who said that what it was wasn't exactly clear. But this is pretty clear: From all walks of life, the social attitude toward digital intellectual property is morphing about as fast as English language usage. At the same time, the skills to circumvent intellectual property are easier and easier to come by. Technology is a moving target, while most of the attempts to contain, restrain, or stop it simply aren't traveling at the same speed. The tide is not in favor of John Law. Pirates are enterprising, clever, hard to find, and sometimes ingenious. They seem always one step ahead of the gendarmes.

▪ *Item:* the sequel to the popular PC action game Half-Life, produced by a company called Valve and distributed by Vivendi Universal, is found in pirated form on gamer Web sites in Sep-

13.  Mike Brunker, "Mystery Shrouds Arrest of Accused Software Pirate," MSNBC, September 30, 2003, available at www.msnbc.com/news/968178.asp?0sl=-12.

tember 2003, months before official release. The theft of code prompts Vivendi to postpone launch until after the Christmas holidays.

■ *Item:* A team of researchers from AT&T and the University of Pennsylvania finds that over 75 percent of the top 50 movies of 2002 and 2003 uploaded illegally to the Web were leaked from industry insiders;[14] movies like *The Matrix Reloaded* and *Finding Nemo* are available on the Web within days of release, despite tough controls over distribution and audiences at premiers. (For *Finding Nemo,* premier theaters used metal detectors and night vision glasses to deter and detect bootlegging.) To prevent piracy, the MPAA says late in the fall that members wouldn't support sending out the year-end movie screeners to Academy Award voters, although the MPAA backtracks within three weeks as a result of protests from independent filmmakers.

■ *Item:* An entire cottage industry of "mod chippers" has sprung up to modify the hardware in video games like Microsoft Xbox and Sony PlayStation so they can play pirated software by circumventing chips inside them that prevent playing copied games. Ironically, modifying the hardware is not illegal, only violating copyright.

■ *Item:* Weeks before it is released in the spring of 2002, *The Eminem Show*, distributed by Interscope, is the second-most played CD on PCs—meaning it had been purchased from bootleggers or passed from CD burner to CD burner.[15]

How can law enforcement catch up? What's a cop to do?

---

14. Simon Byers, Lorrie Cranor, Eric Cronin, Dave Kormann, and Patrick McDaniel, "Analysis of Security Vulnerabilities in the Movie Production and Distribution Process," in Proceedings of the 2003 ACM Workshop on Digital Rights Management, October 27, 2003, Washington, D.C. (Paper also presented at the 31st Research Conference on Communication, Information and Internet Policy, September 19–21, 2003, Arlington, VA.)

15. John Borland, "Eminem CD Spotlights New Piracy Pattern," CNETNews.com, May 28, 2002, available at http://news.com.com/2100-1023-923472.html.

# DEPUTIZING THE BUSINESSMAN

Cops aren't the only ones chasing pirates. Most digital piracy captures fall to privateers—the companies and trade associations with vested interests in clear shipping channels over the digital seas. They do the sleuthing, the legal legwork, and the lobbying, even serving the subpoenas for civil action. They also get the money (less attorney fees) from settlements.

There are several avenues for leads. According to BSA President and CEO Robert Holleyman, his trade organization has several tools for finding pirates, including:

- Employees and ex-employees. They can contact the BSA by phone, email, or an online form on the BSA Web site. The online form asks for particulars on exactly what software is being used illegally, on what machines, whether the CEO or management is aware of it, and whether the company would erase the software if it knew of pending legal action. In the U.S. the BSA gets scores of leads like this every month—more when there are lots of layoffs.

- Customers of counterfeiters and "disk-loaders" (companies that add illegal software to computers before sale to customers) who feel cheated when they find out their software is not authorized.

- Crawlers—software that roams the Internet looking for copyrighted software for sale from unauthorized sources, such as warez sites, known piracy sites, and auctions. Thousands of transactions are found monthly on the Internet.

Once a lead comes in, whether to the BSA, the RIAA, the MPAA, or one of their member organizations, the spadework begins. Lawyers and investigators either interview or correspond with the source to ascertain if, indeed, there is a case of piracy and if it is egregious or high-profile. Once piracy is discovered, they either turn it over to law enforcement agencies for criminal prosecution or prepare their own civil action. Under the DMCA, litigators can obtain search warrants to go on a suspect's premises. There they can commandeer computers, inventory software on machines, and ask to examine license agreements.

"These are the exceptions, though," says the BSA's Holleyman. "In many more cases when we get a report from our hotline, we'll investigate, determine that it's credible, but also that we can resolve it by going directly to the company. We send them a letter and 99% of the time those cases are resolved."

At any one time, he points out, the BSA might have 500 cases going in the U.S., and maybe 20,000 enforcement actions worldwide.

The 19,500 cases outside the U.S. make the BSA's life interesting. Each of the 80–100 countries involved operates under different laws and cultures; each has a different view of how to enforce the international treaties and local laws that enforce copyright protection.

"There are many countries outside the U.S.," notes Holleyman, "where the civil court mechanism is wholly ineffective. And in those cases, even for end-user piracy (usually businesses using unlicensed software on their company systems), we rely more on the criminal courts."

## NOTICE AND TAKEDOWN

Perhaps the most useful tool in the antipiracy campaign is what's called the notice-and-takedown provision of the DMCA. As you will recall from Chapter 5, *Inside the Sausage: The Making of the Digital Millennium Copyright Act*, this allows a copyright holder who believes someone using the Internet has infringed on his or her copyright to contact the carrier providing access (notice) and order the carrier to block access (takedown) to the offending content with haste.[16]

---

16. If the carriers cooperate with takedown, they fall under the safe harbor provision of the DCMA and aren't liable for the copyright violations of their customers.

The origin of this provision, according to Brad Smith, Senior Vice President and General Counsel of Microsoft, was a particular focus after the development of the WIPO treaty and in the formative years of the Digital Millennium Copyright Act, in balancing the rights and interests of the content industry and the ISPs (Microsoft is both). The content industry wanted the carriers to do more to protect copyrights, while the carriers were worried about the cost of doing so.[17] In the end, according to Smith, Senator Orrin Hatch, a sponsor of the DMCA, asked Holleyman and the BSA to broker a compromise. The notice-and-takedown provision was born from that deal.

Microsoft lobbied in favor of the notice-and-takedown provision. "Being both a content company but also having an online network in MSN was helpful to us in seeing both sides," says Smith.

The notice-and-takedown provision of the DCMA gives some civil libertarians the willies. In practice, what can happen is that content owners can send a notice, such as the one in Figure 8–4, to a carrier (including college and university network administrators) and the carrier, in order to retain safe harbor status, will take down the offending material or block access to it without question. This can all happen without prior notice to the person or company responsible for the alleged copyright-infringing content.

This is a good deal for content owners, at least those with the resources to pursue copyright infringement on this scale; it gives the carriers, a normally risk-averse bunch, some insulation from the shenanigans of their customers. Needless to say, it doesn't make their customers happy.

"There are thousands of takedowns a week," remarks Smith, "but in any given week the number of people who actually feel they were taken down inappropriately can be counted on one hand, or perhaps a finger or two. And companies are very sensitive to the fact that these are customers, paying customers, so they tend to respond quickly to customers who raise an objection."

---

17. From an interview with Brad Smith on September 24, 2003.

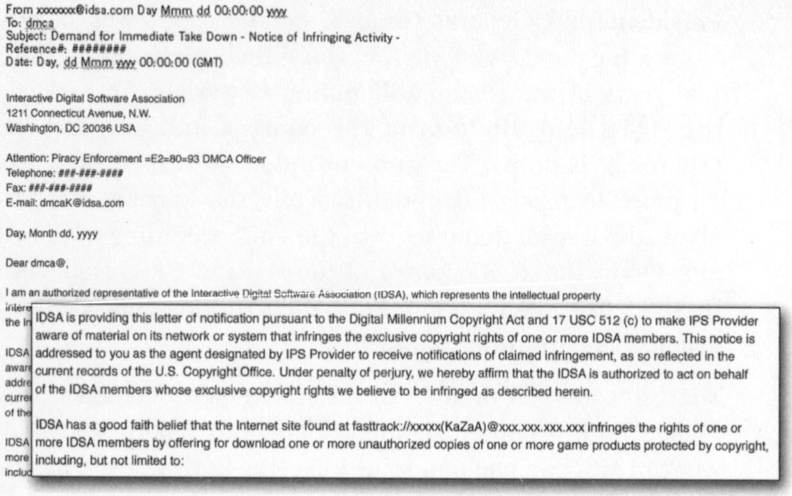

From xxxxxxx@idsa.com Day Mmm dd 00:00:00 www
To: dmca
Subject: Demand for Immediate Take Down - Notice of Infringing Activity -
Reference#: ########
Date: Day, dd Mmm www 00:00:00 (GMT)

Interactive Digital Software Association
1211 Connecticut Avenue, N.W.
Washington, DC 20036 USA

Attention: Piracy Enforcement =E2=80=93 DMCA Officer
Telephone: ###-###-####
Fax: ###-###-####
E-mail: dmcaK@idsa.com

Day, Month dd, yyyy

Dear dmca@,

I am an authorized representative of the Interactive Digital Software Association (IDSA), which represents the intellectual property

IDSA is providing this letter of notification pursuant to the Digital Millennium Copyright Act and 17 USC 512 (c) to make IPS Provider aware of material on its network or system that infringes the exclusive copyright rights of one or more IDSA members. This notice is addressed to you as the agent designated by IPS Provider to receive notifications of claimed infringement, as so reflected in the current records of the U.S. Copyright Office. Under penalty of perjury, we hereby affirm that the IDSA is authorized to act on behalf of the IDSA members whose exclusive copyright rights we believe to be infringed as described herein.

IDSA has a good faith belief that the Internet site found at fasttrack://xxxxx(KaZaA)@xxx.xxx.xxx.xxx infringes the rights of one or more IDSA members by offering for download one or more unauthorized copies of one or more game products protected by copyright, including, but not limited to:

**Figure 8–4**   This is an actual notice-and-takedown email message sent on behalf of the RIAA and its client record labels to a four-year educational institution's network administration department in the fall of 2003 (identifying information has been removed).

But the guilty-until-proven-innocent nature of the process can lead to abuse, intentional or otherwise. Invocations of the DMCA have ranged from disclosing sale prices in advance to attempting to block competitors from selling accessories for another company's product to barring televised sports events in public venues to stifling legitimate scientific research to suppressing book-writing projects that explain how to "hack" various consumer electronics products such as TiVo and gaming consoles.[18]

So far, notice-and-takedown has worked for the BSA, the MPAA, and the RIAA. Or perhaps it just seems to be a useful tool against overwhelming odds. Sort of like a Keystone Kop disguised as *The*

---

18.  For an exhaustive essay on DMCA abuse, see "Unintended Consequences: Five Years under the DMCA" on the Electronic Frontier Foundation Web site at http://www.eff.org/IP/DMCA/unintended_consequences.php.

*Matrix*'s Neo, fending off thousands upon thousands of Mr. Smiths with a stick.

# THE INTERNATIONAL BLACK HOLE

Oh, you don't believe the odds are overwhelming? Got no sympathy for the music, movie, electronic gaming, or software companies? .

In that case, maybe you should check out the annual "Special 301 Report,"[19] published by the Office of the United States Trade Representative (USTR), headed by Robert B. Zoellick, the country's top trade negotiator and trade policy advisor to the President.

The annual report details the state of intellectual property protection in over 70 countries. The 2003 report focused specifically on counterfeiting and piracy, "with particular emphasis on the ongoing campaign to reduce production of unauthorized copies of 'optical media' products such as CDs, VCDs, DVDs, and CD-ROMs." The section that discusses the problem is entitled: "Global Scourge of Counterfeiting and Piracy."

Got that? Global *scourge*!

Let's check the rap sheet on some of the biggest offenders, whose lax enforcement has resulted in this global scourge:

■ The Ukraine is first on the list and suffered $75 million in U.S. sanctions in 2002 for failing to comply with some previous agreements. "Although enforcement efforts have resulted in a significant decline in the production of pirated media within the Ukraine, there is still substantial traffic in illegal optical disc media, both in street sales to consumers as well as larger distribution to Western Europe, the Baltics, and elsewhere."

---

19. Available at http://www.ustr.gov/reports/2003/special301.htm. The name comes from the provision (# 301) in the U.S. Trade Act of 1974 that charges the USTR with identifying countries that have inadequate intellectual property protection and to use the information to effect certain trade policies or sanctions.

What was that software piracy rate we read about in Chapter 6, *Global Fallout*, 91 percent? Sounds about right.

■ In China, the issue seems not to be the laws and international agreements, which have been put into law the last 10 years, but enforcement. "The lack of transparency and coordination among Chinese government agencies, local protectionism and corruption, high thresholds for criminal prosecution, lack of training and weak punishments all hamper enforcement of IPR." Wait until the 2008 Olympics—think of the deals you'll be able to get on new releases of *The Matrix ReReReReRe-Loaded, John Madden NFL 2008, Microsoft Office 2008*, and the Rolling Stones' *Golden Jubilee* album.

■ Paraguay, it seems, has difficulties with both internal and border enforcement, organized crime in the piracy business, and a general judicial and constabulatory lack of interest in the whole matter. Ciudad del Este, a town on the border of Argentina and Brazil, is alleged to be an international haven for software pirates.

■ Brazil has a Dr. Jekyll and Mr. Hyde problem: It is at once one of the largest global markets for legitimate copyrighted products and also one of the largest global markets for *pirated* products. "Virtually all audio cassettes sold are pirated copies," the report states.

■ India, on the priority watch list, pirates books and software and counterfeits not just CDs and DVDs, but also medicine, auto parts, clothing, and consumer goods. The USTR "urges" India to do something about all this.

And that's how it goes. The Bahamas allow cable providers to retransmit premium cable programs. In the Philippines, optical media piracy has "exploded," and in 2002, the country began exporting more pirated material than it imported. Poland doesn't seem to want to shut down its open-air market in government-owned Warsaw Stadium. While Russia made some token moves to shore up its IPR defenses, "the number of optical media facilities has doubled since 2001." Korea looks the other way as firms obtain rights to register and distribute bootlegged U.S. movies. In

Thailand, one of the problems is "the impunity accorded well-connected figures involved in infringement."

Piracy isn't going away, any more than globalization.

## THE ONGOING ARMS RACE

There is an arms race in the war against piracy. For each step the antipiracy sleuths and enforcers take, the digital pirates counter with a host of new treasons, stratagems, and foils. In October, 2002, the music companies sued Netherlands-based KaZaA, which operates the most popular peer-to-peer file-sharing network since Napster (which has since gone commercial and legitimate). By January 2003, the company had reconstituted itself as an aggregation of corporate entities in Estonia, Sweden, and a mysterious site offshore of Great Britain, and had set up its computer system on Vanuato, a South Sea island tax haven. At last report, KaZaA's owner, Sharman Networks, was headquartered in Sydney, Australia.

Poof, what's to sue?

So the record companies use KaZaA itself to find downloaders pirating copyrighted songs. Then they create "spoofs" of songs that get themselves downloaded at 200 million copies a month,[20] so KaZaA sues the RIAA for misuse of its software and, get this, violating copyright! At the same time, KaZaA has been increasing the amount of legal music it sells and distributes over its own network—morphing into a legitimate music distributor in competition with the major labels.

---

20. Spoofs are fake MP3s that at first appear to be real songs on the list of those available from other peer-to-peer users, but have been engineered to play noise, endless loops of the same notes, messages that tell users not to steal music, or links that redirect them to commercial music sites. In fact, there was an arms race just within the spoofing community. The file-sharing networks developed their own antispoofing software—which was related to the technology used by the RIAA to track downloaders!

Yet while the record companies are trying to sabotage KaZaA, Morpheus, Grokster, and the other peer-to-peer networks with technology and shut them down through the courts, they are also paying top dollar to a company called Big Champagne for instant market research on which songs are hot in which markets at which time. It turns out that by tracking downloads on KaZaA, record labels can find out where radio stations are underplaying their songs and use the data to increase radio play, which, they believe, increases record store sales. Go figure.

In one interesting case, after the RIAA began suing college kids for pirating music, two students from MIT, working for two years on a grant from Microsoft, set up a downloading alternative by piping analog music files onto to the campus network from a library of 3,500 CDs purchased from a company in California.[21] It's called the Library Access to Music Project, or LAMP. Most of the time was spent getting the proper licenses and releases to broadcast. Because LAMP is analog, the rules for broadcasting apply, and not the DMCA. What a coup for the students!

Well, at least for a few days. It took about a nanosecond for the record industry to go after the California company, Loudeye, for illegally ripping the CDs it provided to MIT, which it had assured the university were properly licensed. LAMP was extinguished within a week.

How about Madonna's spoof of her own album, *American Life*? She and Warner Brothers, her label, populated the file-sharing networks with spoofs in the spring of 2003. Try to download cuts from the album and you got Madonna swearing at you, saying "What the f*** do you think you're doing?" The spoof instantly became a cult hit, and some say it was more popular than the album itself. Other musicians then took the spoof and remixed Madonna's words into other songs, some of which still

---

21. Analog is the original form in which a recording is usually published. An example is a WMA file, which can be played by Windows Media Player software. A WMA file is made digital when it is converted to an MP3 file. It can also be played by Windows Media Player. There are *many* analog and digital music file formats.

live on.[22] Plus her site was hacked and a bunch of songs offered for free download along with the words *"This* is what I think I'm doing." Tough crowd.

Besides spoofing, the antipiracy forces have considered more drastic methods, according to *The New York Times*.[23] These include planting virus-like software on file-sharing computers that freeze or stall their systems, programs that search user hard drives for pirated music and delete the tracks, and software attacks that prevent users from accessing a network while trying to download songs. (Senator Orrin Hatch, a Republican from Utah and Senate sponsor of the DCMA, likes these ideas. At a Senate Judiciary Committee hearing in June 2003, he said he favored technology that would destroy or permanently disable the computers of illegal downloaders.)

But the file downloaders themselves are countering as well, by developing their own encrypted file-sharing networks (underground, or "dark," networks) and using services that provide anonymity, like FreeNet, a UK–based service, as well as Blubster and Piolet from Spain. And so it goes.

---

## DOES DOWNLOADING ACTUALLY HURT CD SALES?

The music industry has long maintained that illegal downloading directly cannibalizes CD sales and supports this conventional wisdom with statistics that show the simultaneous rise of downloading and fall of music sales.

Imagine the industry's chagrin, then, when two researchers, Felix Oberholzer from Harvard University and Koleman Strumpf from the University of North Carolina, published a study in March 2004 that

---

22. See The Madonna Remix Project, www.irixx.org/madonna/.
23. Andrew Ross Sorkin, "Software Bullet Is Sought to Kill Musical Piracy," *New York Times*, May 4, 2003; and Saul Hansell, "Crackdown May Send Music Traders into Software Underground," *The New York Times*, September 15, 2003.

drew the conclusion "downloads have an effect on sales which is statistically indistinguishable from zero" and that the research is "inconsistent with claims that file sharing is the primary reason for the recent decline in music sales."

The study was different from most, in that it didn't rely on surveys of users who might or might not provide accurate answers, but on studying actual downloads and CD sales, monitored at the song title level, at the same time. Oberholzer and Strumpf used server logs from OpenNap to track almost 2 million actual downloads for a period of 17 weeks in late 2002 and early 2003 and Nielsen Sound-Scan to study sales of 680 albums over a period of 10,000 album weeks. Even in the most pessimistic scenario, their report says, it would take 5,000 downloads to displace a CD. Projected to the full market, say the researchers, this would be a "rounding error" in total CD sales.

In addition, in an adjunct survey run off the server and administered while respondents were actually downloading, 65 percent of users said that downloading led them to not purchase an album, but 80 percent said they bought at least one album after first sampling it on a file-sharing network. The net effect was positive. Downloading looks to be like radio, where "free" air play helps sales of CDs.

Although the music industry immediately pooh-poohed the research as just one of many studies of the subject, the methodology is unique and research credentials of the study authors impeccable.

The authors themselves said they were surprised by their findings. Imagine the average music industry executive

# AN UPHILL PUSH

In the movie short *Super-Hooper-Dyne-Lizzies*, in one of the most memorable Keystone Kops scenes of all time, the protagonist, played by Billy Bevan, is pushing his car home. But the car keeps bumping into other cars, and pretty soon he's pushing a whole string of cars. Eventually he pushes them up a hill and over a cliff.

For the antipiracy cops, it must sometimes seem that they are pushing a lot more than a half dozen cars up the hill. The whole thing's very Sisyphean. Consider:

- For law enforcement, digital piracy is a complex crime with little in the way of crime scene and no glory for apprehending criminals.

- For the courts, it's an endless morass of tangled, inadequate, or outdated laws, conflicting precedents, and squabbling hordes of intellectual property lawyers.

- For most governments, the immediate benefits of curtailing piracy come mostly from not being clubbed over the head by the U.S. government and its multinationals.

- For pirates, from downloading teens to Ukrainian mobsters, the chances of getting caught are slim and the punishments light.

- The purported victims, whether Microsoft, Disney, or Vivendi, Bill Gates, Adam Sandler, Metallica, or Shania Twain, are viewed as rich monopolists who engender little sympathy from the public.

- For lawmakers, there's no pork to bring home to the home state in intellectual property legislation.

But up the hill our Sisyphuses must go. As we saw in Chapter 6, *Global Fallout*, there are economic costs to piracy. But in a way, they're more like the economic costs of littering than the economic costs of, say, alcoholism or drug abuse. There is little reward for any one individual not to litter—there is no personal price paid, as with drug or alcohol abuse—but there is a big reward for society at large not to be awash in trash. There is little to deter an individual from digital piracy; however, there is a big reward for society at large not to have to pay the costs of piracy.

But there is an asymmetrical tension here: the long-term benefits of lower piracy versus the short-term costs of eduction and enforcement.

So, if you're a legislator or a member of the bar and your constituency does not buy the piracy argument, what is left for you to do? As people have said, maybe about a billion times: There must be a better way.

Stay tuned. We're showing Keystone Kops movies back-to-back with episodes of *The Untouchables*.

# 9

# ANGEL ON MY SHOULDER: WHAT'S IN IT FOR ME?

Daniel Peng, 17, a computer wiz who skipped two grades before coming to Princeton University, ran a campus-wide search engine that could be used to locate and download songs and movies. The music industry slapped him with a lawsuit seeking potentially billions of dollars in damages for distributing copyrighted works. His site was shut down and his life thrown into chaos. Dan, a junior, lived right down the hall from me last semester, and his plight made me rethink the whole issue of sharing music online.

News of Dan's situation exploded on the New Jersey campus. Some students sprinted back to their dorm rooms to wipe their hard disks clean of any record of unauthorized downloads.... Others simply shrugged, opened up KaZaA and went on swapping music.

Dan's experience revolutionized the way I download music: I started paying for it.

Until Dan's case showed us how far the music industry would go to stop Internet downloads, a lot of students thought this was an infraction similar to speeding on the highway. The case against Dan persuaded many to slow down. Still, when I hear a timeless Beatles classic on the radio and then go home to look for it on Pressplay or iTunes and it isn't there, I tend to longingly eye the KaZaA icon that still sits on my desktop, beckoning me to return to piracy. Only fear and Dan Pang's ordeal keep me in line.[1]

**Powell Fraser, undergraduate at Princeton University and intern at CNN.com**

---

1.  Powell Fraser, "Why I've Stopped Sharing Music," CNN.com, July 14, 2003; available at www.cnn.com/2003/TECH/internet/06/27/music.sharing.column/.

Whether digital pirates reflect a culture that has run amok—could a president get away with a sentiment like, "Ask not what your country can do for you, but what you can do for your country" today?—or are simply responding to a complex environment of technology, opportunity, peer pressure, ignorance, interest politics, mass communication, and unheralded youth affluence, digital piracy is the result of individual decisions. At some point, every person, company, or country asks, either implicitly or explicitly, "What's in it for me?"

Call it the WIIFM factor.

---

## TECHNOLOGY OR PEOPLE: WHO'S RUNNING THE SHOW?

Based on the odds of getting caught, digital piracy seems like a no-brainer: pirate, pirate, pirate. Download, copy, steal, borrow, or as in the infamous Apple advertisement, "Rip. Mix. Burn" (see Chapter 3, *Us Against Them?*). That's the message we're getting from the devils on our shoulders whispering in our ears: It's okay to download. It's like building your house at the 100-year flood line. What are the chances that *you* will be in it when the river beats the record from 1905? As we saw in Chapter 8, *Eliot Ness or Keystone Kops?*, the rate of convictions for intellectual property crimes is quite low, and the number of subpoenaed music downloaders lower still, given the number of transgressors.

Meanwhile, today's technology cornucopia—MP3 players, MPEG4 software,[2] DVD burners, multigigabyte disk drives, software cracking algorithms, the Internet—acts as a megaphone for our digital devils.

Consider the Apple iPod, the world's most successful portable MP3 player. Apple has sold millions of them; this single device increased Apple's bottom line by 20 percent in 2003. Even

---

2.   MPEG4 is the newest emerging standard for digital video and interactive multi-media, but just you wait: MPEG7 is just around the corner. Technology never sleeps.

though Apple created the iTunes Online Music Store to sell tunes for iPods at a buck apiece, who knows how many people are loading up their iPods with illicitly obtained MP3s? Nowhere in the iPod's 54-page instruction manual is the legal or ethical behavior of downloading copyrighted content mentioned. It's in the fine print, of course, the asterisk.

At the start of the digital millennium, that is pretty much where the observance of intellectual property protection remains in daily life: in the fine print.

If there is one thing our research for *Pirates of the Digital Millennium* has taught us, it's that human motivations aren't so simple. There is a mix of reasons people and companies—and countries—do or do not pirate music, movies, games, and software. They include culture, attitudes toward big business, laziness, convenience, sense of fair play, and that ever-elusive sense of right and wrong.

As we discussed in Chapter 3, *Us Against Them?,* there are a zillion arguments, or at least justifications, for digital piracy. The record labels rip off the artists ... Microsoft won't miss a few hundred dollars ... I only listen to the music on my PC, I don't burn CDs ... all information should be in the public domain ... software licensing is too complex ... "they" must want us to pirate; since "they" sell us MP3 players, CD burners, and DVD recorder decks ... the laws are too restrictive ... and so on.

But this chapter is a quest to understand the creatures on our other shoulders—the angels whispering in our ears not to pirate.

## ASKING TOUGH QUESTIONS

In the course of our focus groups, interviews, and cocktail conversations with friends and colleagues on the matter, we heard the same refrains over and over. The same arguments offered by the leading academics pushing freer access to copyrighted material were paraphrased by high school seniors. We found teenagers who understood the economic dynamics of the record industry as keenly as the sharpest MBA; we found parents who had downloaded more songs than their kids; we found retirees lamenting the bankruptcy of Napster. In every focus group, we also found that there was always at least one participant who *wouldn't* download because he or she felt it was wrong.

And that seemed to be the key issue. Not whether pirating is illegal, but whether it is *wrong*. When you get down to it, the decision to pirate is a personal one. What might be surprising is that, from all walks of life, income level, and age, the average digital pirate we talked to or surveyed:

a. Knew pirating was wrong.

b. Did it anyway.

Our research found that among the 1,000+ people we talked to or surveyed, most did not see right or wrong as an either/or question. Instead, they made value judgments not just on whether an action (such as downloading) was wrong or not, but *how* wrong.

To get a better picture of this right/wrong spectrum, we asked each focus group and survey respondent to respond to a values survey, ranking a number of questionable acts that are illegal, unethical, or socially frowned upon, yet commonly occur in daily life. The nine acts:

1. Buying a term paper on the Net and passing it off as your own.
2. Stealing a CD from a record store.
3. Downloading a copyrighted song from KaZaA.
4. Speeding 20 mph over the limit on the freeway.
5. Buying a pair of obvious knock-off Oakley sunglasses from a street vendor.
6. Copying from someone during a midterm exam.
7. Using a fake ID to get a drink at a bar.
8. Buying a six-pack of beer and selling it to some 13-year-olds.
9. Smoking one marijuana cigarette (joint).

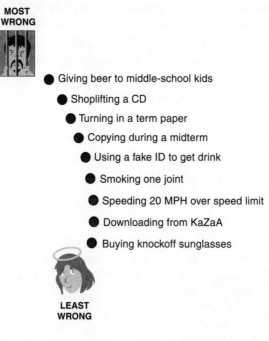

**Figure 9–1** How wrong is it? Across the survey population, this is the ranking of transgressions from "most wrong" to "least wrong." While some of the sins in the middle of the list were controversial—some rated them high, some low, which is why the average is in the middle—those at the ends of the spectrum, including downloading, were not.

Figure 9–1 shows the relative ranking in the values survey by our entire sample.[3]

Not shown in the chart is the consistency among respondents as to the relative unimportance of downloading on the list of sins presented to them. While some questions were controver-

---

3. Focus groups were conducted in the summer and fall of 2003 with incoming college freshmen from a suburb of Boston and students at two four-year colleges in Massachusetts, a four-year college in Pittsburgh, and a community college in Portland, Oregon. The survey was conducted via email invitation to a Web site, with emails going to friends and colleagues of the authors. The survey was managed by IDC and conducted in October 2003.

sial—meaning the average score was the result of a lot of high and low scores added together—the downloading one was not. The only transgressions with less debate over position on the scale were buying knockoff sunglasses from a street vendor (not that wrong) and selling beer to 13-year-olds (very wrong). People took varying positions on speeding, cheating, plagiarizing, and even shoplifting, but not on downloading.

What we also found surprising was the consistency of responses regardless of age, educational level, or gender.

Figure 9–2 takes just two of the nine transgressions and looks only at kids 18 or under and people over 50. In all but these two sins—smoking pot and downloading copyrighted music—there was little difference between the two age groups. Credit where it's due, but the "Say No to Drugs" campaign has been effective: The elders see a smoking a joint as somewhat less harmful than the kids!

## AN ETHICAL QUANDARY

If you don't really believe what you're doing is wrong, what would convince you not to do it? The majority of our survey respondents and focus group attendees simply did not think that downloading, or sharing, music and movies was unethical. As the survey questions point up, even when people confessed that downloading was a breach of copyright law, many did not feel it was *that* wrong—certainly not wrong enough to warrant not doing it.

Historically, the few—the constituted sages, philosophers, priests, and rulers, some purportedly descended from the gods—have established mores and laws for the many. Mass conformity and obedience was assured by the rule of law. Yet more and more we see the authorities, both moral and legal, looking the other way at scofflaws who speed, who smoke an occasional joint, who fail to report all their income on the tax returns, or who possess some form of pirated media.

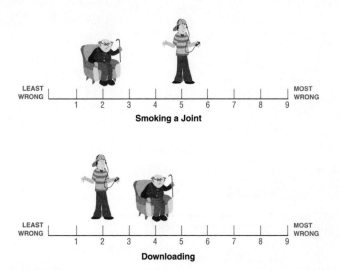

**Figure 9–2**   Which is worse? Across all age groups the ranking of transgressions was remarkably consistent. Only between kids under 18 and people over 50 was there much difference. Kids ranked smoking a joint worse than downloading. Those over 50 ranked downloading worse. In fact the over 50 crowd felt that smoking a joint was barely worse than buying a pair of knockoff sunglasses. The survey also showed us that 55 percent of respondents knew that downloading a copyrighted song from KaZaA was illegal, but that 70 percent thought it shouldn't be.

Have you ever wondered where all the used CDs, DVDs, and computer games you see in retail media shops come from? If so, did it occur to you that people are buying these media, copying them to their computers, and then turning around and selling them? Is that legal? Sure it is. You can buy and sell used books or digital media whenever and however and to whomever you feel like. So, say some, what's so different about downloading the same stuff from the Internet?

If you call copying media you buy or are given for free by a friend (even if that friend is someone you have never met, sitting at a computer hundreds or thousands of miles away) digital piracy, then it is rampant. This is one of the reasons the RIAA was so public with its subpoenas in the fall of 2003, as we talked about in Chapter 8, *Eliot Ness or Keystone Kops?* And it's one of the reasons the BSA spends so much time educating companies about

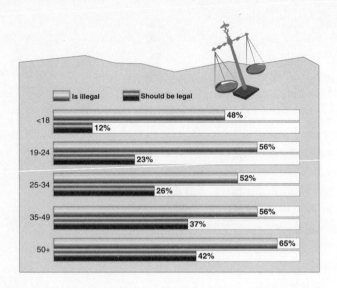

**Figure 9–3** Attitudes about music downloading.

the penalties and problems of using unlicensed software. It's one of the reasons the MPAA began putting antipiracy announcements at the beginning of movies and TV shows in 2003—ads that have the people behind the movies, such as technicians, stunt people, set painters, grips, and make-up artists talking about what they do and why it's wrong to pirate a film or TV show.

But the fact remains that the technology is there to make your own copies, and by virtue of its very existence, people feel entitled to use it. "Everyone else is; why shouldn't I?" asked one student in a focus group. Like the ape in the opening sequence of *2001: A Space Odyssey*, who begins playing with an animal bone, then starts smashing other bones, and soon realizes it would make a great weapon. We play with technology and realize that it makes digital piracy easy. Figure 9–3 shows the survey results of people's attitudes toward downloading.

Getting the genie back in the bottle will be tough. Based on our research, educating the populace that it's illegal to copy or download copyrighted media is going to be a long, hard sell. The names behind the content—Warner Brothers, Sony, Bertelsmann, Microsoft, Disney—don't exactly evoke images of the downtrodden. Moreover, pillorying offenders is unlikely to have the desired effect; as the English Parliamentarian John Viscount Morley, said, "You have not converted a man because you have silenced him."[4]

One of the questions that got us thinking about writing a book about digital piracy was the question, "Why?" Why would kids who wouldn't think of plagiarizing or even shoplifting a pack of gum think nothing about downloading copyrighted material? What *could* they be thinking? After all, these are our kids, too. There was parental concern for their values as well as their legal well-being. What began at the personal level evolved to the global level: Why do governments and businesses condone piracy or allow their people to pirate? What happened to all that stuff about setting a good example for the citizenry and writing corporate credos?

## WHAT'S IN IT FOR GOVERNMENTS?

Some argue that Third World countries, the worst intellectual property pirates, can *only* catch up to the developed world through piracy. In an article in *Harvard Business Review*, world-renowned economist Lester C. Thurow argues the point this way:

> Increasingly, the acquisition of knowledge is central for both "catch-up states" and "keep-ahead states." Smart developing countries understand that reality. Operating as a monopsonist (a buyer that controls a market) and dangling access to its domestic market as an enticement, China demands the sharing of technology from companies such as Boeing and Reuters that sell into its markets. It doesn't need their capital...but demands their knowledge in return for the right to operate in China. Americans deplore China's demands but remember fondly from their high school history classes the clever Yankee engineers

---
4.    www.bartleby.com/100/604.3.html.

who visited British textile mills in the early 1800s and reconstructed them in New England. Initially, Americans were amused in the aftermath of World War II when Japanese businessmen with their cameras were ubiquitously touring U.S. factories. They are no longer amused. Few today will let third world visitors into their plants.

Yet copying to catch up is the only way to catch up. Every country that has caught up has done it by copying. Third World countries know that unless they can acquire the necessary knowledge, they will never make it into the First World. They cannot afford to buy what they need—even if those who have the knowledge were willing to sell, and they are not. So they have to copy.[5]

So, yes, China will create intellectual property protection laws in accordance with the treaties it signs to become a member of the World Trade Organization, but it has no real compelling interest in enforcing them. As we pointed out in Chapter 6, *Global Fallout,* digital piracy impedes the growth of local industry—as with packaged software in Russia, pharmaceuticals in India, or literature in the U.S. in the 1800s—but that may be a trade-off that's worth it.

Or maybe it only seems worth it.

Take Ghana. Along with other African countries that entered the digital era with intellectual property laws that replicated those of their original colonizing countries, Ghana found that its antipiracy laws, authored in 1961 and updated in 1985, were most significant in their breach. And a majority of what patents, trademarks, and copyrights were registered was held by non-Ghanaians. According to estimates by the Ghana Ministry of Justice, piracy of copyrighted music, literature, and art was 90 percent entering the 1990s. Despite its copyright laws, and even an organization to distribute royalties, Ghana's music, literature, and film industries went into decline in the 1980s as a result of that

---

5.    Lester C. Thurow, "Needed: A New System of Intellectual Property Rights," *Harvard Business Review*, September–October 1997.

piracy. Artists, writers, and musicians left the country or gave up their artistic pursuits, local culture stagnated, and the government lost the benefits of a vibrant industry.

The story is easiest to see in Ghana's music industry. The country has always had a rich musical tradition, and with the advent of tape recorders and cassettes in the 1970s and 1980s, indigenous music flourished. The technology made it possible for the music to be heard across the land. Yet the same technology also made piracy easy, and musicians, composers, and producers found it harder and harder to make a living both because their own work was pirated and because they had to compete with pirated imports. The creation of original works ceased.

In a document published by the U.S. State Department, Betty Mould-Iddrisu, Chief State Attorney, International Law Division, for Ghana's Ministry of Justice says:

> It became evident to Ghanaian authorities that when one copies, one does not, in any way, encourage national authorship, national culture, or national creativity. If we in Africa pursue such a course of copying blindly all that comes from developed countries, we would forever be trapped in a cultural negation of our own making that would undoubtedly retard both our economic and our cultural progress.[6]

Realizing this—how rampant piracy was "retarding" its own music industry—in 1992 the government mandated a new system of certifying the legitimacy of musical works. The system requires all legitimate musical works—indigenous or imported—to be affixed with a special stamp, called a banderole, that asserts its authenticity. Banderoles are numbered sequentially and issued to music producers; the copyright office affixes them to

---

6.   "A Developing Country's Perspective," by Betty Mould-Iddrisu, Chief State Attorney, International Law Division, for Ghana's Ministry of Justice, on the U.S. Department of State Web site, http://usinfo.state.gov/products/pubs/intelprp/perspect.htm. The system was based on one used in Portugal. It was also tried in Nigeria and Kenya but with mixed results.

imported prerecorded music with the help of the customs department, and the tax department relies on the banderole system in collecting prepaid income tax.

What a turnaround! According to Mould-Iddrisu, piracy has dropped to 10–15 percent, and the Ghanaian music industry is back in business. Where once only 2,000–3,000 legitimate copies of a hit record might sell, now the number is up around 200,000–500,000. Producers are more accountable to artists and composers, since the copyright office requires copies of contracts before issuing banderoles, and artists and composers can find out how many of their works have been sold. Meanwhile the government has a new source of tax revenues. The local music production industry is booming as artists and composers from other countries come to Ghana to record.

So this is the angel that sits on a government's shoulder when it comes to enforcing intellectual property protection: Yes, you may copy the knowledge of more successful countries (the Thurow argument) and avoid the cost of the work it took to get that knowledge,[7] but then you will miss the economic base of a legitimate local knowledge industry, and the economic and cultural progress that goes with it (the Mould-Iddrisu argument).

## WHAT'S IN IT FOR BUSINESSES?

The angel on the shoulder of business whispers a simpler message than that of the angels on the shoulders of governments or individuals. Run the numbers; it's a cost-benefit equation. Do some risk analysis.

Let's see, there's the cost of buying properly licensed software versus the cost of buying bootleg. There's the benefit of buying a single copy of Microsoft Office and installing it on 10 or 20 computers. But then there's the risk of getting caught (should be some known probability here, right?) and the costs of fines, lawyer

---

7. For the sake of argument, we'll consider music, software, games, and movies forms of knowledge.

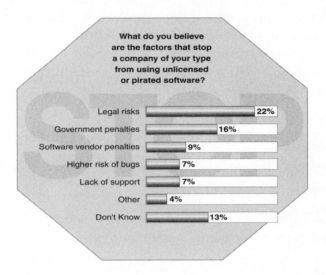

**Figure 9–4**  Factors that inhibit piracy.

fees, and public humiliation that might follow. Given all that, the math should be simple, right?

Not quite. The problem is that the risks, costs, and benefits are not that well-known. If they were, perhaps more senior management in business might consider setting down some guidelines regarding the ethical and legal use of software resources on the company computers.[8]

Let's look at software piracy, which is the most common form of digital piracy for most businesses. In the fall of 2003, IDC interviewed over 1,200 companies in Europe on their attitudes on software piracy[9] and came up with the ranking of reasons not to use unlicensed software shown in Figure 9–4.

---

8. The Ethics Resource Center, a nonprofit organization, is in the business of helping enterprises set up ethical and moral guidelines for their businesses and employees. Visit their Web site at www.ethics.org.

9. Custom study on piracy and software licensing practices and attitude in France, Poland, Italy, and Sweden, conducted by IDC in December 2003, with over 1,400 companies. Used with permission from IDC.

On the face of it, there is more stick here—government penalties or legal risks—than carrot—fewer software bugs or better quality of software. At the same time, 53 percent of the respondents said they didn't *know* what the penalties were for using unlicensed software. Perhaps if they did, they would change their ranking.

The responses in the highest rated category—other—also seemed to be more related to costs than benefits. Companies wanted to "respect government" or "not lose business or their jobs" or "maintain an ethical image" or "have good control over their operations."

Boiled down, the responses indicated that there are really three main reasons companies refrain from piracy:

- Fear of the penalties or legal risks.

- Desire to have a well-managed operation.

- Desire for better and easier-to-maintain software.

Companies need to assess each of these reasons before condoning (often through inaction) piracy in the ranks. In terms of penalties and legal risks, the costs are not just the fines but the cost of disruption of the business. Robert Holleyman, President and CEO of the BSA, says that once the BSA enters an organization to audit its software (in the U.S. on a warrant issued by a judge; see Chapter 8, *Eliot Ness or Keystone Kops?*), companies generally become compliant as quickly as possible.[10] Which is worse, paying a few hundred dollars per seat for a few software licenses that haven't been kept up to date or having all the computers and employees in a department idle for half a day?

The BSA has also found that license abuse and piracy often stem from sloppy business practices, lack of clear policies, and generally messy operations. Many of the companies the BSA finds violating copyright, especially in developed countries with strong traditions of intellectual property protection, don't do so intentionally. They're just bad at paperwork. In the IDC study, which looked at a projectable sample of businesses in Europe, over half

---

10. Interview with Robert Holleyman by author Gantz, September 2003.

the respondents had only a vague or limited idea of what constituted piracy, and barely half had a policy for employees specify-
ing that they should use only legitimate software.

What research has found is that if a company is one that has a
well-articulated and well-implemented policy on the proper
licensing of software, it probably has well-articulated and well-
implemented policies on a lot of other business practices, too,
such as customer support, pricing, cost management, and so on.

The last cost in the equation, the cost of using pirated software, is
difficult to determine only because there is generally no one individual in the organization whose job it is to track the total cost of
ownership of computing. For many years vendors and consultants have talked of the "total cost of ownership" (TCO) and
"asset lifecycle management" and, in fact, quantified these costs.
IDC studies, and those of other consulting companies, show that
most of the cost of using computers comes not from the software
or even hardware, but from the people and infrastructure, such as
training, networks, security, and the support it takes to operate
everything.

Figure 9–5 shows how piracy affects system costs over a five-year
period based on IDC's total cost of ownership studies. In the first
year, most costs are related to the acquisition of hardware and
software, but by the end of the fifth year, the real cost is in support, maintenance, application development, and overhead on
the operation (assuming all other costs of doing business remain
relative)—in other words, salaries. Using pirated software saves
on those initial acquisition costs but actually adds to the cost of
maintenance and support. Over a five-year period, these people
costs outweigh the savings from using pirated software.

The economic arguments against piracy are logical and the numbers are real. The problem for software vendors is that few companies actually look at their computing costs from this
enterprise-wide perspective. Consider:

■  In many companies, software and hardware are obtained by a
   hodge-podge of people from a hodge-podge of sources. In the

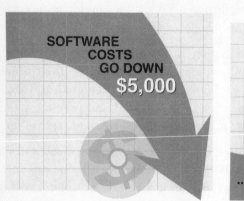
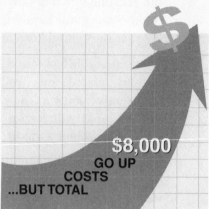

Total cost of ownership: $100,000
**NO PIRACY**

Total cost of ownership: $107,612
**100% PIRACY**

**Figure 9–5**    Total cost of ownership and piracy. Because most of the costs of operating computers systems are in the labor associated with installing, managing, and supporting them, using pirated software can be counterproductive. According to IDC, in a situation where the total cost over five years of owning a computer system might be $100,000, using pirated software might eliminate $5,000 in licensing costs...but would add close to $8,000 to support and maintenance of the overall system.

IDC survey, we found dozens of different job titles with responsibility for software acquisition. Fully a quarter of the companies had no one person in charge of software deployment, and half never really audited their software installations.

- Companies—especially small ones—often look only at first-year cash outlays and subsequently make short-term decisions.

- Finally, in countries where labor costs are low or labor policies inflexible, the cost of letting people sweat and slave to support pirated software may be marginal compared to countries where labor is more expensive.

Another problem: the cost-benefit tradeoffs change when you mix licensed with unlicensed software. If, for example, you have a license for 100 users of Microsoft Office and the infrastructure to support that, actually running an additional 50 illegal copies isn't going to add that much more in staff costs.

Unless, of course, Microsoft finds out.

For the software vendors, then, perhaps the best they can do is make sure the angels on the shoulders of corporations acquiring software are really well-educated on both the economic benefits of using 100 percent vendor-supported software and the costs of disruptions and penalties if they don't. It also makes sense for them to realize that there is a law of diminishing returns: beyond a certain point, the costs of lowering piracy will outweigh the gains. There will always be *some* pirating and license abuse.

---

## BSA'S RECOMMENDED CORPORATE SOFTWARE POLICY NOTICE

Here is an example of a recommended document that enterprises can use to assure that employees are aware of software licensing agreements and that rights are being respected in their organization. The **(My Organization)** convention would be replaced by the enterprise's rightful name.

- **(My Organization)** licenses the use of computer software from a variety of outside companies. **(My Organization)** does not own this software or its related documentation, and unless authorized by the software developer, does not have the right to reproduce it except for backup purposes.
- **(My Organization)** employees shall use the software only in accordance with the license agreements and will not install unauthorized copies of commercial software.
- **(My Organization)** employees shall not download or upload unauthorized software over the Internet.
- **(My Organization)** employees, learning of any misuse of software or related documentation within the Company, shall notify the department manager or **(My Organization)**'s legal counsel.
- According to applicable copyright law, persons involved in the illegal reproduction of software can be subject to civil damages and criminal penalties including fines and imprison-

ment. **(My Organization)** does not condone the illegal duplication of software. **(My Organization)** employees who make, acquire, or use unauthorized copies of computer software shall be disciplined as appropriate under the circumstances. Such discipline may include termination.

■ Any doubts concerning whether any employee may copy or use a given software program should be raised with a responsible manager.[11]

# FACING UP TO THE ETHICAL ISSUE

Say what you will about digital piracy being a teensy-weensy crime, not even as bad as shoplifting. Say what you will about how Third World countries must pirate to catch up economically, or that businesses can build spreadsheets justifying the risk versus return for pirated software. No matter how much we spin fancies, rationalizations, or justifications, we must come back to the pervasive but thorny issue of ethics. Is it okay to download? Is it okay to use copyrighted material you haven't paid for? Which creature on which shoulder decides if it's okay or not?

In researching *Pirates of the Digital Millennium,* we went looking for the psychology that might explain why normally upright citizens could have little or no compunction about downloading copyrighted material. Sure, there are cultures, countries, and even religions where violating copyright laws wouldn't be seen as an ethical breach. Yet most countries have a social structure that coheres people in a bond of mutually assumed trust and appropriate behavior. How have we gotten to the point where 60 million people all believe it's perfectly legitimate and ethical to use KaZaA?

We spoke with psychologists and sociologists, scanned research archives, and Googled for hours on the topic, but came away with little enlightenment or explanation. We found ethical canons about

---

11. The BSA offers a number of resources and tools for learning about and assessing software policies, including auditing tools and a clever Dilbert campaign, at www.bsa.org.

copyright sanctity written for businesses, librarians, software programmers, Islamic and Jewish scholars, students, teachers, kids, IT
professionals, graphic artists, and even church choir directors. We
found mathematical equations from game theory describing the
equilibrium between piracy and the cost of catching pirates. All the
shouldas and oughtas were covered. But we found precious little to
explain *why* it still goes on, despite all the ministrations.

In our quest, we were offered articles on how young people feel
invincible (and thus immune from RIAA lawsuit). We saw technical
studies showing that "choice options influence decisions under
risk" (i.e., the easier it is to download, the more likely it is to happen) and that "backward inhibition" is different from "negative
priming" (i.e., those who *did* get subpoenaed probably wouldn't
download again).

We were even referred to the experiments of Stanley Milgram, the
assistant professor at Yale who conducted a controversial experiment in 1961 showing how willing average people were to inflict
pain on others when a figure of authority seemed to approve.[12] His
previous work was on the degree to which humans seek to conform
to those around them (which we translated into: if everybody's
downloading, it must be okay).

Finally, our research even led us to an intriguing analysis of the
music downloading issue in the context of classical ethics theory.
The work of four students in a business ethics class at Santa Clara
University (SCU) in the fall of 1999, this project mapped the arguments of a music publisher versus a music pirate against the ethical frameworks of John Locke, Immanuel Kant, Jeremy Bentham,
John Stuart Mill, and Plato.[13] The case was real: A student at SCU

---

12. The experiments had subjects participating in a faked experiment that was supposed to link punishment with learning. The subjects were instructed to deliver
electric shocks of increasing voltage by pressing a lever on a black box to a
learner each time he made a mistake matching words on a list. The learner was,
in fact, an actor and there was no electric shock, but the subjects didn't know
that. Under the authoritative eye of the supposed lab director, a majority of the
subjects had cranked the voltage up to the max (450 volts) by the time they were
done. For more information, see Thomas Blas, "The Man Who Shocked the
World," *Psychology Today*, March/April 2002.

had made MP3s from a CD of a local band that he'd bought legitimately at a street fair. Later, one of the band members noticed it available for download on Napster, but the band let it ride, hoping increased popularity would lead to increased income. Three months later, though, the band signed with a record label to promote and distribute the CD. When record sales didn't materialize as rapidly as downloads did, the publisher contacted the RIAA, which contacted SCU to ask the university stop the student pirate from sharing the CD.

Using this as a backdrop, the students placed the actions and motivations of the publisher and the band on the one hand and the student on the other against four ethical constructs:

- Locke (Reason): Property and ownership rights accrue based on invested effort.

- Kant (Deontology): One's actions should follow from duty to and obligations of the law, seeking to follow those that are universal laws.

- Bentham/Mill (Utilitarianism): One's actions should strive to promote the most happiness.

- Plato (Virtue Ethics): An action should help us strive for moral excellence within ourselves, with virtues like justice and courage outweighing others, such as gentleness.

What was interesting about the exercise was that under each ethical system, there were arguments to be made on both sides. Was the happiness of those getting free music over Napster greater than the happiness of the band and record label at achieving higher record sales? Was the effort invested in ripping a CD and putting it into MP3 format on a computer more than the effort of creating the CD in the first place? Is there more justice in charging $16 for a CD that cost a fraction of that to make than in making the song available to others for free?

After wrestling with all the pros and cons within the four ethical theories, the students in their final analysis, determined that

13. *An Investigation into the Ethics of Music Piracy in the Information Age*, available at http://itrs.scu.edu/mcalkins/fall99/EthicsMP3/index.htm.

three out of the four supported the record company. And perhaps this is what ethics boils down to: Through enlightened discourse, an individual wrestling with the angel and devil on his or her shoulders, or in a social group, must form his or her own interpretation of right ethical behavior, as each of these four philosophers did.

---

## STREET ETHICS

*What follows are unedited quotes from the six focus groups we conducted on the ethics of digital piracy in the fall of 2003, along with email responses from some of those we surveyed in October 2003.*

"Is it wrong?    No. Well, yes, maybe a little, but not very much. Everybody does it...." —*college freshman*

"I would never download, it's just not right...." —*high school senior*

"My 2 cents on downloading music: It's awesome! I have not done nearly as much downloading as most people, but I do know that it's convenient, cheap/free, even enjoyable; it should definitely be legal. Also, the fact that it is currently illegal makes virtually no difference in the amount of downloading people do. I read in *Wired* that you only have something like a 1/90 millionth of a chance of getting caught and punished. So basically, there's no way to stem the tide of downloading...." —*urban professional*

"I'll buy CDs from certain artists, like I'm collecting them, but I'll download most of my music...." —*college sophomore*

"I am a singer/songwriter with a CD I try very much to get paid for, but I also provide several MP3 downloads through my website. From my own experience, there seems to be a disconnect surrounding the 'morality' of free music download/sharing depending on the level of success of the artist. Major label artists make such a small percentage of each CD sale, it's really the labels that are feeling the financial pains in diminishing CD sales. Strangely enough I was in the process of downloading 'Tighten Up' by Archie Bell and the Drells when I got the link to your survey. I found it for free on someone's random personal site. Unethical and illegal but a fine song I needed for a personal CD compilation I am making...." —*professional musician*

"How can it be wrong? Don't they *want* you to download MP3s? Look how they advertise the players...." —*college freshmen*

"The average consumer can care less if some huge record label makes a few million less a year. If I want to support an indie label or band I buy the CD. I personally do not listen to MP3s. I want my music to be CD quality. Plus I like to buy CDs of bands that are actually good and have more than one song I want to listen to. If the record companies want to end this then stop producing shitty one-hit-wonder crap..." —*young business executive*

"Look, there are a lot worse problems out there than music piracy...."—*college senior*

"Every time I download I fell like I'm striking a blow for freedom...."—*post-graduate student*

"I am struck by the massively out-of-value the current music/voice CD business model compared to video/movies. Two hour movies are from $5.00 to $20.00.The music industry wants to charge the same range for 1.2 hours of songs. They are so out-of-their minds. The $0.99 on-line pricing is an extension of this nonsense...."
—*middle-aged professional*

"The only music I download is music I have already bought in one or more forms. I bought a lot of music on 45s in my youth and often bought albums. Later, when cassettes became popular I often bought duplicates of the music I owned on a 45 or album/LP. Then, when CDs came out I bought the same music once again! Now, with Peer-to-Peer, I have the opportunity to DL [download] the music I've bought one or more times in the past...." —*high-tech executive*

"I'm not buying that it's wrong. I'm not going to buy a CD when it's a one-hit wonder. They have one good song and seventeen crappy tracks, I'm not spending $20 on that. I'm going to download the one and not feel bad...." —*college junior*

"My brother is a musician and a lot of my friends are musicians. So to hear that all this downloading is going on makes me bullshit, because if you're not a musician putting yourself out there, sweating, working your butt off, going without everything to make it big, you don't know how much it hurts...." —*college sophomore*

"I could care less about the record companies or Microsoft. Screw 'em. I just hope my daughter doesn't get caught..." —*mother of three college and post-grad students*

"Hey if my neighbor's apple tree grows over into my yard and I eat an apple, am I stealing?..." —*high school student*

"My 14 YO granddaughter is the one who burns my music for me, and I'll be honest—I'm just not sure how I feel about it, so I usually don't. I think I'm leaning toward: There is so very much smart technology out there—allowing us to kill the enemy on a single particular corner of a block halfway around the world, or allow even a 9 YO to save music from someone else's CD from a single particular computer halfway around the world, or however it's done. The point being—if there's enough technology to allow us to do this, there should be enough technology to stop us. And there probably is. Why isn't it in place. This just might be something us grownups don't really understand the ethical point of, but our kids do. And maybe it would be nice for us to stay out of it for once, because music is beautiful, and sharing is nice. That's what we teach our kids. Why do the government and lawyers have to muck up everything nice?" —*grandmother of a teen*

"There's nothing better than speeding on the highway smoking a joint and listening to music I downloaded from KaZaA...."
*—56-year-old contractor-jokester*

## THE ETHICAL CLIMATE

We were surprised in our survey by how widespread piracy was within the ranks of the well-informed and highly educated. We can't say how many ministers, ethics professors, musicians, software developers, or cops might have answered our survey, but we can tell you that a majority of the responses were from college graduates, with a full 40 percent holding graduate degrees. Our findings were borne out in the Ipsos-Reid study of software piracy in higher education we mentioned in Chapter 7, *Dude, Where's My MP3?* To wit:

- While over 50 percent of students felt it was okay to swap or download software without paying for it, 15 percent of professors and administrators felt the same way.

- Only about a quarter of the time did professors admonish students about copying or downloading software.

- More professors and administrators thought there should be no penalties for students caught with unlicensed software than thought they should be suspended or put on probation (53 percent felt they should lose computing privileges).

- One in five professors/administrators simply wished the software vendors would leave students alone.

- Half felt the software was overpriced, and almost a third thought the software companies should be happy the students used their software, whether purloined or not (presumably so they will buy it when they get real jobs).

For those who would stop illegal copying of digital media, the ethical climate is harsh. Having done our research, we believe it's safe to say that almost everybody either intrinsically senses or genuinely knows when they're pirating copyrighted intellectual property, and that it is wrong. For the publisher, however, that's not much help. Changing the ethical climate—which means sliding digital piracy up a few notches on our values survey—is a challenge.

So, if the experiments of Stanley Milgram tell us anything, it's that ethics can be molded by conformity. It's situational ethics. Everybody else is doing it, so I might as well jump in and do it, too. In a nation of scofflaws, even setting an example seems futile. The technology is there to do all kinds of things and, for better or for worse, it has warped personal values. Classical ethics teaches that making a morally and ethically appropriate decision is based on asking oneself what a fair, honest, truthful, and equitable person would do in the circumstance. The objective is to arrive at a just decision.

Even taking the unbalanced DMCA law and the obnoxious and insensitive measures of the RIAA into account, it's still hard to imagine that most people would not conclude that digital piracy is unethical. And when they come to that conclusion, they seem to follow with a silent, "So what?"

Those concerned with protecting their digital media (software, music, movies, games) have to realize this. Changing climates is a long-term proposition. We've been conditioned by the Lay's potato chip mindset: Just as we don't want to eat just one, neither do we want to download just one piece of digitized stolen property. The technology is addictive—it's so easy to download another and another, not just songs but movies, too; who cares if the quality isn't that great, neither is the movie; and maybe I won't even watch the whole thing but I saved nine bucks, so what? And look over here, somebody's actually put my bio textbook online; I'm gonna download that too. Hey, there's a copy of Adobe GoLive, think I'll grab that so I can build my Web site, and look! here's Grand Theft Auto III. I'll burn a copy of that for my little brother....

For now it seems the devils on our shoulders are shouting down the angels. As one focus group student said, "It can't be that wrong. My mom downloads."

# 10

# THROUGH THE FOG: THE FUTURE OF INTELLECTUAL PROPERTY

The prevailing wisdom among those who earn their living within our system of intellectual property protection is that some minor tweaking here and there will fix the problem. The prevailing wisdom is wrong. The time has come not for marginal changes but for wide-open thinking about designing a new system from the ground up.[1]

**Lester Thurow, MIT Economist**

The ethical discussion starts with the admission that intellectual property exists and that making off with it is theft. I've heard lawyers establishing that there is no such thing as IP. Copyright is a granted privilege, not a form of property. That there are draconian laws enforcing copyright is one thing. That media industry lobbyists and executives think they have "property" and try to spin the public debate is another. But the whole thing is based on a handshake agreement to benefit industry interests. If that ends up enriching more people than are stolen from (in terms of profit margins) then fine and good. But if it's just a form of welfare by legal fiction, then does not the whole stack of ethics relating to civil disobedience apply? Artists make their money from concerts, not albums. No set designer was ever put out of work because his shitty, class-C, two thumbs down, car chase movie was copied on the Internet after it was done filming, editing, and being released. And Rosa Parks and I refuse to sit in the back of the RIAA bus.

**Comment from Josh Rochester (author Rochester's son) after reading this manuscript**

---

1.  Lester C. Thurow, "Needed: A New System of Intellectual Property Rights," *Harvard Business Review*, September–October 1997.

Here it is, twenty years (since the CD was introduced) and prices haven't come down. The record companies dish up crappy artists like Britney Spears…and then get the radio stations to play the same crappy songs over and over again. For those three reasons—they're screwing us, they're screwing the artists and they're giving us a crap solution—that's why people pirate. They think, "You don't care about us, so why should we care about you?"

**Student comment from focus group**

All futurescapes are shrouded in fog—a fog of possibilities, random events, roads not taken, and quantum probability. The futurescape fog surrounding intellectual property swirls and eddies with the countervailing currents. If technology makes digital piracy as easy as a click of the mouse, it can also wrap digital content in locked containers. Economic power that favors publishers and copyright holders is countered by market power that favors consumers and the pirating public. History repeats itself in cycles of pirating and counterpirating offensives, from the Statute of Anne in 1710 to the Digital Millennium Copyright Act of 1998. The interests of fat-cat artists and developers compete with those of starving artists and startup software writers.

What *is* the future of copyright, fair use, and digital media rights management? Tomorrow's intellectual property futurescape will surely evolve out of today's landscape—one event, one new law, one technology, one social trend, one upheaval, at a time. Is there any clarity on what, at least, these individual events, laws, technologies, or trends might be? Truth be told, the technology is moving so rapidly that any short-term prognostications on our part could be hopelessly passé by the time you see these words in print. We know. We saw some of our major theories become reality during the time it took to write this book.

Following the individual events and issues, we can extrapolate a view of the trends and possible outcomes of the various digital rights issues. In the preceding nine chapters we've given you soup to nuts, from the history of copyright and the psyche of downloading teens to the current state of intellectual property law enforcement and the costs of pirating. Let's embark upon this journey to the future of digital media by reviewing the key lessons from those same chapters, and see where we might be by around 2010.

## LESSON ONE: WE'RE LOCKED IN A WAR NO ONE CAN WIN

The public, after all, is the pirate's customer (and in some cases the pirates themselves). It could be said that over the past couple thousand years, the public has not worried too much about the legality or morality of copying books and other written material, buying low-cost pirated books, copying sheet music, borrowing tunes or musical phrases from others, making audio tapes from records and other tapes, videotaping TV content, or burning CDs from downloaded MP3s today. It's been rip, mix, burn even before the printing press was invented. Yet the governing bodies—first the Church and then the State—have attempted to protect copyright interests with laws. Has it worked? How much has slipped through the cracks? Who knows? What we do know is that laws, even when enforced (which is seldom), do not have much bite.

A possible exception has been the RIAA's deployment of the DMCA in 2003 and 2004 to sue file-sharers for lost royalties. The net result has been the nearly absolute loss of the fair use clause in copyright law, which has reached far and wide with the ever-blossoming definition of intellectual property. Most people enjoy getting something for nothing, and often have only a vague sense of value when it comes to digital media. It's always been a tough sell that a software program is worth hundreds and hundreds of dollars. Whether food, songs, or games, people innately love to share something they like. Will people stop downloading, copying, and file-sharing? Probably not.

But the worldview of digital piracy is a bit different. We're not talking about you making a copy of Alicia Keys' "You Don't Know My Name" or the computer game Samurai Jack. We are talking about warehouse-sized operations run in many cases by big-time gangsters and criminals. Remember, three-quarters of the world comes from regions or cultures—the Orient, Islam, tribal Africa, former communist countries—with no tradition of intellectual output as personal property. Perhaps the BSA, the RIAA, and the MPAA can change the culture and mores of the world, but to do so, they'll need the moral authority of an organized religion, the charisma of a Mahatma Gandhi, and the organization of a thousand thousand Interpols. It probably won't happen.

## LESSON TWO: COPYRIGHT LAWS WON'T GO AWAY, EVER

From Finnian of Moville's appeals to the King in 557 to force the monk Columba to return an unauthorized copy of Finnian's prayer book, to the English booksellers who pressured the Queen to institute the first copyright law in 1710, to Lexmark's use of the DMCA to protect its toner business, the interests that hold copyright have always waged a war of progressively more control, ownership, and rights management. The course of copyright owner behavior seems to go like this:

- *Step One:* Sound the alarm (with proper spin). Let others know that a problem is occurring that threatens (a) the livelihood of English authors, (b) the creation of an American literature, (c) the entertainment industry, (d) the U.S. leadership of technology innovation, or (e) the livelihood of authors, artists, actors, software developers, musicians, sound technicians, record store clerks, and startup garage bands. Leave out the part about where it also threatens the livelihood of the executives, publishers, or booksellers that have made a living exploiting authors, artists, actors, software developers, musicians, sound technicians, and startup garage bands.

- *Step Two:* Appeal to the Crown, Parliament, or Congress. Use trade groups and lobbyists to get laws passed that protect the status quo. If you're lucky, the political stars will align and you will get a Statute of Anne or Sonny Bono Copyright Extension Act. Use the legislative version of the quarterback sneak to get your legislation passed when others aren't paying attention.

- *Step Three:* Aid and abet enforcement. The printers' guild of London helped pay for police enforcement of copyrights, the sheet music publishers hired detective agencies and then conducted raids with their own well-muscled squads, and the RIAA and BSA use their own staff to chase pirates under the DMCA. In the modern age, this also means devising technological methods of enforcing the law, with the burden of investment on the publishers.

- *Step Four:* Market your position. Use anything and everyone who can support your position to convince the public and lawmakers of the sanctity of your rights. As soon as you have them on your side, get more laws passed that favor your interests. If things don't seem to be going well, throw any monkey wrench you can find in the works to buy time—the time needed to deal with the next lesson.

Given that this is the case, the only recourse available to citizens is *Step Five*: Lobby for change in the copyright laws. Lobby back against these interests with your own. Write your Representative or Senator. Keep abreast of pending legislation that concerns your rights. Get involved in the one of the many rights groups.[2] Form a blog, group or coalition to repeal copyright laws that are unreasonable. Put some weight behind your efforts and keep it there, because it's one of the most important things you can do. Once one constitutional right gets abrogated, more end up on the slippery slope as well.[3] This probably sounds pedestrian and trite, but it's about the only thing that works. It really does: democracy, one voice at a time.

One such voice is that of William W. Fisher, a professor of intellectual property law at Harvard. As part of the Harvard Berkman

---

2.  For example, The Alliance for Digital Progress, http://alliancefordigitalprogress.org/; Copyfight: The Politics of Intellectual Property, www.copyfight.org/; Digital Consumer, www.digitalconsumer.org; Digital Future Coalition, www.dfc.org; Electronic Frontier Foundation, www.eff.org; Respect Copyright, www.respect-copyright.org. Many of these sites have links to other kindred sites.

3.  Web sites such as www.keepmedia.com provide a wealth of information from hundreds of periodicals, organized by topics, so you can form your own opinions about current issues.

Center's Digital Media Project, Fisher has conducted research into copyright law and fair use based on the Apple iTunes music store business model, concluding that:

- Media companies are using contract law in the form of license agreements and "terms of service" provisions to overrule copyright law, in an attempt to prohibit lending, reselling or transferring digital media.

- There is a strong trend toward using technological protection schemes (see Table 10–1, Knights on White Horses, later in this chapter) to limit the ability to transfer digital content from one computer, device, or type of media, to another. Fisher cites the iTunes FairPlay technology, which limits the number of times a song can be copied, or burned, to a CD.

- Digital convergence from a technology perspective is in general beneficial to consumers; however, a parallel trend in legal convergence is being used in the U.S. and Europe to negate the doctrine of first sale (see Chapter 5, *Inside the Sausage: The Making of the Digital Millennium Copyright Act*), stating the doctrine applies only to tangible goods, not downloaded digital media from the Internet.

This is a fascinating study, well worth reading by anyone concerned with the increasing erosion of our individual rights to use digital media.[4]

## LESSON THREE: PIRACY HAS CHANGED THE RELATIONSHIP BETWEEN MEDIA BUYERS AND SELLERS

There really isn't anything fair about how copyright works. Neither is there anything fair about pirating someone else's creative intellectual property. But then, what's really fair in life? At a certain point, it boils down to bare survival of the fittest, and over time, fitness has been redefined from brute strength wielding a

---

4.    "iTunes: How Copyright, Contract, and Technology Shape the Business of Digital Media" at http://cyber.law.harvard.edu/media/uploads/53/GreenPaperiTunes041004.pdf

club to more sophisticated political and economic strength. So be it. Just don't complain about "them," whichever side you're on.

There are two ways "they" battle "us." One is by direct attack, as the RIAA demonstrated in 2003. The other is the use of technology dodges, which is going on all the time, more or less successfully (usually less or, if more, for only about 15 minutes). Concessions and temporary armistices must be made by both parties from time to time. But both are still committed to their ideals, which are diametrically opposed to one another's.

Similar to how the British booksellers had to give up their perpetual monopoly and actually pay artists in order to get lawmakers to pass the Statute of Anne, media publishers will have to continually come up with new schemes to minimize the appeal of piracy. At the same time, some of the pirating organizations are becoming (or are being compelled to become) legit. Napster is no longer a pirate but a partner in digital commerce, and KaZaA offers a version where songs can be had for a fee. Producers of pirated software CDs are now also doing legitimate distribution under agreement with the publishers.

In other words, over time the publishers will bend with the evolving economics and co-opt the "pirate" activities as much as possible. Another way to say this is that media companies, used to having business their way, will have to learn how to please their customers. They have too long called the shots, dictating the form (who among us has ever liked the plastic CD jewel box and that security sticker tape on top?) and content, the price, the groups themselves—the works. That's all over. Times change—fast. The media industries must face up to the fact that it's insanity to keep serving up the same goods and terms and expecting customers to go blithely along. Today it's all about personalization: my media, my way; what I want, when I want, in the format I prefer, and only the content I desire.

## LESSON FOUR: IT'S ABOUT CAPITALISM, STUPID

No matter what you think or do, at the end of the day someone has to pay and someone has to be paid for that media you use. Even unestablished artists, singing their hearts out in the subways below Boston, put the hat out for contributions. If we all simply download and nobody pays, all the artists, moviemakers, software writers, and game designers simply go out of business.

The argument that media is overpriced is only partly correct. Swiss wristwatches and SUVs are overpriced, too, but like everything, market forces determine value and pricing. Back on point: Yes, the CD disc and the plastic case are cheap, but as the Microsoft Office story illustrates, that's just the barest tip of the economic iceberg. A story is told about a businessman interviewing two consultants. One's fee is five times the other's; when asked why, the consultant replied, "Because I've been working in your industry for 20 years. You're paying for my knowledge and my accumulated expertise."

Just as corporations do not want you to use their logo or marque unless it's on an approved product,[5] the music industry does not want you to listen to a song in any manner it does not control. Yet in May 2004, the very industry that claims to be protecting the earnings rights of its artists (and itself) was found to be not paying artists all the royalties it had collected. Eliot Spitzer, New York State Attorney General, found that over $50 million had gone unpaid by the likes of Vivendi Universal's Universal Music Group, Sony Corp.'s Sony Music, EMI Group Plc, Bertelsmann AG's BMG Group, and Warner Music Group. "We have this misperception that artists have all gained enormous wealth by virtue of their success," said Spitzer at a press conference. "But there are many artists who struggle, who have one successful song and

---

5.   The sports leagues are notorious for their logo control with holographic serial numbers on T-shirts and baseball caps, but perhaps one of the most ludicrous examples was in the 1980s, when Chrysler Corporation wrote to a man whose nickname was Jeep from childhood, and which had nothing to do with the Jeep vehicle, to remove the name from his bar in a small Wyoming town because it violated their trade mark.

they depend on those royalties. We have found that there has been an accumulation of royalty payments that were not distributed to the artists." The RIAA said many of the artists' addresses were difficult to obtain, but that hardly accounted for not paying David Bowie, Sean "P. Diddy" Combs, or Dolly Parton.[6]

On the other hand, when you don't pay for copyrighted material you have obtained, you might just be putting a friend or neighbor out of work. Somebody's got to pay, and it's often with their livelihood. And sometimes that's us, not them. Is that a price with which you're comfortable?

But in all your financial transactions, consider that a higher principle can prevail: You're getting good value and fair return for your money. Fair return is what makes software and computer games in particular such a good value: With each new version, they just get better and better.[7] Conversely, this is why so many are disgusted with music and its relatively poor quality-to-value ratio. The bottom line is this: *You* must make some decisions about what *you'll* pay for, as well as what you won't. The "everybody's doing it" argument doesn't hold water. It's unrealistic and unreasonable to expect to get *all* your media for free. You owe it to yourself and the forthcoming flow of media product to pay for some of it, some of the time. If you don't, you lose. We all lose.

---

6.   "Artists to Get $50 million in Unpaid Royalties," Reuters news, May 4, 2004. http://www.reuters.com/newsArticle.jhtml?type=entertainmentNews&storyID=5038300&section=news. And remember that banderole system in Ghana that we mentioned in Chapter 9, *Angel on My Shoulder*? One of the side benefits was that it made the whole royalty business transparent to artists, which meant they could actually get paid.

7.   Jonathan Blow, a game developer and columnist for *Game Developer* magazine, wrote an article entitled "Game Development: Harder than You Think" for the online 'zine *ACM Queue* (Vol. 1, No. 10, February 2004) that described how game development has changed in the past 10 years. In 1994, a typical game had five linked programming modules. In 2004, a massively multiplayer game (MMG) has 30 or more modules, a complexity factor six times greater. "Keep in mind that each node in these graphs is itself a complex system of many algorithms working together, and that each of these nodes represents somewhere between six thousand and 40 thousand lines of source code," Blow advises in the article.

## LESSON FIVE: LAWS AND CASE LAW WILL SEE-SAW

Just as the laws and customs couldn't keep up with the printing press, photolithography, the copier, or the tape recorder, neither will they be able to keep up with lightning-fast digital technology. Legislative changes in the law will hopscotch around the new, developing issues, and case law will have to fill in the empty spaces. There will be a large, permanently gray area around intellectual property protection.

We all know the Washington drill: The lobbyists and special interests will push for new legislation. The laws Congress passes will attempt to color in the gray areas, and will tend to favor the moneyed interests, but by the time the legislation is actually enacted, it will be at least partially obsolete. The DMCA was written before Napster. The case law on copying movies onto tape was written 20 years before DVD burners were invented. Laws are almost always written for cats already out of the bag, and when it comes to technology-based issues, the cat is halfway down the block before Washington even knows there was a cat in the first place.

In this respect, technology can serve you. Just as Howard Dean, running for President of the United States, made extensive use of the Internet in 2003, more and more of the democratic process is moving there as well—Web sites, blogs, news and information on issues, and various coalitions and organizations to help you express your views. Bookmark pertinent Web pages with news and information about the issues you're most concerned about, and refer to them often. *Contribute.* Start a blog, get the word out, start a revolution. You won't be the first, but you could be the best.

## LESSON SIX: GLOBALIZATION CREATES THE COMMON DENOMINATOR

The global nature of the Internet, of modern commerce, of major publishers, and of music, movie, game, and software markets means that digital piracy really needs to be approached—dare we say attacked?—on a *global* scale.

We see globalization at work in pricing. In countries where there is high piracy (and usually low per-capita income), media producers have to compete with lower-priced pirated goods. Today, a DVD of Disney's *Finding Nemo* sells in the WanFungYan Bookstore in Beijing for under $3—in competition with pirated versions costing closer to $1.50. And as if that were not bad enough, the amount of software transported across international borders in Internet chat rooms and newsgroups is staggering and uncountable.

We see globalization at work in value as well. It may be a given that most people in most countries covet American products— especially our media—but it is *not* a given that they can afford them. Street prices are not always adjusted to the local economy because of (a) inflexible pricing and (b) the need to restore profits lost to piracy. So you see, it's another Catch-22: If you're a media publisher, how do you win without losses? Factor in the criminal element (remembering that running digital media contraband provides a higher return than running pot), and you have no chance. There may be an acceptable level of loss to a Microsoft, but not to a young, growing computer gaming publisher. We promulgated the concept of a free market economy, and this is one form of fallout it produces, like it or not.

Pirated media is going to leak across the borders. The thing is, all kinds of stuff leaks across borders these days: SARS, mad cow disease, software, cigarettes, drugs. Perhaps the only real and persistent solution is an international trade sanctions force—a cross between the United Nations peacekeeping force and Interpol— with no vested interest in preserving any one nation's illicit trade.

# LESSON SEVEN: DECRIMINALIZING THE KIDS SHOULD BE A TOP PRIORITY

For the good of our children, ourselves and our society, we can't have an entire generation or two running around breaking copyright laws. Downloading music today leads to downloading software tomorrow, and before you know it, all the lines between right and wrong, legal and illegal, misdemeanor and grand larceny are blurred beyond distinction. It seems easier to go astray in the digital world, which to the brain can be just as real as the so-called real world. From scofflaw to real criminal: It's happened again and again, as the U.S. Government's Cybercrime Web site proves.

The solution is not to fine, subpoena, or arrest youth for their seeming indiscretions, but to first educate them and then motivate them to make the social changes needed to redress the problem. They can be educated on many levels—by the public service announcements the movie industry is playing in theaters,[8] or more effectively, by teaching the ethics and legalities of digital copyright in high schools and colleges. If our research and that of Ipsos-Reid bears out, we may need to educate a few college professors as well—first to the fact that it is most assuredly not okay to advocate free downloading.

But more importantly, we need to convey to youth that they are a powerful force for change. For example, if every download was accompanied by a message to a member of Congress urging action to, say, repeal the DMCA, what a chorus that would be. Concomitantly, what if every downloader contributed a dime or a quarter to lobby against the RIAA and the MPAA? Who would have more money and power? Clearly this requires moving away from the sheer self-gratification model and into a social conscience stance, but it could be done.

It could be done.

---

8. Remember the TV ad, "This is your brain...this is your brain on drugs?" Envision this media equivalent: "This is you, sitting at home listening to your favorite tunes that you downloaded legitimately" (picture of Maxell guy in front of stereo)...fade to guy living in a cardboard box: "This is you, unemployable because of your criminal record for intellectual property theft."

# LESSON EIGHT: GIVE A LITTLE TO GET A LITTLE

Another radical idea is for both sides—the downloaders and the media moguls—to compromise a little with each other. We're not talking about the real pirates, the criminals who have added software to their portfolio of drugs, contraband, and sex, but rather the—shall we say *innocuous*—digital pirates whose purposes are not for profit.

For example, in return for file-sharers laying off new CD, game, or software releases and first-run movies, the media companies could make their legacy collections available for inexpensive (or, shock of shock, free) download. This is the "nice price" model Columbia set up for records and CDs years ago—its older catalog, those albums that had probably paid for themselves at least once over—applied to the digital, Internet world.

Similarly, software and game publishers might offer older versions of their programs for short bucks. It's a travesty when Microsoft is still selling its Windows Millennium Edition (circa 1999) for roughly the same price as Windows XP, its most current version.

An alternative to purchasing an expensive licensed copy is the rental or consumables model, sometimes called *meterware*, where you only pay for what you use. You download the full version and post your credit card number; then you only pay a fee for how much you actually use the program.

We don't presume to offer the last word in how equanimity can be reached. What we do advocate is an end to the acrimony and bitter feelings expressed on both sides. When youth read that the head of a motion picture studio says, "It's grand larceny,"[9] they are not likely to be cowed into submission. In fact, they're likely to download more with a vengeance. Look what happened as a result of the Madonna spoofs. The media industries surely must recognize that turning customers into criminals is not in their best interests.[10] Downloaders and file-sharers who vow they will

---

9.  Barry Meyer, chairman of Warner Bros., quoted in *Time* magazine, said of digital piracy, "It's theft. It's shoplifting. It's grand larceny." (January 26, 2004, p. 58.).

never pay for media they can get for free must realize that they are killing the goose that lays the golden eggs they so desire. There is no agreed-upon transactional base for a relationship, and that must change, so that each side feels it's getting a fair deal.

## LESSON NINE: ETHICS ARE IMPORTANT

Quite frankly, we worry about the state of personal ethics in the U.S.[11] It's one thing to say you have ethics, and to feel strongly that killing, selling liquor to minors, or being a Yankees fan are wrong,[12] but quite another to say that your own personal guilty pleasures are not. Or at least to say they are only a little bit wrong and yet still okay to enjoy. Ethics, properly executed, are an unwavering basis for rational and responsible living. They make one the kind of person others can depend upon. They help us make consistent sense of life. But good ethics aren't applied unevenly across the spectrum of human endeavor. In other words, you say you're an ethical person. You download media even though you know it's wrong, but it's only a little bit wrong, not as wrong as murder or shoplifting. Bzzzzzzt! You're unethical. At least admit it.

Study life in ancient Rome or Greece, Babylonia or Persia, some 2,000 to 3,000 ago, and you'll see they dealt with the same moral

10. Media reports in December 2003, indicated that file-sharing was down; the RIAA crowed that its prosecutorial campaign had succeeded. Then in January, it was back up; turned out the dip was due to college students going home for the Christmas holidays, where they apparently were either distracted or didn't have a high-speed, high-bandwidth Internet connection.

11. David Callahan, author of *The Cheating Culture: Why More Americans Are Doing Wrong to Get Ahead* (New York: Harcourt, 2004), tells gruesome stories of unethical and illegal behavior, ranging from ATM theft by firemen and policemen during 9/11 to college students pirating MP3s to Jayson Blair at *The New York Times*. Callahan writes, "...available evidence strongly suggests that Americans are not only cheating more in many areas but are also feeling less guilty about it. When 'everybody does it,' or imagines that everybody does it, a cheating culture has emerged."

12. The authors hail from Boston, Massachusetts, home of the Boston Red Sox, where it is a known fact that the New York Yankees are the emboidment of evil.

and ethical issues we do today: Where does personal pleasure give way to the public good? Which sins are worse than others? The difference is we have more outside stimuli that affect clear judgment. And technology is a big one. We love to tout how technology has made our lives better in so many ways, yet we often overlook some of its most egregious downsides: its utter lack of moral, ethical, altruistic, or emotional character. We can kill others with sophisticated technological weaponry and never feel a thing. Similarly, we can commit various intellectual property crimes with computers and, because we have no perception of the other people involved, can claim no one was hurt—even if every download is striking a knife into our favorite artist's heart. It's time to get real with ourselves and our own value system. Walk the walk.

## THE NEXT FEW STEPS

So, from what we've learned in these lessons, it seems pretty easy to predict the outcome of the next few battles in the war over intellectual property.

- The content publishers will offer new online delivery mechanisms and adjust their content to fit—selling songs, and not whole albums, over the Net, selling on-demand movies, and selling software and computer games as an ongoing service. They'll design products for the new conditions. The software industry is well down this path, and the music industry is there except for pricing and the dismantling of physical distribution. Internet media distribution companies like iTunes and Musicmatch are doing well because they are built upon solid but progressive business models. The movie industry, however, seems headed for perilous times. Movies will soon be as plentiful as music on the Internet, and there seems to be little experimentation with new business models that might counter the eventual cannibalization of the market.

- The content publishers will turn to technology fixes to protect content (see Table 10–1) even while admitting that for every content-locking technology there will be hackers poised to crack it and distribute the keys on the Internet—probably in five minutes or less.

- The media hardware companies will continue to introduce products that allow people to make or copy media into their own formats. In 2003, we saw a portable DVD recorder introduced that connects to home theater systems, which means you can ostensibly make a copy of your favorite television show or movie from your video service provider. The proprietary MP3 players keyed to a specific media downloading service such as Rhapsody or Musicmatch will soon fade away as people spurn them in favor of nonrestrictive playback formats. Once people get a taste for personalizing their media experience, it is impossible to roll back the technology.

- The industries will continue to lobby for more and stricter laws, but the laws currently on the books are more likely to be rolled back than extended. It's pretty clear that the DMCA and the Sonny Bono Copyright Extension Act—and their international legal and treaty-based brethren—have stacked the deck on the side of producers to the detriment of the public's constitutional right to gain access to new "knowledge."

- Digital piracy will reach some equilibrium—probably a different one for each media type—and fluctuate around that center point. It will come down in high-piracy countries and stay flat in low-piracy countries. It will generally float upward as more and more people use the Internet (IDC expects the number of Internet users to double in 10 years to over 2 billion) and as Internet connections get faster.

In other words, in the short term—until mid- to late-decade—the war over intellectual property will rage on, with posturing on all sides by the same old players. Perhaps the whole system should be rebuilt from scratch, as Lester Thurow suggested, but it's hard to envision from where the intellectual property messiah needed to make that happen will come. So expect entropy and enmity to continue to build in the current system as the pirates continue pirating and the media moguls continue moguling.

The Committee for Economic Development released a thoughtful, provocative analysis of the situation in March 2003. Entitled "Promoting Innovation and Economic Growth: The Special Problem of Digital Intellectual Property," the report confirms a number of ideas we have put forth in this book, namely that legislation to prevent digital piracy is not a good idea; that digital intellectual property has to be regarded differently than tangible property; that the short-term (profit-motivated) interests of media distributors are not necessarily in the best interests of long-term creative and artistic innovation; and that digital pirates are not necessarily callow thieves without personal values or ethics. In its conclusion, the report states:

> We are sympathetic to the problems confronting the content distribution industry. It is beyond question that this industry faces real problems that deeply affect its future. But these problems—perfect copies of high-value digital works being transmitted instantly around the world at almost no cost—require clear, concentrated thinking, rather than quick legislative or regulatory action. As Thomas Edison said: "There is time for everything." Given the present limitations on bandwidth, the immaturity of many technical protection systems, and the inevitable unforeseen consequences of governmental actions, there is time to lay a stable foundation for intellectual property rules in the digital world.[13]

## POSSIBILITIES FROM THE FRINGE

Technology really is the culprit. It's always been a double-edged sword, whether a pen held in the hand of a copyist monk, Gutenberg's movable type, the magnetic tape recorder, or the recordable DVD. It's almost like there is some deep, unconscious need buried in humans to possess the means to own a copy of something they desire. We love to collect things: Think Hummel figu-

---

13. The report can be found at www.ced.org/docs/report/report_dcc.pdf.

rines, No Fear T-shirts, bestselling Stephen King novels. Is it the copying itself or the means to copy that people desire?

We also love to play with ideas, by virtue of which people and all the things we create and collect grow and evolve. Ideas, according to the old prescripts of copyright law, cannot be copyrighted. Yet with the ever-increasing threat from the contemporary definition of intellectual property, it can often seem that any idea that wiggles is someone's property. This is a dangerous thing, capable of stifling innovation and creativity on a massive scale. Consider just the personal computer industry: Had Apple's Steve Jobs not appropriated several key ideas from the Xerox Palo Alto Research Center, there would be no Macintosh, no graphical user interface, no mouse, no computer network. Had not Bill Gates appropriated several key ideas about the graphical user interface and the operating system from Apple, there would be no Windows.

We need ideas, no matter what their original source, to innovate and evolve. Ron Rosenbaum, a columnist for the *New York Observer,* wrote that it's possible Vladimir Nabokov may have "stolen" the idea for his 1955 novel *Lolita* from an eponymous short story written by Rainier Schelling in 1915. Rosenbaum goes on to say Nabokov may not have realized he had usurped the idea, being a victim of "cryptonesia," or the inability to remember when one originally got an idea for a work. Similarly, George Harrison might have suffered from cryptonesia when he wrote "My Sweet Lord" and later found himself charged with plagiarizing "She's So Fine." But we cross a very dangerous and innovation-stifling line when ideas themselves can be appropriated and owned by the misuse of copyright, license agreements, or other forms of intellectual property law.

While we've been discussing the main battles of the war over intellectual property rights, there are some other efforts underway to undermine the status quo without direct conflict. These are the digital utopian communities, Shaker villages, and hippie communes dotting the landscape. Whether they survive and prosper into the futurescape is anyone's guess. Some of the more promising:

■ *The open source movement.* This is the gathering of content, mostly software (e.g., Linux, Apache, and Perl) today but increasingly information compilations (e.g, Wikipedia[14]) and written works (e.g., The Public Library of Science and The Gutenberg Project[15]), from diverse volunteers who can use the open source material, as well as add to it, as long as they agree to let others use their contributions as well.

■ *Copy-free zones.* As the name implies, these copyrightless Web sites are collections of content, such as that being assembled by the University of Maine's media lab "pool," Swarthmore's Digital Commons, or the Creative Commons.[16] These are basically variants of the open source movement where contributors donate their music, art, writing, movies, images, and software to the collective. Some restrictions are often put on the content, usually at the request or discretion of authors.

■ *Contractual copyrights.* Artists often think a publishing contract (regardless of the media) is a take-it-or-leave-it deal. It's not; as the old saw goes, everything's negotiable. That's why contractual copyright or license agreements between creators and publishers that are less restrictive than existing copyright law, but place some conditions on use—such as attribution or what rights are assigned—are becoming more popular. When Brazilian singer Gilberto Gil released a new CD in early 2004, for instance, it had a notice that buyers were free to make derivative works, a contractual right he requested and received from his label.

■ *Copylefts.* Promoted by the Electronic Frontier Foundation, these are legal agreements that allow users of the copyrighted

---

14. Wikipedia (www.wikipedia.org) is a free online encyclopedia project begun in 2001, now with over 150,000 entries.

15. The PLOS (www.plos.org) was created by three research scientists as a repository for scientific research. Rather than charge libraries and other scientists for access, the PLOS charges contributors. The objective is to make scientific research (often funded by taxpayer dollars) more available to the public. The Gutenberg Project (www.gutenberg.net) is a library digitization project where volunteers type in the classics.

16. See http://newmedia.umaine.edu/stillwater/; http://scdc.sccs.swarthmore.edu/; www.creativecommons.org.

material to use it freely and to modify or improve it—but not then to copyright proprietary versions based on the "copy-lefted" material. Harvard Business School professor Deborah L. Spar says copyleft ideas are getting more attention and believes it might pave the way to developing an approach to copyright that encompasses the Internet and new interactive media.[17]

- *Value-added media.* This idea has been hyped nearly into extinction, but still there is hope if the media outfits stop trying to fool the public. The music industry's Super CD, with purportedly higher sonic quality (remember the "gold" CDs?), was by and large an attempt to resell CDs with copy protection at a higher price. The movie industry's value-add of director or actor commentaries (and previews for other movies) has been less than spectacular, appealing to a few but often panned by reviewers. Given that the sound quality of MP3s and low resolution of downloaded video are a stigma, perhaps a better value-add would be high-quality downloads. Computer gaming has been somewhat more successful with its value-add by linking games to the online experience: You insert the CD, log on a companion Web site, and play, chat, and horse around with a multitude of other players. The software industry, on the other hand, could add value by decreasing the features and complexity of certain applications, for example offering stripped-down versions of Word or Excel for $29.

- *ISP service fees.* This concept—so far, still a concept—proposes that you pay a flat fee, say $5 a month, to your ISP to download whatever you want. Ostensibly, you do not file-share. The fee is divided up and parceled out to the various media companies. Among our focus groups, this solution was met with the most approval of any. Not everyone downloads, so some will pay who don't play, but it's a better alternative to the government imposing a value-add tax and getting its fingers into the mix.

---

17.  John Schwartz, "Report Raises Questions About Fighting Online Piracy," *The New York Times*, March 1, 2004.

The future of media use may in fact be an intersection, a synthesis, of many, most, or all the above. Begin with the premise that personalization is what the technological media mavens (in other words, most young people) want. That means being able to select just what you want to hear or see and the time, place, and device of choice. Then apply open source technologies that allow personalization and customization (today's capability to cut or skip commercials in TV shows, for example), stir in copyleft and value-add, publish to copy-free zones (or wherever in cyberspace you want to go—even someone's cellphone), and pretty soon anybody can be modifying content to his or her own taste and becoming an artist and copyright owner in the bargain—Everyman and Everywoman as Artist.

## WHAT SHOULD HAPPEN?

After spending a year immersed in the subject, we'd like to share concluding thoughts on who should do what about digital piracy.

■ *Create new distribution channels.* The suppliers need to create alternatives to pirated content—alternatives that are better, easier to use, and if not cheaper than pirated material, at least cheaper than what's being pirated. Think of an iTunes with a music library the size of KaZaA. A Napster filled with old, out-of-print tunes. A downloadable movie vault the size of Ted Turner's TNN channel. A smart industry service might actually find a way to solicit songs from file-sharing customers, test them for quality, and resell them, collecting a royalty along the way. Hey, maybe they could put ads for their media on the downloading services.

■ *Develop new business models.* Media industries, especially the music business, need to look outside their own industries to find new ways to do business. Think about promotions, such as getting a free T-shirt or baseball cap for every 20 downloads. Or offer a free oldie with the purchase of five for-sale works. Most importantly, rethink some preconceived attitudes about crumbling distribution channels. Randy Nicolau, president of Playboy.com, believes that sharing Playmate photos brings more customers to

**TABLE 10–1**   Knights on White Horses: Technologies for Copyright Protection

| Technology | What It Does | Problems with It |
|---|---|---|
| Broadcast Flag | This is a coded signal in digital TV broadcasts that is recognized by DTV reception equipment (as mandated by law as of November 2003) to prevent what the FCC calls "indiscriminate redistribution of DTV signals" (e.g. uploading to the Internet). Broadcasters and movie companies had been reticent about converting to digital TV for fear of piracy. This will help the FCC achieve its goal of migrating analog broadcast to digital, which will free up spectrum. | Digital signals can still be recorded using the analog recording functions on players, and the content will find its way onto the Internet in other ways. DTV tuners built after July 2005 will be incompatible with older devices because of the broadcast flag. Which signals on which devices can be viewed will be determined by content providers. |
| Copy Protection | This is the existing technology for scrambling unauthorized recordings on CD, VHS, and digital audio players. A system created by Macrovision has been used for years to inhibit copying of VHS tapes. It also includes enhancements to Serial Copy Management (SCM) systems that inhibit PC copying of CDs by adding deliberate errors on the media (see below). Audio players can read over the errors; PCs can't. | Sometimes even legitimate copying is stymied, and error codes can be blanked out, say with a magic marker, if the user knows where on the disk (usually the outer edge) it is. These schemes don't prohibit analog copying. In one case (BMG's implementation of SunnComm's MediaMax CD-3 system), a PC user only had to hit the shift key to be able to rip an audio CD. |
| Digital Rights Management | This is software that takes copy protection to the next level, giving the content publisher the means to tailor (or restrict) the content user's rights. Apple's iTunes "FairPlay" system allows unlimited download to iPod players and copies to reside on up to three computers. It is also okay to burn CDs, but not to upload to the Internet. Microsoft Office 2003 has "permission templates," so authors can determine who is allowed to view their documents. | DRM gives significant control of content playback to authors, but libertarians worry that publishers will be able to institute copy control—e.g., prohibit even fair use—beyond that allowed by existing copyright law. It will also cost money to implement. And, it, too, can be circumvented. In 2004 the Norwegian teen (Jon Johansen) who published DeCSS published a workaround to the iTunes FairPlay system that disables it. |

**TABLE 10–1**   Knights on White Horses: Technologies for Copyright Protection  (Continued)

| Technology | What It Does | Problems with It |
|---|---|---|
| Encryption | This is the method used to scramble entire electronic files, or at least the portions of them that provide copy protection, such as those commercially distributed DVDs. The most widely used is the Content Scramble System (CSS), which the 1998 Digital Millennium Copyright Act made illegal to circumvent. | A decryption program for CSS, called DeCSS, was long ago put on the Internet by a 16-year Norwegian, Jon Johansen, who developed it so he could watch a DVD he purchased on his computer. In 2003, he was acquitted of criminal charges in Norway, and acquitted in a lower court in the U.S., but prosecutors have appealed. |
| Music Finger-printng | This software, which lives inside a network switch and copies all traffic flowing through it, can, using filtering and matching techniques, single out the content of stolen songs. System administrators can see exactly which people are transferring what files over the network. The first company to market this software, Audible Magic, is targeting universities primarily worried about overconsumption of network resources caused by downloading, and, to some degree, about copyright protection. | So far the software only identifies songs being shared on the network but doesn't block them (the next step). Executing the programs it would take to block pirated songs would consume almost as many computing resources as file-sharing. In addition, the blocking algorithms often block legitimate transfers, and encrypting the content would make them useless. Then there is the creepy Big Brother aspect to it. |
| Serial Copy Management | This is the system that inserts a few key control bits into the bit stream of a CD or digital audio tape that must be properly read by the playback device. To do so, the device must be designed to prevent second-generation copying. | SCM systems apply only to audio devices and don't prevent PCs from copying. |
| Watermarking | Here specific identifying information is encoded in each frame of a DVD movie and remains recognizable even after analog copying. Recording devices designed to support this form of copy protection recognize the watermark and refuse to record the content. Home movies are unaffected. | This technology will be expensive to implement, and there are issues of visibility of the watermark. The technique inhibits casual copying, but is still vulnerable to counterfeiting. |

his site, who then become subscribers. "It's direct marketing at its finest," he says.[18]

- *Keep the government out of it.* Legislators and elected officers of the court are too often easily swayed. For example, according to the nonprofit Center for Responsive Politics, the Disney enterprise shoveled more than $6.3 million in 1997–1998 into promoting passage of the Sonny Bono Copyright Term Extension Act. Once legislation is passed, it's difficult to repeal or reverse. Congress' record on protecting the public's interest in copyright is at best questionable (see Table 2–1, A Political History of Copyright, at the end of Chapter 2). The same might be said of how the Federal Communications Commission has botched up HDTV, mandating in 2004 the broadcast flag, an antipiracy measure mentioned in Table 10–1. Much easier to let the free market correct aberrations and let the government that governs least govern best.

- *Educate the educators.* The media industries need to enlist the support of high school and college educators in explaining the ethical consequences of their actions to casual pirates. The amount of time and money that has been put into notice-and-takedown efforts could be redirected in a positive direction, providing educational materials or support for teachers to educate students on copyright.[19] The amount of time most consumer digital pirates have spent thinking about the ethics of what they're doing is infinitesimal. Students themselves told us this at our focus groups. Pirates need to know that piracy is not a victimless crime; they need to know that their small acts of piracy add up with those of others and that (if the content suppliers do *their* thing) there are attractive alternatives. They may *still* decide to pirate, but if so, they do it with eyes wide open. No lame excuses. As we have said before, we advocate the equivalent of sex or drug education: Give people the information and let them at least make informed decisions.

---

18. John Schwartz, "The Pornography Industry vs. Digital Pirates," *The New York Times*, February 8, 2004, p. B1.

19. The educational resource on the Respect Copyrights Web site is a good start; see www.respect-copyright.org/junior-achievement.html.

■ *Reopen the public domain.* Today, no material copyrighted in a person's lifetime will ever enter into the public domain while they are alive. That is ludicrous. Waiters should be able to sing "Happy Birthday" and the Girl Scouts should be able to sing "God Bless America."[20] Steamboat Willie's squeaky voice should be freely downloadable over the Internet. This *should* happen, but it's hard to see how it will. It would take a populist politician with a public-domain bent who also has power and influence in Congress. Unless the voters care passionately about rolling back the length of copyright—and they don't—it's hard to see such a politician emerging.

■ *Stop prosecuting customers.* It may have seemed like a good publicity stunt at the time, but the RIAA's notice-and-take-down campaign of 2003 was an ill-founded idea that left everyone with a bad taste in the mouth. Better to spend those dollars going after the crooks, counterfeiters, and thieves, of whom there are many right here in River City,[21] selling home-made copies on the streets.

■ *Take back the night.* Downloaders might consider amassing their purchasing power to outmanipulate the music industry. It's conceivable that by pitching in a dollar apiece, they could affect the behavior of the entire business. Then they could have the music their way while restoring the *art* to artists. Another alternative is for the software industry to merge with the music, movie, and computer gaming industries, since they all have the same concerns and, more or less, the same customers.

---

20. In 1996 the American Society of Composers, Authors, and Publishers (ASCAP) informed summer camps in the U.S. that many songs commonly sung around the campfire were copyrighted material for which royalties should be paid: songs like Woody Guthrie's "This Land Is Your Land," Bob Dylan's "Blowin' in the Wind," and Irving Berlin's "God Bless America." Although ASCAP was willing to settle for a blanket royalty fee as low as $257 for some camps (and others as high as $1,500), after a summer of bad press the society backed off, saying such "public performances" were okay if they weren't for commercial gain.

21. With apologies to *The Music Man*.

- *Get tough on global criminal piracy.* International antipiracy laws need to be trimmed down so that they can truly be enforced, and then we need to truly enforce them. Let's go after the hardcore Mafia and contraband types who are really costing our economy a great deal of money. At the same time, there should be an expanded definition of fair use that lets honest people remain honest (compare to medical marijuana). These two actions should cut down on unprosecuted violations. We believe that having no law is better than having a law that can't be or won't be enforced. Who needs a nation, an entire world, of scofflaws?

- *Scale media pricing to the local economy, and then stimulate product development in the country.* Software piracy was big in Ireland until it got its own software industry going, which now ranks as second only to that of the U.S. as a software exporter. It's unrealistic to demand a poor country to pay the same prices for media as a well-to-do country. Publishers need to create a new business model that makes it more attractive for locals to buy a homegrown version of the media than a pirated or counterfeit one.[22]

There are legitimate arguments that intellectual property protection is actually stifling the free flow of information and the flowering of innovation. Yet some of the greatest ideas and innovations have never been owned or sold: for example, in 1953 Bell Labs gave the technology of the transistor away, for free, to any who wanted to work with it and extend its uses. This led to one of the greatest waves of technological innovation the world has seen.

The Internet is a similar technology, capable of radically transforming the way we work with ideas, their expression, and media technology. It is conceivable that by 2010 it will be commonplace to mix your own ideas and their expression into another artist's

---

22. Of course, this can be a delicate issue for vendors. In 2004, when Microsoft began offering a regionalized, stripped-down version of Windows XP in Thailand for $38 to first-time users, it got complaints from corporate customers, including some in the U.S., who resented subsidizing others by paying higher prices and not having access to the stripped-down version.

work. Multimedia technology makes this possible now: altering photographs, music mixes, using film clips within other films, and so forth. Technology is driving more and more multimedia personalization, and we as individual artists, as well as societies, need to appreciate and, indeed, embrace this change.

Technology is disruptive for media industries. Those who rely on the past to suppress the technological future take a greater risk than those who embrace change and run with it. Is there a reward in taking the short-term solution, built on past business models, outmoded laws, and regressive thinking? Or is there a greater reward in moving with the social and technological flow into a wealth of future potential?

No risk, no reward. No time to lose. Time to take some chances, and begin to move things forward.

# AFTERWORD

## MY PERSONAL JOURNEY: JOHN

As we began the book, I had just completed a project for the Business Software Alliance on the economic impact of software piracy, so I knew that piracy was not a victimless crime. At the same time, I had been an early user of Napster (my wife and kids showed me how to use it) and had come to believe that it truly was a better way to find music than rooting through record bins or searching in vain on fee-based services. I found old jazz and rock and roll on the disk drives of Napster users that weren't available in any industry catalog. The rapid growth of Napster's user base—to millions in a few months—convinced me that there was a phenomenon taking place driven by much more than simply the availability of free music. At the same time, having seen how record labels chew artists up and spit them out, I had little respect for music industry executives. Whatever happened to Frankie Lyman, Cindy Birdsong, and Clarence "Frogman" Henry?

As we started interviewing people—specifically teens—regarding their attitudes about music, game, and software downloading, however, it began to bother me that they didn't see anything wrong with what they were doing. Maybe it's splitting hairs, but I wanted them to at least admit to themselves that what they were

281

doing was wrong. When I downloaded a song from Napster that I knew I could buy in a store, I knew it was wrong. I didn't try to justify it; I just did it. I speed sometimes, too, and I once owned a radar detector.

Now I have more sympathy for the music and movie industries; they are in the middle of a cataclysmic technology-driven change in their way of business and should be forgiven for staring straight into the fireball and letting it burn their retinas. It took the Eastern hardcover publishers years to figure out how to compete with paperbacks; the software industry has been experimenting with licensing and electronic delivery models for 20 years. It took the Web five years to get to 50 million users; Napster only 18 months. Technology accelerates everything to dizzying speeds.

I would like the music industry to build a better KaZaA than KaZaA (at reasonable fees), I would like the movie business to let me burn first-run movies to DVD so I can watch them on airplanes, and I would like the software industry to make it 10 times easier for companies to comply with their licenses. I would like everyone who downloads a copyrighted movie, song, software package, or game to spend at least as much time as it takes for the download thinking about whether what he or she is doing right or wrong.

As for those guys with the factories in the jungles of Asia or Latin America or the cities of Eastern Europe pumping out counterfeit media? Bust 'em.

What about this book? I have been asked how I would feel about people reading copies without paying for them. Well, if they read it cover to cover, I'd feel pretty good. The prospects of getting rich off a book on digital piracy, where the bulk of revenues go to cover the publisher's costs, is slim; but good things have got to come from having lots of readers, a wider audience. Opportunity down the road.

So, like in many aspects of copyright protection and digital piracy, I find I must take advantage of that peculiarly human ability to hold two conflicting views at one time. Buy the book. Read the book. Maybe even do both!

## MY PERSONAL JOURNEY: JACK

My interest in computer technology and ethics dates back almost 20 years, to a newsletter called *Conscience in Computing* and a story *BusinessWeek* did about my idea for deterring kids from hacking into corporate computers. When John and I first discussed writing this book, I was still waging The Good Fight in the college classroom, trying to convince my students that downloading tunes was unethical and plagiarism was grounds for dismissal.

At the time, I had exactly four songs on my computer that I had downloaded from the Internet: "What I Like About You" by the Romantics, Elwood's 60-second version of "Sundown" from the Gateway commercial, John Klemmer's "Touch," and Alana Davis' special version of CSN&Y's "Carry On" recorded for a Sony television commercial, which I actually had bought on Sony's Web site for a dollar. Yet I was no stranger to downloading and MP3s: I have thousands of old-time radio dramas, now long in the public domain, which I've ripped, mixed, and burned. When I listened to new music, it was on the Musicmatch Jukebox, to which I had a full subscription. When I heard something on Musicmatch that I liked, such as the new Kathleen Edwards album *Failer*, I went out and bought it.

So much for my not living in the real world.

As we finish this book, I am disappointed and angry—disappointed in youth and others who rationalize their illicit and unethical digital behaviors, and angry at the media companies for their unmitigated greed and ill-considered retaliation against hapless children. I am sick at heart over seeing citizens ripping off musicians and artists, and equally sick at the music business for doing the same thing to their customers. I am saddened that people live in the selfish denial that it's okay to download because they want media that costs nothing or is hard to find.

I also fully empathize with teens and youth who rage against the media machine.

But I do not condemn; rather, I seek to understand. I have taught computer ethics in my classes and textbooks for nearly 20 years, and it's a tough sell. I understand that there's a cheap thrill in doing illicit, immoral, or unethical things on the Internet. I understand that it's hard to think you're stealing when you're only making a copy of a file for yourself. I understand that technology has changed everything, including the way we conduct commerce, the definition of intellectual property, and the way we conduct our lives.

I'm sick of seeing business preying on youth and their buying power—or lack thereof. Textbooks, music, movies, software— they're all priced out of the typical college student's reach, and have been for years. Business knows that youth is a captive market, and they exploit it, just as surely as they exploit the Third World. No wonder the kids have rebelled. I don't want to see teen- agers with criminal records over this, but I would like to see them accept some responsibility for their acts, respect copyright, and pay a small fee (not a dollar a song). I don't want to see the media companies go out of business, but I do want them to follow Uni- versal Vivendi's lead and get the price of music CDs down where it ought to be, like the industry did with vinyl records.

I don't want to see the government get involved in digital rights management because whenever it gets involved, we lose some rights or control over our lives. We've seen it happen with OSHA, child car carriers, warning tags on hair dryers, local TV channels on cable, you name it. And I don't want to see all the media com- panies encrypting and blocking access to media. What if we end up where you can only play a Sony CD or movie on Sony hard- ware? That's regressive.

The album-with-a-dozen-songs-by-a-single-artist-on-a-CD as we know it is dead. The concept of static media and media-playing devices is disappearing as we go increasingly mobile and online with our lives. While moviemakers strive for higher-definition movies and television, kids who could care less are watching their favorites on computer monitors with mediocre resolution. Software publishers need to better recognize that acquiring a customer in their youth means keeping the customer for life, and that the only option they're faced with today is either selling that customer a less expensive version of their programs or never selling them anything because they'll get it from the Internet. And the Internet itself is about to get bigger, better, faster, and probably cheaper and easier to use. These are some of the realities we face in the new millennium. The rate of technological change is dizzily accelerating: New thinking about copyright and intellectual property, new attitudes about digital media, more customer awareness, and better business models are top priorities.

# INDEX